THE BIG BOOK OF Preserving THE Harvest

Carol W. Costenbader

Storey Publishing

*The mission of Storey Publishing is to serve our customers by
publishing practical information that encourages
personal independence in harmony with the environment.*

Edited by Pamela Lappies, Julia Rubel, and Karen Levy; expert review by Joanne Lamb Hayes
Cover and text design by Cynthia McFarland; text production by Erin Lincourt, Susan Bernier, and Kelley Nesbit
Cover art by Jane Davies
Chapter opener art by Carolyn Bucha, illustrations by Alison Kolesar, except pages 325, 326, 327, and 328 by Wendy Edelson; pages 83 and 290 by Judy Eliason; pages 13, 113, and 287 by Brigita Fuhrmann; page 91 (top) by Charles Joslin; pages 28 (top and center), 31 (left and center), 116, and 245 by Doug Merrilees; and pages 35 (top), 38 (left), 39 (top), 42 (top left and top right), 43 (top left, top right, and bottom right), 44 (bottom), 79, 80, 88 (top), 120, 250, 251 (top left and bottom left), 310, and 312 by Elayne Sears.
Indexed by Susan Olason, Indexes + Knowledge Maps

The information in this book is true and complete to the best of our knowledge. All recommendations are made without guarantee on the part of the author or Storey Publishing. The author and publisher disclaim any liability in connection with the use of this information. For additional information please contact Storey Publishing, 210 MASS MoCA Way, North Adams, MA 01247. Storey books are available for special premium and promotional uses and for customized editions. For further information, please call 800-793-9396. *Note:* Many of the food preservation procedures described in this book are subject to U.S. Department of Agriculture guidelines. Storey updates information upon publication of each edition and encourages readers to check for the most current standards by writing to Cooperative State Research, Education and Extension Service, U.S. Department of Agriculture, Washington, DC, 20250-0900; calling 202-720-7441; or visiting the agency's Web site at www.csrees.usda.com. You may also contact the extension service in your county. In Canada, contact Public Information Request Service, Agriculture and Agri-Food Canada, Sir John Carling Building, 930 Carling Avenue, Ottawa, Ontario K1A 0C5; 613-759-1000; or visit the agency's Web site at www.agr.gc.ca.

The Big Book of Preserving the Harvest was first published in 1997. All of the information in the previous edition was reviewed and updated.

Printed in China by R.R. Donnelley

30 29 28 27 26 25 24 23 22 21 20

LIBRARY OF CONGRESS CATALOGING-IN-PUBLICATION DATA

Costenbader, Carol W.
  The big book of preserving the harvest: 150 recipes for freezing, canning,
  drying, and pickling fruits and vegetables / Carol W. Costenbader. — Rev. ed.
    p. cm.
  Includes index.
  ISBN 978-1-58017-458-9 (alk. paper)
  1. Canning and preserving.   I. Title.
TX603.C763   2002
6 4 1 . 4 — d c 2 1   2002021172

CONTENTS

Acknowledgments to the First Edition

Special thanks to Lynda Spivey, Family and Consumer Educator,
North Carolina Cooperative Extension Service;
Lane W. Byrd, a typist who is also a great cook;
my husband, the gardener in the family;
Pamela Lappies, my editor;
Julia Rubel, production editor;
and Nancy Ringer, editorial assistant.

Deo Sit Gloria.

The second editon is dedicated to the
memory of Carol W. Costenbader.

ONE OF MY FONDEST MEMORIES of childhood is playing in my grandmother's pantry — the smell of the onion bin; the way the air stayed cool, even in the hot summertime. Sometimes the mouthwatering aroma of ham from Sunday dinner wafted out to greet you when you opened the door. The floor space under the bottom shelf made a great cubbyhole for hiding away. There were endless rows of pickles — watermelon rind, green tomato, bread and butter — stacks of colorful jam jars, and rows of mixed vegetables. Granny must have felt rich. In those times, preserving was a necessary economy.

In earliest history, a new age began with the discovery of drying as a way of preserving. How revolutionary to be able to save meat and produce from a time of abundance into the leaner winter months. Around 3000 B.C.E. the Egyptians preserved herbs in their precious olive oils. Fishermen in Biblical times dried their catch in the hot, dry open air. In colonial times, Native Americans shared their methods of drying corn and meat with early European settlers. That help meant the difference between living and dying as winter took its toll.

In the early nineteenth century, Frenchman Nicolas Appert devised a way to preserve food by heating it in a sealed container. From there Louis Pasteur, another Frenchman and scientist, documented sterilization as a way to destroy dangerous microorganisms that spoil food. With these discoveries, preserving food had become a science instead of folklore. The metal can and the glass

To avoid frustrating delays, gather together all the equipment before starting your recipe.

canning jar were improved. Electricity and the advent of refrigeration soon revolutionized food storage. Refrigeration became so popular that the old methods of preserving the harvest were not widely used.

Today's families often turn to food preservation as an inexpensive and time-saving way to have chemical-free food that prolongs the abundance and flavors of summer. Because I have preserved much of the harvest of seasons past, I can serve almost any condiment, relish, chutney, or fancy pickle from my own pantry — and for far less than the cost at expensive specialty food stores.

The Big Book of Preserving the Harvest considers all forms of food preservation for today's busy families. We seldom rely on the methods our grandmothers used because of what we now know about the dangers of bacteria. But we have at our disposal an array of new appliances that make the job of preserving healthy, safe, and simple. Here are the best of Granny's offerings updated into safe, creative, good-tasting recipes everyone can use.

As you might guess, my kitchen is set up for almost any food preservation method, and having the proper equipment makes getting started that much easier. Nothing is more frustrating than realizing in the middle of a recipe that you are lacking a key piece of equipment. The beginner need not invest in every single piece of equipment mentioned in this book, but it's a good idea to purchase everything you will need for the particular method you choose. The good news is that many of the items mentioned are standard kitchen equipment.

When the harvest is rolling in, my philosophy is to gather either enough produce for one recipe of a canned product — usually four to eight jars, or two recipes of a frozen product — one for dinner that night and one for the freezer. Preserving in small batches does away with the long hours of preparation, and frequently you can complete that evening's dinner at the same time. Picking small batches assures impeccable freshness.

I hope this idea of preserving in small batches will motivate even the most timid or inexperienced cook to try food preservation. Small batches make more sense for families that may not have the room to store great quantities of preserved food or that may not even own a large freezer.

TIP
. . . .
Try preserving in small batches, particularly if you are a beginner.

TIP
. . . .
Start as early as possible in the day and allow plenty of time.

CHAPTER 1

Choosing Ingredients

ONE OF THE GREATEST JOYS of growing your own produce is to stand in your garden as you are harvesting, in the midst of all your labor, and eat a just-picked tomato still warm from the sun. Nothing compares, whether because of the time you've put into it, the experience of seeing something grow out of almost nothing, or the incomparable flavor and juiciness. The same is true of harvesting strawberries and other fruit, sun-sweet, ripe, and ready for shortcake. The flavor and nutritive value of just-picked garden vegetables are far superior to those of the produce you encounter in most supermarkets, and the goal of preserving food you've grown yourself or purchased from a local farmer is to lock in that flavor so that you can enjoy it during off seasons.

It's hard to replicate the satisfaction of growing your own fruits and vegetables, but looking at pantry shelves stocked with preserved produce, ready for the cold season ahead, certainly comes close.

Starting out with the very best ingredients is absolutely essential. Choosing the freshest produce, spices, and herbs helps ensure that your final product will be of the highest quality. I check the garden early every morning to see what is ready. Harvesting early in the day before the sun warms the garden heightens the freshness of your produce and gives you plenty of time to start whatever preserving process you choose. Time is of the essence between the harvest and the processing, so getting organized before you pick your fruits and vegetables is important.

Only the Freshest Produce

No book on food preservation would be complete without a word about handling the harvest. You'll want to use only the very-best-quality fruits and vegetables, since no recipe, however elaborate, can make up for ingredients that are inferior in taste or freshness.

Whether you get them from your garden or a farm stand, choose vegetables that are still young and tender. The older they are, the more fibrous and tough they're likely to be. Once again, no amount of processing can change the basic qualities of the original produce.

Vegetables and herbs undergo change immediately after they are picked. Their vitamin C content, for instance, begins to decline. If you must wait several hours between harvesting and starting the preserving process, refrigerate your unwashed bounty. If you pick tomatoes or herbs, however, keep them at room temperature — they actually lose flavor at lower temperatures. Stand herbs in a "vase" of water like flowers until you can use them.

An alternative to refrigerating produce is to submerge it in water and ice cubes in your kitchen or laundry sink. This works especially well for short periods of time (one or two

Stand freshly picked herbs in water until you are ready to use them.

Fruit for Preserving

· · · · · · · · · · · · · · ·

Pectin, the naturally occurring substance found in the skins and cores of fruit, produces a gel when combined with sugar and additional fruit. While commercial pectin can be added to recipes, the natural pectin in fruit can sometimes produce enough gel for jams and jellies. Underripe fruit contains more pectin than ripe fruit. Listed below are fruits that when underripe contain enough pectin to produce a proper gel.

Blackberries	*Currants*	*Oranges*
Blueberries	*Eastern Concord grapes*	*Plums*
Crab apples	*Gooseberries*	*Quince*
Cranberries	*Lemons*	*Sour apples*

hours). When you're ready to begin preserving, drain the water and rinse off any garden dirt. Several sinkfuls of rinse water may be necessary to get your produce perfectly clean and ready for processing. Winter squash, cucumbers, and other thick-skinned vegetables may need scrubbing with a soft brush. When you're sure your bounty is clean and ready, dry it on clean towels.

FARMER'S MARKET PRODUCE

Most cities and towns have farmer's markets that provide fresh produce to urban and suburban dwellers. I find walking the aisles of a farmer's market in spring, late summer, or fall one of life's greatest pleasures. Each time I do, I'm reminded of the bounty of blessings we have in this country. (If you're tired of gardening, you can doubly

Community-Supported Agriculture

• •

One wonderful solution to the dilemma of how to obtain fresh produce without actually gardening yourself is Community-Supported Agriculture. This began 30 years ago in Japan when a group of women realized that more and more of their food was being imported. They organized a group that bought directly from a farmer, inaugurating the system that came to be known as Community-Supported Agriculture (CSA). The Japanese word for CSA is teikei, which means "putting the farmer's face on food."

Most CSAs begin with a farmer and sometimes a core group of members, who draw up a budget that includes all farm production costs, including salaries and overhead, for one year's operation. The total cost is divided by the number of families the farm will provide for, and that determines the cost of one share of the harvest. Each week, shareholders go to the farm or to a pickup site to collect their produce, with one share's worth enough to feed a family of four for a week. Most CSAs offer half shares, as well, and make arrangements for installment payments. The risk of the harvest is shared by the farmer and the members.

The first CSA in the United States began in Massachusetts in 1985, and since then several thousand more have come into being, across the United States and Canada, many in large cities. Almost all use organic methods; not only do they foster a sense of community in the region, but they also encourage good environmental practices and a strong local economy.

appreciate how much effort has gone into growing the piles of spring asparagus or the mountains of ripe summer tomatoes.) The produce at a farmer's market is usually better than most grocery store fare because it's grown locally (or at least regionally) and therefore less time has elapsed between harvest and purchase. I like to eat "close to the earth" and always try to buy produce in season for the region.

Using In-Season Produce

When you plan menus, try to keep in mind when different fruits and vegetables mature. For example, in a recipe that calls for green spring onions and butternut squash, which mature in autumn, something has come from cold storage or isn't locally grown. An eggplant purchased in October in the south or a strawberry in February in the northeast has been grown in another part of the world. Some of this produce could possibly be acceptable for eating, but not for preserving. When you buy locally grown fruits and vegetables, you know you are buying fresh, in-season produce.

Never go to the farmer's market in the hottest part of the day, load up your car with beautiful fruits and vegetables, and continue running errands. Produce in a hot car will wilt very quickly, and you'll defeat your original purpose of preserving fresh foods. If schedules are tight, try taking a cooler with you, pre-iced for storing produce until you can get home.

Fortunately, some produce cellars, or stores, very nicely. Many root crops, such as carrots, onions, sweet potatoes, and white potatoes, because of how easily they can be stored, are perfectly good much of the year (see chapter 8 on root storage). Do experiment, and you'll learn the difference between the tastes of a new-crop spring potato and a cold-storage or root-cellared potato.

TIP

Call ahead to reserve just the fresh produce you need for the exact time you need it. Produce-stand owners are often glad to cooperate.

To keep fruits and vegetables fresh in a hot car, pack them in a cooler.

Fruits ripen at their own pace, and you pretty much have to strike at the decisive moment. However, if you know in advance when you will be on vacation, try planting your vegetables so that they will reach maturity when you return from your trip.

SUPERMARKET PRODUCE

Although there may be times when you need to buy supermarket produce to cook for dinner, there is no good reason to do so for preserving. Big business has forever changed the world of agriculture, and the same is true of the way food is marketed. While common sense supports the notion that locally grown food is the best quality and the least expensive, big business has created wholesale markets that buy in huge quantities and then distribute to chain supermarkets throughout the country.

In "supermarket mentality," foreign-grown produce travels long distances to appear in the bins of your supermarket, while fresh, locally grown produce is left out. In the United States, food travels thousands of miles from its origin before it reaches supermarket shelves, and most U.S. grocers purchase a large percentage of their food from out-of-state sources. Aside from the loss of freshness, foreign-grown fruits and vegetables are often grown under less-stringent controls regarding the use of pesticides.

Another reason for choosing locally grown produce is the higher nutrient content of fresh food. Fruits and vegetables begin to lose vitamins and minerals the moment they are picked. Food that must be shipped thousands of miles contains fewer nutrients by the time it reaches your table than food that was picked 12 hours ago. You can also be more confident that lettuce or apples are indeed chemical-free if they are grown by a local farmer who prides himself on his organic methods than if they are advertised as organic in a grocery store. While organically grown produce has not been proven to contain more nutrients than that grown with chemical pesticides, no one can deny that it's best to consume untreated food.

Aside from economics and nutrition, the difference in taste, appearance, and scent between fresh-picked fruits and vegetables and those sold in the supermarket is the most persuasive reason to avoid supermarket produce. No one benefits from unappealing produce that lies uneaten in the refrigerator bin. When you consider all the arguments for eating locally grown food, you wonder why anyone would choose the alternative.

Much of the produce sold in supermarkets is coated with a protective wax to help prevent mold during shipping. If produce has wax on it, you can be sure it wasn't grown locally. Unfortunately, the wax makes it impossible to properly clean the fungicides off the skins. Before you eat or process such foods, always peel off the skin.

TIP

· · · · · · · ·

Avoid using waxed supermarket produce for preserving.

Caution! Waxed Produce

· · · · · · · · · · · · · · · · · · · ·

One supermarket in North Carolina has a sign over the produce section that reads:

Coated with Food-Grade Vegetable, Petroleum, Beeswax, and/or Shellac-based Wax or Resin:

Apples	Lemons	Plums
Apricots	Limes	Rutabagas
Asparagus	Mangoes	Squash
Avocados	Nectarines	Star Fruit
Beans	Oranges	Sweet Potatoes
Cantaloupes	Parsnips	Tangelos
Cucumbers	Passion Fruit	Tangerines
Eggplant	Peaches	Tomatoes
Grapefruit	Pears	Turnips
Honeydews	Peppers	Yucca Root
Jicama	Pineapples	

Quantity per Quart

Fruit	Quantity per Quart Canned	Vegetable	Quantity per Quart Canned
Apples	2½–3 lbs.	Artichokes, globe	4–10 whole
Apricots	2¼–2½ lbs.	Artichokes, Jerusalem	1–2 lbs.
Blackberries	1½–3 lbs. or 1–2 qt. cartons	Asparagus	2½–4½ lbs.
		Beans — bush green	1½–2½ lbs.
Blueberries	1½–2 lbs. or 1–1½ qt. cartons	Beans — bush yellow	1½–2 lbs.
		Beans — lima, in pod	3–5 lbs.
Cherries	2–2½ lbs.	Beans — pole	1½–2½ lbs.
Figs	2–2½ lbs.	Beets	2–3½ lbs.
Grapefruit	2 lbs.	Broccoli	2–3 lbs.
Grapes	2 lbs.	Brussels sprouts	2 lbs.
Oranges	2 lbs.	Cabbage	2 lbs.
Peaches	2–3 lbs.	Carrots	2–3 lbs.
Pears	2–3 lbs.	Cauliflower	3 lbs.
Plums	1½–2½ lbs.	Corn	3–6 lbs.
Raspberries	1½–3 lbs. or 1–1½ qt. cartons	Cucumbers	6–12 whole
		Eggplant	2 medium whole
Rhubarb	1½–2 lbs.	Kale	3–4 lbs.
Strawberries	1½–2 lbs. or 1–2 qt. cartons or 6–8 cups	Mushrooms	1½–3 lbs.
		Okra	1½ lbs.
		Onions	3–8 whole
		Peas	3–6 lbs.
		Peas, snap	2–2½ lbs.
		Peppers	2 lbs.
		Spinach	3–4 lbs.
		Squash, summer and winter	2–4 lbs.
		Swiss chard	3–4 lbs.
		Tomatoes	2½–3½ lbs.

NOTES ABOUT OTHER INGREDIENTS

Fruits and vegetables aren't the only ingredients used in canning, freezing, or drying. Salts and spices provide the extra zing and variety that make preserving a creative endeavor.

SALT

Salt added to canned foods acts as a flavoring. When used for cured meats and seafoods, it is added as a preservative. Be sure to choose the right kind of salt, for many are unacceptable for food preservation.

Best Choices

Canning salt. Pure sodium chloride, it is the preferred salt to use for processing. You will usually find it in the canning section of hardware and grocery stores. It is also called pickling salt.

Not Recommended

Table salt. This is not the best choice to use for preserving food. It contains a filler that makes it pour easily out of the shaker but will cause cloudiness in the canning process. Also, iodine in table salt can darken foods being canned.

Sea salt. Although it is considered food grade, it is not recommended for preserving because of its high cost and possible mineral content, which can affect the food's color.

Kosher salt. Originally used in the Jewish ritual of food cleaning, it is also acceptable for food preserving. Today kosher salt is frequently labeled as gourmet salt and is usually coarser in grain than table salt. One pound of kosher salt can measure anywhere from 1½ cups to 1⅔ cups.

Must Be Avoided

There are many other kinds of salt on the market, and most should be avoided for food preservation. *Solar sea salt* should never be used for food preservation. It is produced for use in water purification systems and is not food grade. If used for curing meat, it will actually promote spoilage.

TIP

Salt is perhaps the only ingredient in your kitchen that can benefit from being stored over or on the stove. Particularly in a humid climate, the warm, dry air from a heated oven will prevent the salt from caking.

Dairy salt is used as a supplement for animal feed and not for human consumption. *Halite salt,* used for melting ice and snow, is also unsafe. Avoid *salt substitutes* for food preservation; they cause preserved food to have an unpleasant aftertaste and are best suited for use at the table.

SPICES AND HERBS

As with the produce itself, you'll want to choose the finest, freshest, most aromatic herbs and spices available for canning so the final product will be the best.

Spices

Spices age quickly, and using old spices in food preservation is a complete waste of energy. Whole, fresh allspice or this season's fragrant cinnamon bark enhances the flavor of a splendid jar of watermelon rind pickles, while old spices would add little. Mail-order sources offer an excellent selection of spices and herbs, especially for difficult-to-find varieties. Health food stores frequently sell dried herbs and spices in bulk at prices much lower than those the supermarket charges for small cans and jars.

Whole spices are generally preferred for pickling, although a ground spice may be used for some chutneys and relishes. Generally, canned products with clear liquids call for whole spices because ground spices can cloud the finished product. Whether whole or ground, spices left in canning liquid or vinegar continue to intensify the flavor of the preserved food. Sometimes this is desirable, as well as pretty to look at. As the cook, you'll have to decide how strong you want the final flavor to be. (See chapter 7 for more on how to make this decision.)

Herbs

Nothing is quite as appealing as a sprig of rosemary or thyme suspended in a bottle of vinegar, or chopped mint leaves in a jar of jelly. Using herbs to ornament and flavor preserved food gives a personalized touch that will

TIP

· · · · · · · · ·

Tie spices in a cheesecloth or muslin bag so they can be removed after the cooking process and before canning. This prevents darkening of the produce and intensifying of the flavor after it's bottled and sealed.

distinguish your canned goods from others. Fresh herbs impart less intense flavors than dried ones, but a fresh dill sprig or a plump garlic clove looks great in a jar of pickles.

You can find fresh herbs in most supermarkets, but don't forget that you can easily grow them, either outdoors or on a sunny windowsill. Growing them indoors in the winter can be very satisfying. I like to use a huge terra-cotta pot and plant several herbs together, such as chives, parsley, oregano, and thyme. These seem to winter over particularly well in a south- or west-facing window. The large pot keeps the soil from drying out as quickly as it does in the little pots you find in sets of three for hanging in your kitchen window. When warm weather returns, you can place the pot outdoors in the sun or plant the herbs directly in soil in a sunny location.

Herbs for preserving can be fresh or dried, but don't use dried herbs that have been on your shelf for more than six months to a year. Dried herbs lose their flavor quickly when exposed to air, so keep them in airtight containers. (See chapter 3 for herb-drying instructions.)

TIP

Dried herbs and spices are best kept in a cool, dark place. Heat will make their flavors evaporate very quickly. A bouquet of delicate tarragon might look great hanging in your kitchen window, but its essence will dissipate quickly.

Mint

· · · ·

Mint is a prolific grower and one of the easiest herbs to grow outdoors. It doesn't require a lot of sun and thrives in a damp area, for instance under an outdoor faucet or in a low area of your garden. My mother used to place a brick soaked in water next to a newly planted mint cutting to keep the plant moist until it got over transplant shock. Plant mint in a submerged clay pot outdoors to prevent it from spreading too far and wide.

....

Dried herbs are much stronger than fresh herbs, so adjust dried quantities downward by ⅓ to ½ when you're using them in food preservation.

Whether you grow your own herbs or purchase fresh herbs at the market, be sure to choose the best and use them right away. If you pick herbs in the morning, when they are covered with dew, you may wash them right away and then lay them on a towel to dry. Herbs grown with heavy mulch may not even need washing. If that's the case, wait until later in the day to pick them to allow the dew to dry. To choose the freshest herbs in the food market, pick packages that have no condensation to ensure that no mold has formed. Use purchased herbs immediately when you get home.

Choosing Herbs. The herbs that you most like to use in cooking are the herbs to use as flavorings when you preserve other foods. Since the taste of the herb will intensify the longer the preserved food sits, you don't want to rely on herbs you don't enjoy. Experiment with an herb by using it in fresh food before you commit your hard-won harvested produce to it.

One of the favorite herbs for flavoring preserved foods, especially cucumbers, is dill. While it is subtle when used fresh in cooking, preserving allows the flavor of dill to emerge and permeate other food around it. The dill plant produces a light yield, but both foliage and seeds can be used for flavoring. The dill flower, or head, can be used in salads or as a garnish.

Use basil in combination with tomatoes for a somewhat sweet flavor. Other herbs that blend well with tomatoes are parsley, oregano, garlic chives, and cilantro, which is especially good in salsas.

Almost any herb can be used alone or in combination with other herbs and spices to flavor vinegar. A simple process, making flavored vinegars requires little in the way of equipment, and the end result makes a stunning gift. Creating your own blends is fun to do, and anyone who dines with you will appreciate the results. See chapter 7 to learn how to make flavored vinegars.

Sweeteners

Sugar adds to the color, texture, and flavor of foods when used in small amounts for canning, curing, or freezing. With only 16 calories per teaspoon, it is the ingredient almost always called for in the recipes in this book. You'll want to use "table" sugar, white and refined, from cane or beets. Sugar is a preservative and helps form a gel for jams, jellies, and preserves. If you wish to substitute other forms of sugar or sweeteners, the chart below gives substitutions that do not affect consistency or texture.

Artificial Sweeteners

Aspartame. Because heat destroys the components of this artificial sweetener, it is suitable only for uncooked freezer fruit recipes. (See chapter 4.)

Saccharin. This is used in commercially canned products. It carries a U.S. Food and Drug Administration (FDA) warning label as a possible health hazard. It is not recommended for use in home food preservation.

Sucralose. This heat-stable sweetener offers some promise for preserving.

Chart of Sugar Substitutes

Item	To Use as a Substitute	Variation Produced	Calories
Brown sugar	packed; equal parts for equal parts	changes color of food and imparts a distinct flavor	17 per teaspoon
Light corn syrup	replace 25% of sugar called for with this canning syrup	increases richness of color; in jelly helps coat fruits	19 per teaspoon
Fructose (granulated)	use ⅓ less for same sweetening power	much sweeter than table sugar (sucrose)	18 per teaspoon
Honey (mild flavor)	replace up to ½ of sugar called for with honey	has double the sweetening power of sucrose	21 per teaspoon

THICKENERS

Flour. Some recipes call for flour as a thickening agent. The drawback in using flour this way is that the sauce can be runny if it's heated too long.

Agar. This natural seaweed product can be used for thickening uncooked sauces. It's available from health food stores and Asian markets and comes in flakes, powder, or packages of long, thin strands.

ClearJel. This new cornstarch can be used as a thickener. It is a modified waxy food starch and, when used in canned foods, produces a smooth, heavy-bodied sauce that does not set to a gel upon cooling. ClearJel is resistant to breakdown under high temperatures and low pH conditions. It has no starchy taste and makes a clear thickening agent that gives an excellent sheen to the finished sauce. With ClearJel, canned foods have greater shelf life stability, retain a smooth texture, and show no liquid separation upon storage. Although ClearJel is not recommended for frozen food, it is perfect for canned cream-style corn, soups, sauces, gravies, and pie fillings. Use it like regular cornstarch. If you can't find it in your area, see Resources on page 331.

WATER

Large amounts of minerals in your water supply can change the finished product of your preserved food. Sulfur and iron will darken foods. Hard water caused by calcium or magnesium carbonate toughens and shrivels vegetables. Don't ever assume that the heat in a canning process will destroy microorganisms in a questionable water supply. Always have the health department test your water for bacterial levels and mineral content. It may be possible to purify your water supply by boiling, but I prefer to purchase distilled water by the gallon when in doubt. Using purchased distilled water shortens and simplifies the purification step, and rarely is more than a gallon of water needed.

TIP

• • • • • • • • •

Don't use potato or wheat flour or regular cornstarch for thickening sauces that you intend to can, freeze, or refrigerate unless a recipe specifically calls for it. They can make the sauce very liquid.

Choosing the Preservation Method

Those who are new to food preserving sometimes find that choosing a method is as difficult as the process. Is there a reason to freeze berries but not potatoes? Why go through the bother of pressure canning for tomatoes? Can you dry potatoes?

The method you choose depends on a number of factors, with flavor being among the most important. While nothing can top the taste of a freshly picked strawberry, the preserving method that comes closest is freezing. The same, however, is not true of apples, which are much better when kept in a root cellar. The effect of a preserving method on flavor is a very important consideration.

Safety, of course, is the primary consideration. The acidity of a food will be a determining factor in deciding which process you use. The more acidic a food, the more options you have from which to choose. Most fruits are acidic enough to allow canning using the boiling-water-bath canner, while vegetables canned without the acidity of vinegar will need to be canned with the pressure canner to kill bacteria that could otherwise grow to potentially harmful levels.

The charts on the next pages list most fruits and vegetables, the proper time to harvest, and the preferred method of preservation for each. Throughout the book, each food has been included in the chapter that recommends its best preservation technique. For instance, potatoes are a wonderful root-cellar candidate but a poor choice for canning. Therefore, I've included no instructions for canning potatoes in chapter 2. If you don't see a particular food on the chart in the canning chapter, it probably isn't ideally preserved in that particular fashion. However, some vegetables, such as carrots, are good root-cellar candidates as well as excellent for canning and freezing. You'll find carrots in all three chapters.

Preserving Methods for Fruits & Vegetables

Fruit & Best Variety	Best Methods	When to Harvest/What to Look For
Apples, most varieties	cold storage	Late summer or fall. Deep color, firm flesh.
Jonathan, Stayman Winesap	freeze, cold storage, cider, juice, sauce	
McIntosh, Red Rome	cold storage, cider, juice, sauce	
Crab	pickle, jelly, sauce	
Apricots	fruit spreads, can, dry	Summer and fall. Deep color, firm but soft.
Blackberries	can, freeze, fruit spreads	Mid- to late summer. Deep color, sweet, soft.
Blueberries	can, freeze	Spring to early summer. Deep color, sweet, soft.
Cherries, bush and sour	can, freeze, fruit spreads, dry	Spring and summer. Deep color before fully ripe but softening.
Sweet	can, freeze, fruit spreads, dry	Spring and summer. Deep color, sweet, soft, just as they begin to fall.
Currants	can, freeze, fruit spreads	Summer. Deep red or pearly white color.
Figs, most varieties	can, freeze, dry	Late or early summer. Pick before ripe; let soften on counter. Skins can split.
Grapes	fruit spreads, juice, dry	Aromatic, soft and sweet but firm.
Lemons and limes	fruit spreads, dry, freeze the juice	Year-round for lemons, winter for limes. Deep color, juicy in subtropical climates.
Melons	cold storage	Late summer. Deep color, mature on vine, sweet odor, blossom end springy to touch on some melons.
Oranges	freeze sections or juice, fruit spreads, dry, can sections	Check year-round in your region. Tree ripened.
Peaches	can, freeze, dry, pickle, fruit spreads	Late summer and early fall. Deep color, tree ripened, soft, firm and aromatic.
Pears	can, dry, fruit spreads	Late fall. Pick before ripe but fully grown; ripen on the counter.

Fruit & Best Variety	Best Methods	When to Harvest/What to Look For
Pineapple	can, fruit spreads, dry, freeze	Purchase year round. Golden color, leaves pull out easily.
Plums	can, fruit spreads, dry	Late summer. Deep color, soft, sweet.
Raspberries	can, freeze, fruit spreads, dry	Midsummer, some fall producers as well. Deep color, firm, sweet.
Rhubarb	can, freeze	Harvest stalks only in spring. Tender, 1–2'-long stalks. Be sure to discard leaves; they are poisonous.
Strawberries	freeze, fruit spreads, dry, can	Late spring to early summer. Vine ripened, deep color, aromatic, soft but firm.

Vegetables

Fruit & Best Variety	Best Methods	When to Harvest/What to Look For
Artichoke, globe	pickle	Spring. Tender, fully grown; harvest before flowering.
Artichoke, Jerusalem	cold storge, pickle	Dig in late summer or fall after frost.
Asparagus	can, freeze	Spring. 5–10" stalk with closed "rooster head."
Beans: Bush green, yellow	can, freeze	Summer. Thin, pencil-like rods, seeds immature.
Lima	dry, can, freeze	Summer. Tender, green seeds inside, outside is plump.
Pole	freeze, can	Summer. Tender, green.
Black turtle, fava, garbanzo, great northern, kidney, Maine yellow eye, mung, navy, pinto, white marrow	dry	Fall. Dry on vines until seeds inside are dry; pick before wet weather of fall sets in. No pretreatment; shell when beans are shriveled and seeds rattle; freeze 48 hours to kill insect eggs.
Beets: Detroit dark red	can, freeze, cold storage, pickle	Summer. Dig when 1½–2" in diameter or pull by hand.

VEGETABLE & BEST VARIETY . . . BEST METHODS	WHEN TO HARVEST/WHAT TO LOOK FOR
Broccoli, most varieties . . . . freeze	Spring or fall, cool weather. Deep color but closed flower heads.
Brussels sprouts . . . . freeze, pickle, cold storage	Fall or spring, cool weather. Deep color, firm, no yellowing.
Cabbage: green, most varieties . . . freeze, pickle, cold storage, sauerkraut	Spring or fall, cool weather. Firm heads, mature size.
Red . . . . cold storage, sauerkraut, relish, pickle	
Carrots . . . . can, freeze, pickle, cold storage, juice	Fall, cool weather. 3–8" spears, dark brown, deep root color.
Cauliflower . . . . freeze, pickle	Spring or fall, cool weather. Sun blanch the almost mature heads by tying outer leaves over the heads for 5–12 days; heads should be 2–3 inches when picked.
Celery . . . . pickle, cold storage, dry	Cool weather. Pull whole plant when mature, roots and all.
Corn . . . . freeze, pickle, dry, can	Mid- to late summer. When silks turn brown, twist off ears from stalks. Process immediately to preserve sweetness.
Cucumbers . . . . pickle	Mid- to late summer. Small, deep color, firm.
Eggplant . . . . freeze, pickle	Mid- to late summer. Small, deep color, glossy.
Endive . . . . cold storage	Fall. Tie outer leaves over 12–19" plant, wait 2–3 weeks for sun blanching until outer leaves are dry, cut entire head.
Kale	Harvest as needed through winter.
Kohlrabi . . . . freeze	Fall and spring, cool weather. 2–3"-wide stem.
Leeks . . . . cold storage	Leave in ground as needed or harvest all at once in cool weather.
Mushrooms . . . . freeze, pickle, dry	Spring. Harvest when moist, not dried out.
Okra . . . . can, freeze, pickle	Small pods, not tough or fibrous.
Onions . . . . cold storage, freeze, pickle, can	Spring. Harvest green shoots to thin crop; when tops turn brown in fall dig bulb. Allow to dry before storage.

Vegetable & Best Variety	Best Methods	When to Harvest/What to Look For
Parsnips	cold storage	Harvest as needed through the winter; leave in ground.
Peas, green	can, freeze, dry	Deep color in summer. Firm pods well filled out.
Sugar snap	freeze	Spring. Deep color, not full size.
Snow	freeze	Spring. Bright green, 2–3 inches long.
Peppers: sweet	freeze, can	Early to late summer. Deep color, young green or very mature; deep red, green, or yellow for sweetness; hot peppers should be thin stemmed in late summer.
Hot	pickle	
Jalapeño	pickle, dry	
Potatoes	cold storage	New crop when vines flower in spring; for cellaring, harvest in late summer when vines die back and potato skins are hardened off.
Pumpkin	cold storage, can	Deep color in fall. Fully vine ripened.
Radishes	cold storage	Early to late summer. Small globes about 1".
Rutabagas	cold storage	4" bulbs after a light frost in fall.
Spinach	freeze	Pull whole plant before plant bolts or when leaves are tender; pick leaves one at a time in early to late spring or plant as a fall crop; hates hot weather.
Squash, fall and winter,	cold storage, can, freeze	Deep color before heavy frost of fall. Ripen on vine, hard.
Summer, zucchini	freeze, pickle	
Sweet potatoes	cold storage	Dig in fall near first frost.
Swiss chard	freeze, can	Late summer, fall, cool weather, but more heat tolerant.
Tomatoes	can, juice, paste, sauce	Mid- to late summer. Firm, deep color, before they split. Harvest green tomatoes when frost threatens.
Turnips	cold storage	Harvest as needed through the winter or after first frost for root-cellar storage.

CHAPTER 2

Canning

SINCE THE DAWN OF TIME, people have wanted to preserve food to stave off hunger when fresh food was not available. For hunter-gatherers, a successful hunt meant food for the moment, but keeping a supply at hand was difficult during the warm weather. Necessity caused prehistoric families to invent an organized approach to smoking, salting, and drying to preserve their food.

A BRIEF HISTORY OF CANNING

For centuries, the ancient Egyptians preserved foodstuffs in olive oils and made precious, soothing cosmetics from herbs to protect their skin from the power of the sun. Fruits such as figs, abundant in Mediterranean civilizations, were left in the hot sun. Under hot, dry conditions, moisture in the figs evaporated rapidly, and someone noticed that the figs that were dried out didn't spoil as quickly. Today we know that low levels of moisture in foods limit the growth of bacteria and microorganisms that cause spoilage.

In the late eighteenth century, when France was in economic and military shambles, the lack of supplies and fresh food for the troops caused scurvy and malnutrition. In 1795, the French government announced a prize of 12,000 francs to any patriot who could invent a new way of preserving food for longer periods of time. Nicolas Appert, a chef, winemaker, brewer, distiller, and confectioner by trade, took up the challenge and experimented with various methods and equipment. It took him 14 years of experimentation, but in 1810, Appert accepted his prize from the French army for inventing a safe and practical method of preserving food. He stressed the use of airtight glass containers and insisted that applying heat to the filled container eliminated the air, essentially creating a vacuum that kept food from spoiling. He sealed his wide-mouthed glass containers with corks and placed them in boiling water. Although he did not know why this method worked, he was successful in preserving more than 50 types of food. His thesis, "The Art of Preserving All Animal and Vegetable Substances for Several Years," was published in 1810 and translated into English in 1811. He was the first to can food commercially, but his factory near Paris was destroyed during the Napoleonic wars.

Peter Durand, an Englishman who had access to Appert's thesis, obtained a patent for using iron and tin to make cans for preserving food. By 1818, the British navy and army utilized the method, which Durand patented under the name "tin canister." Later refinements were made, and "tin canister" was shortened to "can."

In America in 1858, John Mason invented the glass jar with a threaded top, which replaced the cork-stoppered jars. The early history of home canning culminated in 1874, when A. J. Shriver, also an American, invented a pressure canner for home use.

Pasteurizing Foods

In 1857, when Louis Pasteur refined the process of preserving food by applying heat to destroy the microbes that caused spoilage, he accomplished the same thing that home canners do today. Regardless of which canning method you use, the principle behind it is the same: to destroy microorganisms that cause food to spoil and to create a vacuum in which remaining bacteria cannot grow.

Clostridium botulinum grows in the absence of air (oxygen 2 percent) and the absence of acidity in a moist environment between 40° and 120°F. Although *Clostridium botulinum* is present on fresh food, the conditions are not right for it to be harmful while the food is still fresh. But when the fresh food is canned and the proper conditions do exist for the bacteria to grow, the food could be harmful *if the canning process was not properly carried out.*

This is the axis upon which all canning principles turn. The acidity of produce is the determining factor in choosing which final canning process (boiling-water bath or pressure canner) must be used to make the food safe to eat. See the discussions of canning safety found on pages 29, 31, 35, and 47.

Containers and Equipment

The cork-stoppered, widemouthed, handblown canning jars used by Nicolas Appert in 1810 have been replaced by a wide variety of jars. You can choose half-pint, pint, and quart jars; widemouthed pickle and jelly jars; and small-mouthed jars for mixed vegetables, soups, and main dishes. Whether you are using large widemouthed jars for canning whole cucumbers or small jars for grape jelly, you need to use the right kind of jars and lids.

Jars and Lids

Recycling commercial glass jars, such as mayonnaise or pickle jars, for use in home canning may sound practical, especially with today's emphasis on conserving resources. But if you do, you're jeopardizing the preserving process and risking injury. Jars containing commerical products are not the same sturdy quality as jars made specifically for canning and may not be able to withstand the lengthy exposure to the high temperatures of the boiling-water bath or the high pressure of pressure canning methods.

TIP
· · · · · · · · ·
Never use recycled commercial jars for canning. They are not strong enough and can easily break in the canning process.

Commercial jars can shatter, destroying your food and possibly causing you or others in your kitchen injury. Although the United States Department of Agriculture (USDA) allows the reuse of commercial jars in boiling-water-bath processing, I do not recommend it. The last thing you want is to risk ruining the fruits or vegetables by placing them in jars that might break.

Clean, glass canning jars, free of chips and cracks, are the only containers you should use for canning. Each jar must have a two-piece lid that consists of a new metal vacuum lid and a new or used metal screw ring. These are the only acceptable lids to use. Only canning jars and lids manufactured especially for the purpose fill this requirement.

Although jars of other sizes are available, the half-pint, pint, and quart-size jars are the ones most recipes call for and fit best into most home canners. Make sure that you match your recipe requirements with the jar size before you get started. This affects quantity-to-jar ratio as well as processing time. Half-gallon jars can be used for juice canning, and you can consult your county agent for processing times for them.

Your finished product will determine the kind of jar to use. Widemouthed jars are absolutely essential for foods that are packed whole, such as pickled peaches or cucumbers, whereas relishes or jams can easily be ladled into the small-mouthed jars. Follow recipe requirements for jars carefully and use good judgment.

Avoid using recycled commercial glass jars for canning.

Appropriate canning jars must be free of chips and cracks.

Half-pint jar   *Pint jar*   *Quart jar*

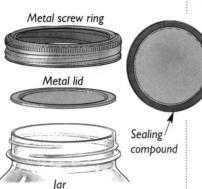

Metal screw ring

Metal lid

Sealing
compound

Jar

Components of a canning jar lid

In canning, the screw ring holds the vacuum lid in place and, unlike the vacuum lid, it can be used year after year. Twenty-four hours after the canning process, when the jars have thoroughly cooled, remove the metal screw rings from the jars before storing your canned goods in the pantry.

Metal screw rings left on jars may rust. If a screw ring is stuck or stubborn, don't force it and risk breaking a seal, but rather leave the ring in place. *Under no circumstances should you tighten the screw ring further after processing.* This action could break the seal and leave the food vulnerable to spoilage.

There are new jars available with differently styled lids that can be used for home canning. While some are quite attractive, don't buy any of them unless they include specific processing instructions that meet USDA guidelines.

Antique jars with porcelain-lined zinc caps are available at flea markets, and new rubber rings to fit them are available commercially. However, I don't recommend using them for modern home canning. It is heartbreaking to have half your recipe not seal properly because of the equipment. Rather than taking a chance, use new canning jars or reuse last year's jars, but always buy new lids.

Old glass jars with bailed-wire seals and rubber rings with glass lids, which look pretty, are also not recommended for use in boiling-water baths or pressure canning. If they are clean, in good condition, and free of chips, these jars can be used for refrigerator storage of fancy sauces and fruits, or for dried products.

Tin cans are not widely used today, as they are difficult to find and unwieldy to use. Special sealing equipment for the cans is also required. The commercial cans we now call "tin" are really made of aluminum.

Regardless of which type of canning jars you use, they must be short enough for the water bath to cover them by 2 inches before the water boils. An additional 2 inches of "pot space" is needed after the boiling begins, so plan to use jars that are at least 4 inches shorter than the height of your canner.

BOILING-WATER BATH

The boiling-water bath is a process that submerges packed canning jars of highly acidic, raw, or blanched food in boiling water long enough for every particle of food to reach a certain temperature. Jars of food are often densely packed, and unless the jars are exposed to the high temperatures of the boiling water long enough, the food in the centers of the jars won't reach the same temperature as food closer to the outsides of the jars. The food needs to reach a temperature that is high enough to kill the molds, yeasts, and bacteria that cause food to spoil. The boiling-water-bath method also drives out any air in the jar, including air in the food itself, creating a vacuum that causes the rubber-coated lid to form a seal.

Only food that is highly acidic can be canned with a boiling-water bath. *Clostridium botulinum,* the bacterium that causes botulism, the lethal food poisoning, exists in the soil and is always on fresh foods, though not in dangerous quantities. For this bacterium to grow to a potentially fatal level, it requires a vacuum and a nonacidic environment. It becomes harmful only when food is improperly canned. Among the highly acidic foods that are suitable for canning using the boiling-water-bath method are pickles; relishes; chutneys with vinegar; most fruits; and heavily sweetened spreads, such as jams, jellies, butters, and preserves.

Boiling-Water-Bath Equipment

Ideally, a newly purchased 21- or 33-quart boiling-water-bath canner with lid and jar rack is the piece of equipment of choice. The better ones are made of aluminum or porcelain-covered steel. The most expensive but durable ones are made of stainless steel. There are also many appropriate alternatives. Any large pot with a lid can be substituted as long as it is at least 4 inches higher than the jars (deep enough to allow 2 inches of water to cover the jars plus the 2 inches of "boiling room"). You will need

---

Standard Equipment for Canning

• • • • • • • • •

Having all the equipment on hand and ready to use will make canning easier and help you feel more confident. If you have extra measuring cups and spoons, keep them handy, too.

Canning jars with screw rings
New rubber-edged vacuum lids
Jar lifter or tongs
Boiling-water-bath canner or pressure canner
Canning funnel
Kitchen timer
Teakettle
Clean kitchen towels
Large wooden and slotted spoons
Nonmetallic spatula or wooden chopstick to remove bubbles
Soft scrub brush
Sieve
Colander
Paring and chopping knives
Measuring cups and spoons
Large bowls
Food processing equipment (grinders, slicers, blender, or food processor)
Heavy potholders or mitts
Food scale
Magnetic wand to lift lids from hot water

A boiling-water-bath canner

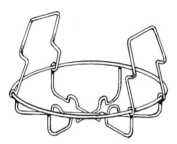

Wire rack used in boiling-water-bath canner

Pressure canner

a wire rack for the bottom to hold jars away from the direct heat and from each other to prevent cracking. In lieu of a rack, you can use towels between the jars to prevent breakage during the canning process, just as Nicolas Appert did in nineteenth-century France. Connect metal screw rings with twist ties to lift the toweled jars off the bottom of the pot.

A pressure canner, though usually small, can also be used for a boiling-water-bath canner. When using it for the boiling-water-bath process, however, do not lock the lid and make sure the petcock is wide open.

PRESSURE CANNING

Because some foods lack high acidity, the bacteria are free to grow in the vacuum created by canning. Using a pressure canner exposes these low-acid foods to high temperatures (240°F), which will sterilize the food by destroying the toughest microorganisms, including the bacteria that cause botulism. Low-acid foods include all vegetables (except tomatoes); meats; seafoods; and all mixtures, such as soups. Only vegetable products with a high vinegar content, such as pickles and sauerkraut, do not require processing with a pressure canner.

Pressure Canner Equipment

Don't confuse a pressure canner with a pressure cooker. A pressure cooker is not as reliable as a pressure canner in maintaining proper pressure and is not recommended for use in canning.

A 16- to 22-quart-size pressure canner is ideal. Check the petcock and safety valve opening of your pressure canner before each canning season begins. You can clean the petcock and safety valve easily by passing an ice pick or string through the holes to free them of food bits and other matter. Wash the valve in hot soapy water and set it out to dry.

There are two types of pressure canners, weighted and dial gauge. Weighted gauge models regulate pressure

Unsafe Canning Methods

You may hear of canning methods used by previous generations that are no longer recommended. They may not produce tainted food every time, but even a small risk should be avoided. After all, the consequences could prove deadly. Do not use the following canning methods.

Atmospheric Steam Canner. Not considered proper equipment for canning; it cannot produce the high temperatures necessary to destroy dangerous bacteria.

Open-Kettle Canning. Once the preferred method, open-kettle canning is now considered dangerous. If an old recipe calls for packing boiling-hot foodstuffs in clean sterilized jars, beware. Bacteria and mold can get inside the food or the jar at any point in the process. Even if the jars should seal, the temperatures are often not raised high enough for long enough periods of time to create the vacuum and properly process the food. Don't process jams and jellies by open-kettle canning in combination with paraffin wax seals. The USDA recommends that a boiling-water bath be used for processing all jams and jellies.

Conventional oven, microwave, or dishwasher. These methods are not safe.

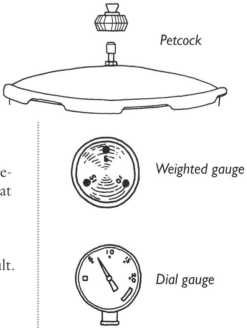

Petcock

Weighted gauge

Dial gauge

precisely, and they don't need to be checked annually for accuracy, as dial gauge canners do. They are also less fragile than dial gauge canners.

The single advantage of dial gauge over weighted gauge canners is that because each pound of pressure is marked on the dial, you can increase the pressure in increments of 1 pound. This is essential for pressure canning at high altitudes.

Dial gauge canners should be checked annually for accuracy. If the gauge is high by more than 1 pound at 5, 10, or 15 pounds of pressure, overprocessing can result. It also indicates that the overall accuracy of the gauge is un-reliable. Dial gauge canners may be checked at most Cooperative Extension offices.

Converting Granny's Recipes

If your favorite recipe is left over from Granny's time, it is still possible to enjoy it safely today if you use modern methods. Frequently, that simply means adjusting the pack method from merely hot packing and hoping jars will seal to adding a short boiling-water bath as is done in some pickle recipes. As long as the product is acidic enough, as in pickles with plenty of vinegar, this is possible. But never rely on this method with low-acid foods, including all seafoods, vegetables (except tomatoes), and meats. They must be canned in a pressure canner even if there is one low-acid ingredient in the recipe — for instance, tomato soup with corn in it.

All canning revolves around the axis of acidity — low or high. Low-acid food, as stated — all seafoods, vegetables, and meats, or combinations — must be pressure canned to kill harmful bacteria. See pages 24, 28, and 33 for discussions of this. High-acid foods, such as pickles, fruit spreads, relishes, and chutney, can be canned in a boiling-water-bath canner. The vinegar and fruit acid in these foods make them acidic enough to preserve by that method.

You can also get information on canning from your county Cooperative Extension office. In some cases, if you add enough vinegar to a low-acid food, such as black-eyed-pea salsa, it can be safe to use the boiling-water-bath canner. (If you put it in a pressure canner to kill bacteria, you would have mush, or at best baby food.) Consult your local Cooperative Extension office before adapting old recipes for today's methods.

A foolproof method to test acidity (pH) is to dip a strip of litmus paper, available at drugstores, into a sample of the liquid (then discard the sample). A reading of below 4.0 is required to ensure proper acidity and canning safety. It is better to over-compensate than undercompensate where acidity is concerned.

The lids of both types of pressure canners should be handled and stored carefully to prevent dents or warping that could compromise the seal. Clean canner lids and gaskets according to the manufacturer's directions. To protect the accuracy of a dial gauge, never immerse it in water, but clean the lid carefully with a cloth.

OTHER EQUIPMENT FOR CANNING

To remove the hot jars from the boiling-water-bath or pressure canner, you'll need either a pair of home-canning tongs or a jar lifter. You'll also need a timer and a funnel that will fit the opening in the size jars you are using. Most other equipment is already on hand in a well-stocked kitchen. A large supply of clean dish or tea towels is essential.

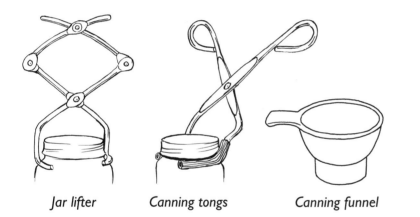

Jar lifter   Canning tongs   Canning funnel

THE IMPORTANCE OF SAFE CANNING METHODS

Safety in canning cannot be overstressed. Fresh food contains high percentages of water, active food enzymes, bacteria, molds, and yeast, all of which cause spoilage. *Clostridium botulinum* exists in the soil and is always on fresh foods, though not in dangerous quantities. Because this bacterium multiplies and produces toxins to a potentially fatal level only in a vacuum, it becomes harmful only when the food is improperly canned. The correct canning process sterilizes the food with heat and holds it in a sterile state in the canning jar until you are ready to eat it. (See General Principles of Safe Canning on page 35.)

Significant Temperatures for Preserving

Temperature	What Happens
240°F	• Minimum temperature for pressure canning.
212°F	• Boiling point (sea level).
165°–240°F	• Temperature range that destroys most bacteria. Kill time decreases as temperature increases.
170°F	• Air exhausts from jars and cans in raw-pack method.
140°–165°F	• Bacterial growth stopped but some survive.
120°–140°F	• Bacteria may grow; many survive.
60°–120°F	• Danger zone: allows rapid growth of bacteria and toxin production.
40°–60°F	• Food-poisoning bacteria may grow. Do not store raw meats for more than 5 days or poultry, fish, or ground meats for more than 2 days in the refrigerator.
32°–40°F	• Some food-spoilage bacteria will grow slowly. • Chill meat, fish, game, and poultry under 40°F and as close to freezing (without freezing) as possible.
32°F	• Freezing point for most liquids and foods.
0°–32°F	• Bacteria stop growing but may survive.
0°F	• Store frozen food.
-10°F	• Minimum for fast freezing.

Partially based on USDA Home & Garden Bulletin No. 162.

Tomatoes Are a Special Case

New information has caused food scientists to disagree about the acidity of some tomatoes and the proper method of processing them. To ensure complete safety in preserving tomatoes, use the pressure canner method. This method also results in higher quality and nutritional value since less processing time is required in a pressure canner than in a boiling-water bath. However, the boiling-water-bath method can be safely used provided more acidity is added to the tomatoes. To acidify and thereby ensure safety when using boiling-water-bath canners for tomatoes, use 2 tablespoons of bottled lemon juice or ½ teaspoon of citric acid per quart of whole, crushed, or juiced tomatoes. It is possible to use 4 tablespoons of vinegar, but the vinegar may impart undesirable flavors to the tomatoes.

The safest way to can all tomatoes is by using the hot-pack method instead of the raw-pack method. (See Raw Pack versus Hot Pack, page 36.)

High- and Low-Acid Foods

Choose your canning method carefully, based on the acidity of the food and the actual food type. Always follow recipe directions and use the canning method prescribed.

High-acid foods, such as most fruits and pickles, can be processed by the boiling-water-bath method. Because of their acidity, they do not provide an environment conducive to the growth of Clostridium botulinum, the bacterium that causes botulism.

Low-acid foods, such as most vegetables, meats, and seafood, need canning temperatures higher than that of boiling water to destroy the deadly bacteria so that they won't grow in the vacuum created by canning. Those foods must be processed by the pressure canner method.

TIP

Simplify the cooking time for thick tomato-based sauces and avoid burning by using a slow-cooker. A less labor-intensive procedure, and my favorite to avoid stove-top burning, is to use an oven for slow, long cooking. Use an ovenproof container, uncovered, in a 350°F oven, stirring occasionally until the sauce is thickened (about 1 to 3 hours).

Regardless of which method you use to process tomatoes, be sure to choose only vine-ripened, undamaged fruits. Do not pick from dead vines or from frost-killed vines. The tomatoes that have fallen from a vine may have already begun to spoil.

ACID STRENGTH OF VEGETABLES AND FRUITS

	1		
	2	Cranberry, pickle, gooseberry, plum, apple	
High Acid	3	Blackberry, sour cherry, rhubarb, prune, apricot, grapefruit, orange, strawberry, sauerkraut	Process at 212°F in boiling-water bath
	4	Peach, blueberry, sweet cherry, pear, pineapple, tomato	
	5	Fig, pimiento, okra, pumpkin, carrot, cucumber, turnip, cabbage, pepper, squash, parsnip, beet, snap bean, sweet potato, greens, asparagus, cauliflower	Process at 240°F in pressure canner
Low Acid	6	Brussels sprout, mushroom	
	7	Lima bean, white potato, pea, corn, olive (ripe)	

Adapted from Ball Blue Book, Ball Corp., *1974.*

General Principles of Safe Canning

Perhaps the most important step in canning food occurs before you even begin. Preparation can make or break a canning session. Before you begin, line up your equipment on the counter and read through the recipe. Mentally check off each ingredient and piece of equipment needed. Canning is a precise science, and it is important to keep the time between harvesting and processing as short as possible. This method ensures that there will be fewer surprises, especially for the beginner.

Preparing Food for Canning

Always start with clean hands, equipment, and food. You can thoroughly scrub sturdy produce with a soft vegetable brush using warm water. Delicate fruit, however, fares better when soaked in several sinkfuls of water, lifting the fruit out each time with a strainer or colander so the grit sinks to the bottom. Be certain all the food you are going to preserve is properly washed or peeled and is free of grit. You don't want gritty tomato sauce!

Pit or peel the produce, if necessary (potatoes must be peeled) and cut into pieces of uniform size. Keep prepared raw fruits and vegetables from acquiring unsightly dark spots by submerging them in a gallon of water with either 1 teaspoon of ascorbic acid or 1 teaspoon of lemon juice added. This acidified water will also prevent cut fruits and vegetables, especially potatoes and apples, from darkening.

Prewashing Jars

Start with clean jars. If the recipe calls for a processing time of less than 10 minutes, you must use a boiling-water-bath canner to sterilize the prewashed jars. If the processing time is longer than 10 minutes, washing the jars

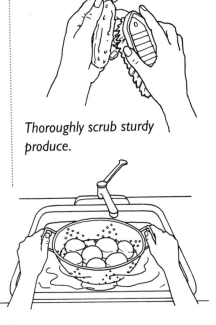

Thoroughly scrub sturdy produce.

Rinse delicate produce in several sinkfuls of water.

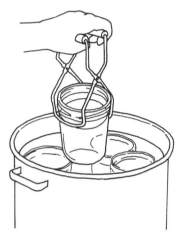

Sterilize jars in boiling water.

in the dishwasher or in hot soapy water will be sufficient to process your produce using either the pressure canner or boiling-water-bath method. Be sure to thoroughly rinse the jars and be careful to remove all traces of soap before filling. Keep the lids hot in a large saucepan of gently boiling water. However, you should always read the manufacturer's directions and follow them to the letter.

Sterilizing Empty Jars

Sterilize clean, prewashed jars for processing times less than 10 minutes by submerging them in a boiling-water bath. Fill the clean jars with hot water and lower them, right-side up, onto the rack in the water-filled pot, making sure that there is at least 2 inches of water above the rims of the jars. At sea level, boil the jars for 10 minutes. At higher elevations, boil them 1 additional minute for each 1,000 feet of altitude. Remove the sterilized jars one by one as you need them, using the jar lifter, and fill them immediately with foodstuffs. Quickly top each jar as it is filled with the lid and metal screw ring. (Save the boiling water for the canning process.)

Cleaning Other Equipment

Make sure the boiling-water-bath canner or the pressure canner gauge and petcock are clean and unclogged. Make sure you are organized and have everything you need ready to complete the process before you actually get started.

Raw Pack versus Hot Pack — Which to Use?

Many foods can be packed in their canning container raw, or cold. This method, called the *raw-pack method,* is also referred to as cold pack. Cleaned, trimmed, peeled raw produce is packed into a warm jar and hot liquid is added. Then the jar is sealed and is ready for processing in a warm, not-yet-boiling water bath.

In the *hot-pack method,* hot vegetables are added to a clean, warm jar and hot liquids are added. The lids are sealed and the jars are ready for processing.

Raw Pack. In the raw-pack method, which is used mostly for high-acid foods, including delicate fruits — apricots, berries, grapes, peaches, plums, and pears — and pickled foods, jars are packed *firmly,* allowing, of course, for headspace. (See the sections on headspace and altitude, pages 39–41.) The raw, room-temperature food is cut up uniformly and cleaned. Pack one jar at a time, allowing for headspace (see the chart on page 50). Add very hot liquid. Generally add 1 to 1½ cups of liquid for each quart jar and ½ to ¾ cup of liquid for each pint jar. Apply the lid and secure it with the screw ring. Raw-pack foods usually have longer processing times. You will put the filled jars in hot, but not boiling, water one at a time and bring the water to a boil. This will help prevent cracking the jars.

One disadvantage of using the raw-pack method is that in 2 to 3 months the upper inch or so of food may become slightly discolored (gray or brown), possibly because of minerals in the water or on cooking utensils. As unappealing as this may be, it does not affect the quality or safety of the food. Another drawback of the raw-pack method is that fruit frequently floats to the top of the canning liquid.

Raw pack is also suitable for some vegetables processed in a pressure canner. Consult the chart on page 50 to determine which vegetables can be raw packed for pressure canning.

Hot Pack. The hot-pack method is required for low-acid foods, such as vegetables, meats, and seafoods. It is the safest method because it kills the bacteria with heat, and more and more authorities are recommending its use. When using the hot-pack method, prepare the food as with other methods: Place it in a pan, cover with water, and bring to a boil. Reduce the heat and simmer for 2 to 5 minutes. Pack the food loosely in warm jars, allowing for headspace (see the chart on page 50 or refer to your

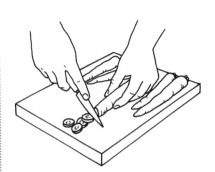

Cut food into uniform pieces.

Finding Your Local Cooperative Extension Office

• • • • • • • • • • • • •

Look in the telephone directory under "local government" or call the nearest land-grant university. You can also go to http://www.reeusda.gov on the Internet and click on "state partners." Or call the USDA information line at (202) 720-2791.

Filling the jars using the hot-pack method.

Run a nonmetallic spatula or chopstick along the sides of the jar to remove bubbles.

recipe). Add boiling liquid, generally 1 to 1½ cups for quarts and ½ to ¾ cup for pints, put on the lid, and secure with a screw ring. Processing time for hot-pack foods in a pressure canner will be the same as for raw-pack foods. There's no need to worry about cracking jars, since the food will not be cold, as it is in the raw-pack method.

FILLING THE JARS

When you have chosen the method and prepared the equipment and food, fill the jars one at a time. The canning funnel and a ladle are invaluable for this stage. Be careful of drips when you remove the funnel from each filled jar. Drips can burn the cook, but they also can spoil a seal if left on the mouth of the jar. Precision is the word here. Be sure to pack each jar for the proper density and headspace according to your chosen processing method (see page 39).

If bubbles appear in the liquid, gently tap the side of the jar with a nonmetallic knife handle to help settle the contents. Or run a clean plastic spatula along the sides in several places to help remove bubbles between pieces of food. Don't stir, which creates more bubbles.

I like to use a clean, thin, wet tea towel over my index finger to rub around the rim of each jar — it picks up the smallest drip of food or liquid. (You will be able to feel the slightest chip on the rim as well. If the jar is chipped, discard it and choose another. The chance of contamination is too great.) A wet paper towel works for this job, too. Place the lid and the metal screw ring on the jar and secure. Then begin on the next jar. Put each jar to the side until they have all been filled. Then process them together.

Headspace

Regardless of whether you use raw pack or hot pack, it is important to leave a space between the jar lid and the level of the liquid. This headspace is necessary because the heat of the canning process expands the food and allows a vacuum to form, thereby sealing the jar.

Too *much* headspace can cause discoloration on the top level of food. Too *little* headspace will cause the food to be forced out of the jars during processing and prevent sealing. (See the chart on page 50.) Consult your local county agent, especially if you are a high-altitude cook, and always follow the recipe carefully. Remember that density of food plays an important role in headspace.

Wipe the rim of the jar with a clean, damp towel.

Seal the jar securely.

Headspace
. . . .
In a pressure canner for low-acid foods, leave 1 to 1 1/4 inches of headspace. In a boiling-water-bath canner, leave 1/3 inch for jams and jellies, 1/2 inch for fruits, tomatoes, and pickles.

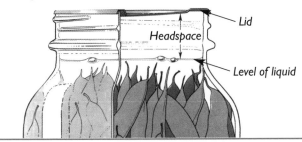

Lid

Headspace

Level of liquid

ALTITUDE ADJUSTMENTS FOR BOILING-WATER-BATH CANNING

When stating processing time for boiling-water-bath canning, all recipes assume an altitude of less than 1,000 feet. If you live higher than 1,000 feet, you must adjust your processing time as shown.

ALTITUDE IN FEET	PROCESSING TIMES OF 20 MINUTES OR LESS, ADD	PROCESSING TIMES OF MORE THAN 20 MINUTES, ADD
1,000	1 minute	2 minutes
2,000	2 minutes	4 minutes
3,000	3 minutes	6 minutes
4,000*	4 minutes	8 minutes
5,000*	5 minutes	10 minutes

*At this altitude you may want to consider pressure canning, which will accomplish the same thing without overcooking your food.

Altitude Adjustments for Steam-Pressure Canning

Altitude (Feet)	Weighted Gauge	Dial Gauge
0 – 1,000	10	11
1,001 – 2,000	15	11
2,001 – 4,000	15	12
4,001 – 6,000	15	13
6,001 – 8,000	15	14
8,001 – 10,000	15	15

ALTITUDE AND BOILING-WATER-BATH CANNING

Water boils at 212°F at sea level. As altitude increases, water boils at *lower* temperatures (which is less effective for killing bacteria). Therefore, you must determine your local altitude and increase the processing time as given above. If you have questions, consult your canner instructions or your county agent for information specific to your area.

ALTITUDE ADJUSTMENTS AND THE PRESSURE CANNER

At higher altitudes, steam expands more in the head-space of the canning jar as it sits in the pressure canner. To allow for this expansion, some sources advise increasing the headspace by ⅛ inch for every 1,000 feet of altitude above sea level, not to exceed ¾ inch for a half-pint jar, 1 inch for a pint jar, and 1¾ inches for a quart jar. The chart on page 50 specifies the headspace at sea level. You may wish to adjust headspace according to your altitude.

Selecting the Correct Processing Time

When you're canning in a boiling-water-bath canner, you'll need more processing time for most raw-pack foods or quart jars than for hot-pack foods or pint jars.

To destroy microorganisms in low-acid foods processed in a boiling-water canner, you must:

- Process jars for the correct number of minutes in boiling water.
- Cool the jars at room temperature.

The food may spoil if you fail to add extra processing time for the lower boiling-water temperatures that occur at altitudes above 1,000 feet, if you process for fewer minutes than specified, or if you cool jars in cold water.

To destroy microorganisms in low-acid foods processed with a pressure canner, you must:

- Process the jars using the correct time and pressure specified for your altitude.
- Allow the canner to cool at room temperature until it is completely depressurized.

Your canned food may spoil if you fail to select the proper processing times for specific altitudes, fail to allow the canner to exhaust properly before weighting or closing the petcock, process at a lower pressure than specified, process for fewer minutes than specified, or cool the canner with water.

Two serious errors in temperatures obtained in pressure canners occur because:

1. The internal temperatures of canners are lower at higher altitudes. To correct this error, canners must be operated at the increased pressures specified for appropriate altitude ranges (see box on page 40).

2. Air trapped in a canner lowers the temperature obtained at 5, 10, or 15 pounds of pressure and results in underprocessing. The highest volume of air trapped in a canner occurs in processing raw-pack foods in dial gauge canners. These canners do not vent air during processing. To be safe, all types of pressure canners must be vented 10 minutes before they are pressurized.

TIP

• • • • • • • • •

Even though the water is rapidly boiling away in your canner at higher altitudes, because of reduced atmospheric pressure it is boiling at a *lower* temperature. You will need to adjust your processing time upward at higher altitudes.

Preparing Food and Jars for Canning

1. Clean the food and, if needed, cut it into uniform pieces. For the raw-pack method, set prepared food aside. For the hot-pack method, place food in the large saucepan, cover with water, and bring to a boil. Simmer 2 to 5 minutes.

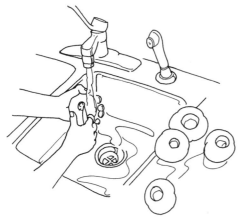

2. Sterilize the clean jars by filling them with hot (not boiling) water and lowering them onto a rack in a water-filled pot. Make sure there's at least 1 inch of water above the rims. Bring the water to a boil and boil for 10 minutes (see altitude chart on page 50). Keep jars hot.

3. Remove a jar and fill it immediately with food. If using the raw-pack method, pack it tightly. If using the hot-pack method, fill the warm jar loosely.

4. Add very hot water, syrup, or juice, according to the recipe, to the jar until it covers the food. Allow for proper headspace (see chart on page 50).

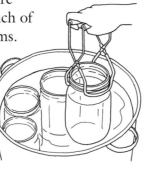

5. Remove air bubbles by inserting a nonmetallic utensil and firmly pressing the food.

6. Using a clean towel, carefully wipe the jar rim to allow a good seal.

7. Apply the lid and secure it with the screw ring.

8. Repeat steps 3, 4, and 5 until all jars are filled. Reserve the water used to sterilize jars for the canning process. Continue on page 44 for boiling-water-bath canning or page 45 for pressure canning.

Boiling-Water-Bath Canning

Place the jars in the canner.

Add hot water until the water level is at least 2 inches above the jar tops.

Remove the jars from the canner to a clean towel.

The steps below are based on USDA recommendations.

1. After packing the jars and fitting them with lids and screw rings, fill the canner halfway with water (or use half the water reserved from sterilizing jars) and heat it to 140°F for raw-pack food or to 180°F for hot-pack food.

2. You may either put the empty rack in the canner and then load the jars onto the rack with the jar lifter or place the packed jars on the canner rack first and then, using the handles, lower the rack into the hot water.

3. Check the water level to make sure it is at least 2 inches above the lids of the jars. Add more hot water, if necessary.

4. Heat the water to a full boil.

5. Once the water is rapidly boiling, set a timer for the number of minutes specified in your recipe. Cover with the lid and reduce the heat enough to keep the water at a gentle boil during the processing. Be sure to adjust for altitude.

6. Check the canner to make sure the water level is still 2 inches above the jars, and add boiling water, if necessary.

7. When the specified time is over, turn off the heat and remove the lid, keeping your face back to avoid the hot steam that will escape.

8. Place a folded towel on the counter near the canner. Use a jar lifter to remove the jars, placing them on the towel. Keep them at least 1 inch apart to allow air to circulate.

Pressure Canning

The steps below are based on USDA recommendations.

1. Reread the user's manual for your pressure canner.
2. After packing the jars and fitting them with lids and screw rings, put the rack in the canner and fill it with 2 to 3 inches of water. Place the filled jars in the rack with the jar lifter, or fill the rack before placing it in the canner. Put the lid on the canner, fastening securely.
3. Open the petcock or remove the weight. Heat on high until steam flows.
4. Continue to heat on high for 10 minutes before closing the petcock or placing the weight on the vent port. During the next 3 to 5 minutes, the pressure will build.
5. When the dial gauge shows the recommended pressure, or when the petcock begins jiggling or rocking, set the timer for the time specified in the recipe. At high altitudes, increase the pressure $\frac{1}{2}$ pound for each 1,000 feet above sea level.
6. Maintain a temperature at or just above the specified gauge pressure. Weighted gauges will jiggle two or three times per minute or rock slowly, depending on the brand. Avoid large variations in temperature, which may cause liquid to be forced from jars, jeopardizing the seal.
7. When the time is up, turn off the heat, remove the canner from the burner, if possible, and let it depressurize. Don't use cold water to speed depressurization. This risks losing liquid from the jars, breaking the seals, and possibly warping the lid. Don't open the vent port. Let it sit for 30 minutes (for pints) or 45 minutes (for quarts). Newer models cool more quickly and have vent locks that indicate when pressure is normal.
8. When the pressure is normal, remove the weight or open the petcock. Let it sit for 2 minutes before unfastening the lid and removing it. Keep your face back to avoid escaping steam.
9. Using the jar lifter, remove the jars and place them on a folded towel. Keep them at least 1 inch apart to allow air to circulate.

Place filled jars on the rack.

Fasten the canner lid securely.

CHECKING THE SEALS

After the filled and finished jars of canned goods have cooled, in 12 to 24 hours, use your thumbs to test the seal of the metal lids. Press hard on the center of one. If the lid does not move downward or give, your jar is complete. If one or two aren't sealed, you can refrigerate these faulty jars and consume the contents within a day or two.

Another method for checking the seals is by lifting your newly canned jar by its lid without the screw ring, using the weight of the jar to test the strength or weakness of the seal. (Protect yourself and the jar by doing this over a sink prepared with a towel to pad the possible fall.)

Check the seal on a jar by applying pressure to the center with your thumbs. It should not give at all.

Questions to Ask Yourself

1. Did I properly execute the processing method called for in the recipe?

2. Did I fill the canner with the correct amount of water to cover the jars properly?

3. Did I figure the altitude adjustment and headspace correctly?

4. Did I check to make sure that the jar rims were free of cracks and chips, and did I use new lids?

5. Did I fill the jar to the proper density and cap it in the prescribed manner?

6. Did I cool the jars naturally at room temperature and in a reasonable amount of time, about 12 to 24 hours?

7. Did I remove the screw rings before storing? If they could not be removed, did I avoid tightening them, which could disturb the seal?

STORAGE

Home-canned foods do not require special storage equipment, just a cool shelf in a dry, dark place. You can tuck canned foods in all sorts of nooks of your house or apartment. Just don't forget where you stored them! Keeping a location chart is a good idea: I tape mine to the inside of a kitchen cabinet door.

The best temperature for storing canned goods, and the one recommended by the USDA, is between 50° and 70°F.

Canning can be a source of safe, economical, chemical-free, quality food all winter long. You'll want your labor to be efficient and precise to fully enjoy the bounty of all your efforts. Attributes of home canning are lost when food spoils, jars break or don't seal, or poor-quality food is used.

Canning Safety

Examine jars carefully using the guidelines on the next page to detect signs of spoilage. If you suspect that canned food has spoiled, don't hesitate to throw it out, but be careful about how you dispose of the spoiled jar and its contents. If you flush it down the drain or toilet, it could contaminate the water supply. To protect you, your household, and your pets, detoxify the jar and its contents before you dispose of them.

Disposing of Spoiled Food and Equipment

To detoxify a jar of spoiled food, place it unopened in a pot of boiling water for 30 minutes, then put it in a garbage bag and dispose of it properly.

If the jar has been opened already, remove the lid and empty the contents into a saucepan. Place the empty container, the lid, and the ring (if it remained on the jar during storage) in a second pan that is filled with water. Bring both pans to a boil. If the spoiled food is thick, thin it with

TIP
· · · · · · · ·

Keep a chart that gives the location of canned goods posted on the inside of your kitchen cabinet or pantry door.

Warning
· · · · · · ·

Clostridium botulinum — the bacterium that causes botulism — grows in the absence of air. It is deadly. Never taste even a tiny bit of canned food you suspect may be spoiled.

1. The jar has mold on it
and/or food has leaked out
during storage. The lid has
mold inside.

2. The food in the jar is completely and very darkly discolored. (Uniform light gray
or brown discoloration may
be caused by minerals in
the water, in which case the
food is safe to eat.)

3. The food looks shriveled,
spongy, slimy, or cloudy.

4. The liquid in the jar is not
static and seems to bubble.

5. The jar's contents "shoot"
out when the lid is opened.

6. The food has an "off" odor.

water to make it boil more easily. Add to the pot of water
any other equipment that has come into contact with the
food. Make sure all items are completely covered by at least
1 inch of water. (The jar can lie on its side.)

When both pans have been brought to a boil, boil hard
for 30 minutes. While they boil, gather any sponges, towels, rubber spatulas — anything that has touched the
spoiled food and can't be boiled — and wrap them in a
heavy plastic bag.

When the contaminated items have boiled for 30 minutes, place them in the garbage bag with the other things
and tie tightly. Dispose of it on the day your county collects
hazardous materials. Call your county agent if you have any
questions or need further guidance.

Remember to wash your hands thoroughly with hot,
soapy water immediately after having contact with any
spoiled food or contaminated item.

SERVING LOW-ACID HOME-CANNED FOOD

The traditional safety precaution when heating home-
canned, low-acid food before eating was to boil it for
10 minutes to eliminate the possibility of dangerous bacteria. The USDA now says that this is no longer necessary as
long as the following guidelines were observed when the
original canning took place.

1. You processed the food in a pressure canner.

2. You checked the gauge of the pressure canner for
accuracy.

3. Times and temperatures for processing were correctly
used for the size jar, method of packing, and food canned.

4. You made proper altitude adjustment for your recipe's pressure and processing time.

5. The jar lid passed all the seal tests.

6. The contents have not leaked from the jar.

7. No unpleasant odor can be detected.

8. No liquid shoots from the jar when opened.

Canning Meats and Poultry

The scope of this book does not deal with canning wild game, duck, bear, and so forth, but I have included several recipes for today's cooks that use meats to make family favorites that will be convenient to have on hand. Detailed instructions are given with each recipe.

Successful home-canned meat-only recipes can only be hot packed then processed in a pressure canner. Fifteen pounds per square inch (psi) is recommended to be certain all bacteria are killed. It is most convenient to use wide-mouthed jars for this.

If you are starting with fresh-killed meat from your own stock and have a large supply for canning, refrigerate right away whatever portion of meat you are not canning. Bacteria start to grow immediately on fresh meat.

Recipes that contain meat products in combination with produce will still need to be pressure canned, but they may require less processing time in the canner than meat-only recipes, depending on the acidity of the added produce (as in tomato sauce with meat, for instance). Combination meat-and-produce recipes may require 10 psi. Always follow canning directions carefully.

TIP
• • • • • • • • •

If you have concerns about canning meats and poultry, you can get help by calling the USDA Meat and Poultry Hotline at (800) 535-4555.

Low-Acid Foods for the Pressure Canner

Unless otherwise indicated, all vegetables must be processed with 10 pounds of pressure.

Produce	Pack	Processing Time (Minutes*)		Headspace (Inches*)
		Pint	Quart	
Artichoke	hot	25	30	½
Asparagus	raw	30	40	1
	hot	30	40	1
Beans — bush and pole	raw	20	25	½
Yellow, green, wax	hot	20	25	¼
Beets	hot	30	35	½
Carrots	raw	25	30	1
	hot	25	30	½
Corn — cream style	hot	85	no quarts	1
Whole kernel	raw	55	85	1
White	hot	55	85	1
Okra	hot	25	40	1
Peas — green	raw	40	40	1
	hot	40	40	1
Snow	raw	20	25	1
Peppers — sweet	hot	35	no quarts	½
Spaghetti sauce — meatless	hot	20	25	1
With meat	hot	60	70	1

*At sea level. Use the chart on page 40 for times at higher altitudes.

Vegetables for Pickling

• • • • • • • • • • • • • • • • • • • •

Not all vegetables are suitable for canning. Cucumbers, eggplants, and hot peppers, for example, lose their crunch and flavor when exposed to the high temperatures of pressure canning. Pickle them instead. The addition of vinegar provides enough acidity for these vegetables to be processed at lower temperatures than those required for standard pressure canning.

HIGH-ACID FOODS FOR THE BOILING-WATER BATH

PRODUCE	PACK	PROCESSING TIME (MINUTES*)		HEADSPACE (INCHES*)
		Pint	**Quart**	
Apples	hot	20	20	½
Apricots	raw	25	30	½
	hot	20	25	½
Berries — black, blue, and raspberry	raw	15	20	½
	hot	15	15	½
Cherries	raw	25	30	½
	hot	15	20	½
Currants and grapes	raw	15	20	½
	hot	10	10	½
Figs (use 2 tablespoons lemon juice per 1 quart)	hot	85	90	½
Grapefruit, oranges, tangerines	hot	10	10	½
Peaches	raw	25	30	½
	hot	20	25	½
Pears	raw	25	30	½
	hot	20	25	½
Plums	raw	20	25	½
	hot	20	25	½
Purées — fruit, applesauce, baby food	hot	20	20	½
Rhubarb	hot	15	15	½
Strawberries (see chapter 5, Jams & Jellies)				
Tomatoes** — juice	hot	35	40	½
Juice and flesh blend	hot	35	45	½
Crushed, no liquid added	hot	35	45	½
Sauce	hot	35	40	¼
Halved or whole, in juice	raw or hot	85	85	½
Halved or whole, no liquid	raw	85	85	½

*At sea level. Use the chart on page 40 for times at higher altitudes.

**Add 1 tablespoon lemon juice per pint, 2 tablespoons per quart. If even one other vegetable is added (potato, squash, peppers, etc.), pressure canning is required.

RECIPES FOR CANNING

Easy Autumn Apple Cider

Not only is this recipe an easy beverage, but just ½ cup can add zip to pumpkin soup, cooked beets, or beef stew.

Boiling-water-bath canner; six 1-quart jars

Purchase cider fresh from the mill during apple season. I like to process this in quart-size jars — 6 quarts or 1½ gallons at a time. Strain it through a dampened jelly bag. Please read about jelly bags on pages 182–84.

1. In a large kettle, bring cider to a slow simmer but not a hard boil.

2. Pour into hot, clean jars, leaving ½ inch of headspace. May be packed into pints or quarts.

3. Cap, seal, and process in a boiling-water-bath canner for 30 minutes. Adjust for altitude (page 40), if necessary.

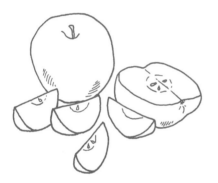

YIELD: 6 QUARTS (TWENTY-FOUR 1-CUP SERVINGS)
NUTRITION PER SERVING

Calories 117		Total fat <1g	
% from fat	2	Saturated	0g
Carbohydrates	29g	Cholesterol	0mg
Fiber <1g		Sodium 7mg	

Green Tomato Dip

Is it a dip for fresh vegetables, a salad dressing for mixed greens, or a sandwich spread? Any way you use it, it is remarkable.

Boiling-water-bath canner; four 1-pint jars

- 8 green tomatoes, washed and cored
- 4 red bell peppers, washed, halved, and seeded
- 4 large onions, peeled, cut in half
- 3 cucumbers, peeled, cut into chunks
- ½ cup pure granulated pickling salt
- 2½ cups white wine vinegar
- 1 cup sugar
- 2 teaspoons celery seed
- 1 teaspoon dry mustard
- ¼ teaspoon freshly ground black pepper
- 1 teaspoon mixed pickling spice
- 2 eggs
- ½ cup flour
- ¾ cup vegetable oil

YIELD: 4 PINTS (THIRTY-TWO 2-OUNCE SERVINGS)
NUTRITION PER SERVING

Calories	108		Total fat	6g	
% from fat		44	Saturated		<1g
Carbohydrates		14g	Cholesterol		11mg
Fiber	2g		Sodium	1,608mg	

1. Grind the vegetables coarsely, using a hand-turned grinder or pulsating motions in a food processor. You may also chop the vegetables by hand. Sprinkle them with the salt.

2. Cover and let stand at least 8–12 hours to allow the vegetables to "sweat."

3. Drain and rinse the vegetables and combine them with 2¼ cups of the vinegar, sugar, celery seed, mustard, and pepper. Add the pickling spice tied in a cheesecloth bag.

4. Pour the vegetables and seasonings into a nonreactive saucepan. Cook, simmering over low heat, for 30 minutes. Combine the eggs, flour, and the remaining vinegar in a food processor. With the motor running, add the oil by droplets in a steady stream until the mixture becomes thick and smooth.

5. Remove the spice bag from the vegetables and stir in the egg mixture. Cook, simmering over low heat, until thick. This should take 5–10 minutes.

6. Ladle into hot, clean jars, leaving ½ inch of headspace.

7. Cap, seal, and process in a boiling-water-bath canner for 10 minutes.

Pepper and Eggplant in Garlic Oil

Serve this delicate dish between split slices of focaccia smeared with goat cheese.

5 small eggplants, unpeeled, sliced ½ inch thick

4 large red bell peppers

2 large yellow bell peppers

1 cup olive oil

¾ cup cider vinegar

3 cloves garlic, peeled and sliced

½ teaspoon pickling salt

¼ teaspoon dried red pepper flakes

10 large basil leaves

1. Broil the eggplant circles on a greased cookie sheet about 4 inches from the flame, turning once, until they are lightly browned, about 15–20 minutes.

2. Broil the whole bell peppers on a cookie sheet 4 inches from the flame, until they are soft and collapsed, about 30 minutes. Turn them occasionally while they're cooking.

3. Place the peppers in a paper grocery bag to trap the heat. When they have cooled, peel off the outer skins, quarter, and remove the seeds.

4. Heat the oil, vinegar, garlic, salt, and red pepper flakes. Simmer for 4–5 minutes.

5. Alternate layers of eggplant, peppers, and basil in two clean, hot pint jars.

Layer the ingredients in the jars.

6. Top off with the hot oil mixture, leaving ½ inch of headspace. Remove any traces of oil from the rim of the jar.

7. Cap, seal, and process for 20 minutes in a boiling-water-bath canner. Let the flavors marry for 10–14 days before using.

YIELD: 2 PINTS (EIGHT ½-CUP SERVINGS)
NUTRITION PER SERVING

Calories 324		Total fat	28g
% from fat	72	Saturated	4g
Carbohydrates	21g	Cholesterol	0mg
Fiber 7g		Sodium	142mg

Green Chile Salsa

· · · · · · · · · · ·

Poblano chiles give this recipe a mild heat but mellow flavor. If poblano chiles are not available, you may substitute Anaheim chiles, or green bell peppers and 1 jalapeño chile, seeded and chopped.

Boiling-water-bath canner; eight 1-pint jars

18 poblano chiles

10 cups (about 80 medium tomatillos, or 4 pounds) coarsely chopped, husked tomatillos with juice

2 cups coarsely chopped onions

1½ cups fresh lime juice (12 medium limes)

1 cup chopped cilantro

1 cup water

6 cloves garlic, minced

2 teaspoons salt

1. Place the chiles on a greased cookie sheet and broil until the skins blister, about 15 minutes.

2. Discard the membranes and seeds from the chiles. (Wear gloves to prevent pepper oils from burning your skin.) Chop the chiles coarsely and combine with the tomatillos in a heavy nonreactive saucepan.

3. Bring the mixture to a simmer and add the onions, lime juice, cilantro, water, and garlic. Cook over medium heat, stirring occasionally, for 10 minutes.

4. Add salt. Stir well.

5. Ladle into hot, clean jars. Cap and seal.

6. Process in a boiling-water-bath canner for 30 minutes. Adjust for altitude (page 40), if necessary.

· ·

YIELD: 8 PINTS (SIXTY-FOUR 2-OUNCE SERVINGS)
NUTRITION PER SERVING

Calories 17		Total fat <1g	
% from fat	13	Saturated	0g
Carbohydrates	4g	Cholesterol	0g
Fiber <1g		Sodium 69mg	

· ·

Corn and Zucchini Salsa

· · · · · · · · · · · ·

Serve this remarkable salsa with corn chips or on top of grilled chicken breasts.

Boiling-water-bath canner; two 1-pint jars

3 medium zucchini, cleaned, trimmed, and diced

1½ teaspoons salt

2 ears yellow corn, husked, silks removed

4 tablespoons olive oil

2 large tomatoes, seeded and chopped

1 cup fresh lime juice (8 medium limes)

½ cup cider vinegar

2 jalapeño chiles, seeded and minced (wear rubber gloves)

¼ cup finely chopped scallions with tops

3 cloves garlic, minced

¼ teaspoon freshly ground black pepper

1. Toss the zucchini with the salt and "sweat" for 3 minutes in a nonreactive colander. Rinse and dry on paper towels.

2. Coat the corn with 2 teaspoons of the oil and roast on a cookie sheet in a 400°F oven for 30–40 minutes. Cool. Cut off the kernels and scrape the cobs.

3. Combine the zucchini, corn, remaining oil, tomatoes, lime juice, vinegar, jalapeños, scallions, garlic, and pepper in a heavy saucepan. Bring to a boil and cook for 2–3 minutes.

4. Ladle into hot, clean jars. Cap and seal. Process in a boiling-water-bath canner for 15 minutes. Adjust for altitude (page 40), if necessary.

Handling Chile Peppers

· ·

The same oils that give chile peppers their heat and spice can cause skin irritation and burning. When preparing chiles for cooking, wear rubber gloves, especially when handling the really fiery peppers, such as jalapeños and habaneros. And always keep your hands away from your eyes, nose, and mouth.

If you cannot wear gloves, try coating your hands with cooking oil, which can provide a protective shield.

If you do suffer from contact with chiles, wash your hands with soap or soak the burning area in milk to relieve the irritation.

When you wash or immerse dried chiles, always start with cold water. Pouring hot water on dried chiles can create strong fumes that may irritate your eyes and nose.

YIELD: 2 PINTS (SIXTEEN 2-OUNCE SERVINGS)
NUTRITION PER SERVING

Calories 61		Total fat 4g	
% from fat	47	Saturated	1g
Carbohydrates	8g	Cholesterol	0mg
Fiber <1g		Sodium 202mg	

Easy Tomato Ketchup

· · · · · · · · · · · ·

This recipe eliminates the need for grinding the tomatoes.
Not only is it easy, but it is also fresh and delicious.

Boiling-water-bath canner; two 1-pint jars

24	medium-sized tomatoes, about 8 pounds
1	medium onion, chopped
1	cup sugar
1	cup distilled white vinegar
4	teaspoons salt
2	tablespoons dry mustard
1½	inches cinnamon stick
1½	teaspoons whole cloves
1	teaspoon celery seed
¼	teaspoon cayenne pepper

· ·

YIELD: 2 PINTS (THIRTY-TWO 1-OUNCE SERVINGS)
NUTRITION PER SERVING

Calories 30		Total fat <1g	
% from fat	4	Saturated	0g
Carbohydrates	7g	Cholesterol	0g
Fiber <1g		Sodium 267mg	

· ·

1. Wash the tomatoes, then dip them in boiling water for 60 seconds, until the skins split. Transfer to cold water, then slip off the skins. Core and quarter them. Squeeze out some of the seeds and juice and discard. This prevents the ketchup from being too runny.

2. Process the tomatoes and onion in a food processor.

3. Simmer the mixture in a heavy kettle until it is reduced by half. (Or you may cook the mixture in the oven at 375°F, which can help prevent burning.) Stir frequently and watch the pot! This will take 1–2 hours.

4. Add the sugar, vinegar, salt, and spices tied in a cheesecloth bag; continue boiling until the sauce "rounds up" on a spoon. There will be no separation of liquids.

5. Remove and discard the spice bag.

6. Fill clean, hot jars. Cap and seal, leaving ⅛ inch of headspace.

7. Process in a boiling-water-bath canner for 15 minutes. Adjust for altitude (page 40), if necessary.

Barbecue Sauce

. . . .

Delicious with pork or beef, this barbecue sauce, adapted from the Ball Blue Book, *should be a staple for your pantry shelf.*

Boiling-water-bath canner; four 1-pint jars

24 large red-ripe tomatoes

3 stalks celery, chopped

2 medium onions, chopped

2 medium red bell peppers, chopped

1 teaspoon whole, black peppercorns

1 cup firmly packed brown sugar

1 cup distilled white vinegar

2 hot serrano chiles, seeded and chopped (wear rubber gloves*)

2 cloves garlic, minced

1 tablespoon dry mustard

1 tablespoon paprika

1 tablespoon salt

1 teaspoon hot pepper sauce

1/8 teaspoon cayenne pepper

*Use rubber gloves to prevent burning hands when cutting any chile. Don't touch your eyes or face after handling chiles. The hot oils on your hands will cause your eyes and face to burn as well. See page 57.

1. Blanch the tomatoes by plunging them into boiling water for 1 minute, then rinse with cold water. Remove the skins, then core and chop the tomatoes.

2. Put the tomatoes, celery, onions, and bell peppers in a large saucepan. Cook until the vegetables are soft, about 30 minutes.

3. Press through a fine sieve or food mill and return to the pan. Continue cooking over low heat until the mixture is reduced by about one-half, about 45 minutes. Stir often and be careful not to burn.

4. Tie the peppercorns in a cheesecloth bag; add with remaining ingredients and cook slowly until the mixture is the consistency of ketchup, about 1½ hours. As the mixture thickens, stir frequently to prevent sticking. Remove the spice bag. Pour into hot jars, leaving ¼ inch of headspace.

5. Adjust the caps. Process in a boiling-water-bath canner for 20 minutes.

. . . .
YIELD: 4 PINTS (THIRTY-TWO 2-OUNCE SERVINGS)
NUTRITION PER SERVING

Calories 61		Total fat <1g	
% from fat	3	Saturated	0g
Carbohydrates	15g	Cholesterol	0mg
Fiber 2g		Sodium 215mg	

. . . .

Chile Sauce

· · · · · · · · · · · ·

This recipe is adapted from the Ball Blue Book. Watch it disappear when served with burgers, or add it to sautéed hamburger along with several varieties of canned beans for an appetite-provoking chili.

Boiling-water-bath canner; six 1-pint jars

24 large red-ripe tomatoes

3 medium onions, chopped

4 medium red bell peppers, seeded and chopped

2 jalapeño chiles, seeded and finely chopped (wear rubber gloves; see page 57)

1 cup sugar

3 tablespoons salt

3 tablespoons mixed pickling spice

1 tablespoon celery seed

1 tablespoon mustard seed

2½ cups distilled white vinegar

1. Combine the tomatoes, onions, bell peppers, jalapeños, sugar, and salt in a large saucepan. Cook over a low flame for 45 minutes.

2. Tie the spices in a cheesecloth bag and add to the tomato mixture. Cook until the mixture is reduced by one-half, about 45 minutes. As the mixture thickens, stir frequently to prevent sticking.

3. Add the vinegar and cook slowly until desired thickness. Remove the spice bag.

4. Pour into hot jars, leaving ¼ inch of headspace. Adjust the caps. Process for 15 minutes in a boiling-water-bath canner. Adjust for altitude (page 40), if necessary.

· ·

YIELD: 6 PINTS (FORTY-EIGHT 2-OUNCE SERVINGS)
NUTRITION PER SERVING

Calories 41		Total fat	<1g	
% from fat	9	Saturated		<1g
Carbohydrates	10g	Cholesterol		0mg
Fiber 1g		Sodium	407mg	

· ·

Cabbage Borscht

This soup makes a meal that is hearty and low in calories. It can be served either hot or cold, with just a dollop of sour cream.

Pressure canner; four 1-quart jars

- 5 pounds tomatoes, washed, peeled, cored, and quartered

- 8 cups red cabbage, coarsely shredded

- 6 cups water

- 4 medium onions, chopped (about 4 cups)

- 3 small tart apples, peeled and sliced

- 2 tablespoons instant beef bouillon granules (or substitute 2 all-natural vegetable cubes available at health food stores)

- 2 tablespoons lemon juice

- 1 teaspoon salt

- Freshly ground black pepper to taste

Shred the cabbage coarsely.

1. Combine all the ingredients in a Dutch oven and gently boil uncovered for 5 minutes.

2. Ladle the hot soup into hot, clean jars, leaving 1 inch of headspace.

3. Cap and seal the jars and process for 75 minutes in a pressure canner. If you're using a dial gauge canner, process at 11 pounds of pressure. If you're using a weighted gauge canner, process at 10 pounds of pressure. Adjust for altitude (page 40), if necessary.

YIELD: 4 QUARTS (SIXTEEN 1-CUP SERVINGS)
NUTRITION PER SERVING

Calories 39		Total fat	<1g
% from fat	4	Saturated	0g
Carbohydrates	9g	Cholesterol	0mg
Fiber 2g		Sodium	510mg

Tomato Sauce

With this sauce on your shelf, you will be a wealthy homemaker. Add sautéed meat, if you wish, or serve it over summer squash topped with cheese or baked chicken.

Pressure canner; ten 1-pint jars or five 1-quart jars

30 pounds farm-ripe tomatoes (½ bushel), peeled, cored, and quartered

2 tablespoons olive oil

1 pound mushrooms, sliced

2 medium onions, chopped (about 1 cup)

2 stalks celery, chopped

4 cloves garlic, minced

½ cup firmly packed brown sugar

2 tablespoons dried basil

2 tablespoons dried oregano

2 tablespoons dried parsley flakes

2 bay leaves

YIELD: 10 PINTS OR 5 QUARTS (TWENTY 1-CUP SERVINGS)

NUTRITION PER SERVING

Calories 179		Total fat 4g	
% from fat	16	Saturated	<1g
Carbohydrates	37g	Cholesterol	0mg
Fiber 8g		Sodium 63mg	

1. In a heavy 16-quart nonreactive saucepan, bring the tomatoes to a boil, stirring often. Reduce the heat and simmer, uncovered, for 20 minutes, stirring often. Process the tomatoes through a food mill and return to the pan.

2. Heat the oil in a heavy skillet; add the mushrooms, onions, celery, and garlic. Sauté, stirring often, until soft, about 8–10 minutes.

3. Add the sugar, herbs, and mushroom mixture to the tomatoes and simmer uncovered until the sauce is thick. Stir often and be careful not to burn the sauce. This will take about 4–6 hours. Remove the bay leaves before canning. You may simplify this process by placing the pot uncovered on the bottom rack of a 350°F oven for several hours. Remove and stir every 30 minutes to prevent sticking.

4. Fill clean, hot jars, leaving 1 inch of headspace, then cap and process. If you are using a dial gauge canner, process at 11 pounds of pressure. If you're using a weighted gauge canner, process at 10 pounds of pressure. If you can this recipe in pint jars, process for 30 minutes. If you can it in quart jars, process for 35 minutes. Adjust for altitude (page 40), if necessary.

Spaghetti Sauce with Meat

No pantry should be without this recipe, adapted from the USDA. A great standby, this sauce requires a very big saucepan and rewards with more than a gallon of sauce.

Pressure canner; nine 1-pint jars

30 pounds tomatoes

2½ pounds ground beef

 1 pound fresh mushrooms, sliced

 2 medium onions, chopped (1 cup)

 2 stalks celery, chopped, or 1 large green pepper, chopped (1 cup)

 5 cloves garlic, minced

¼ cup brown sugar

 4 tablespoons minced fresh parsley

 2 tablespoons fresh oregano

4½ teaspoons salt

 2 teaspoons freshly ground black pepper

Do not change the amounts or ratio of peppers, onions, and mushrooms in this recipe, as it may change the final product regarding acidity, canning safety, and taste.

1. Dip the tomatoes in boiling water for 30–60 seconds. Plunge into cold water and slip off the skins. Core and quarter.

2. In a very large saucepan, boil the tomatoes, uncovered, for 20 minutes.

3. Meanwhile, sauté the beef until brown. Add the mushrooms, onions, celery, and garlic. Cook until the vegetables are tender.

4. Add the beef mixture to the cooked tomatoes. Stir in the sugar, herbs, salt, and pepper. Bring to a boil.

5. Reduce the heat and simmer, uncovered, until thick enough for serving. At this time, the initial volume will have been reduced to approximately one-half. Stir frequently to avoid burning.

6. Fill the jars, leaving 1 inch of headspace.

7. Adjust the lids and process in a pressure canner for 60 minutes. If you are using a dial gauge canner, process at 11 pounds of pressure. If you're using a weighted gauge canner, process at 10 pounds of pressure.

YIELD: 9 PINTS (EIGHTEEN 1-CUP SERVINGS)
NUTRITION PER SERVING

Calories 401		Total fat 18g	
% from fat	38	Saturated	7g
Carbohydrates	50g	Cholesterol	54mg
Fiber 8g		Sodium 645mg	

Mother's Chicken à la King

Childhood memories of great comfort food include this recipe. In the 1940s, it was made with heavy cream! Try adding a can of drained sliced mushrooms at serving time for a special treat.

Pressure canner; two 1-quart jars

- 1 stewing chicken (7 pounds)
- 6 stalks celery, coarsely chopped
- 1 carrot, peeled and cut into 1-inch chunks
- 1 medium onion, chopped
- 2 teaspoons salt
- 2 bay leaves
- 6 whole black peppercorns
- 2 whole allspice
- ¼ cup butter or margarine
- ½ cup flour
- ½ red bell pepper, seeded and chopped
- 1 tablespoon chopped fresh parsley
- ½ teaspoon salt

1. Place the chicken, 2 stalks of the celery, and the carrot, onion, salt, bay leaves, peppercorns, and allspice in a stewpan. Add water to cover. Cover and simmer for 2½ hours. Turn off the heat and allow the chicken to cool in the broth.

2. Defat the broth. Remove the chicken from the bone and cube. Strain the broth.

3. Melt the butter and add the flour, stirring until smooth. Cook for 3 minutes. Slowly pour in 5 cups of the chicken broth, stirring until it begins to thicken. If there is any broth left over, freeze it for another use. Add the chicken cubes, remaining celery, and the red pepper, parsley, and salt. Simmer for 3–5 minutes.

4. Ladle into hot, clean jars. Allow 1 inch of headspace. Can and seal.

5. Process in a pressure canner for 75 minutes at 10 pounds of pressure. Adjust for altitude (page 40), if necessary.

YIELD: 2 QUARTS (SIXTEEN ½-CUP SERVINGS)
NUTRITION PER SERVING

Calories 792		Total fat 59g	
% from fat	67	Saturated	19g
Carbohydrates	15g	Cholesterol	250mg
Fiber 3g		Sodium 946mg	

Chili con Carne

. . . .

*A great one-dish meal to stock in your pantry, this modified USDA classic
is tried and true.*

Pressure canner; nine 1-pint jars

3 cups dried pinto beans or dried red kidney beans, rinsed and picked over

5½ cups water

5 teaspoons salt

3 pounds ground beef

3 medium onions, chopped

1 large green bell pepper, chopped (about 1 cup)

2 quarts crushed or whole tomatoes (15–18 medium tomatoes, about 5 pounds)

3 tablespoons chili powder

1 teaspoon freshly ground black pepper

1. Place the beans in a 2-quart saucepan. Add cold water to a level of 2–3 inches above the beans and soak 12–18 hours. Drain and discard the water.

2. Combine the beans with the fresh water and 2 teaspoons of the salt. Bring to a boil. Reduce the heat and simmer for 30 minutes. Drain and discard the water.

3. Brown the beef, onions, and bell pepper in a skillet. Drain off the fat and add the tomatoes, remaining salt, chili powder, pepper, and drained cooked beans.

4. Simmer for 5 minutes. Adjust the seasonings.

5. Fill the jars, leaving 1 inch of headspace. Adjust the lids.

6. Process in a pressure canner for 75 minutes. If you're using a dial gauge canner, process at 11 pounds of pressure. If you're using a weighted gauge canner, process at 10 pounds of pressure. Adjust for altitude (page 40), if necessary.

. . . .

YIELD: **9 PINTS (EIGHTEEN 1-CUP SERVINGS)**
NUTRITION PER SERVING

Calories 377		Total fat 21g	
% from fat	50	Saturated	8g
Carbohydrates	28g	Cholesterol	64mg
Fiber 10g		Sodium 670mg	

. . . .

Vegetable Beef Stew

This adaptation of old-fashioned beef stew from the Ball Blue Book *is difficult to improve! It is very easy and* delicious.

Pressure canner; seven 1-quart jars

4 pounds stew beef, cubed

2 teaspoons vegetable oil

16 small carrots, scrubbed and sliced

12 small potatoes, peeled and cubed

5 stalks celery, chopped

3 medium onions, chopped

1 teaspoon dried thyme

½ teaspoon salt

Freshly ground black pepper

1. In a large saucepan, brown the meat in the oil.

2. Add the vegetables and seasonings.

3. Cover with boiling water and ladle into hot, clean jars, leaving 1 inch of headspace.

4. Process in a pressure canner for 75 minutes at 10 pounds of pressure. Adjust for altitude (page 40), if necessary.

YIELD: **7 QUARTS (TWENTY-EIGHT 1-CUP SERVINGS)**
NUTRITION PER SERVING

Calories 226		Total fat 6g	
% from fat	24	Saturated	2g
Carbohydrates	26g	Cholesterol	36mg
Fiber 3g		Sodium 102mg	

Spicy Asparagus

*Wrap a crêpe around these tangy asparagus pieces, or add them
to your favorite green salad.*

**Boiling-water-bath canner;
fourteen 1-quart jars**

28 pounds asparagus, washed, trimmed,
  and cut evenly to fit into a 1-quart jar

3 quarts white wine vinegar

1 quart water

2 tablespoons sugar

Per Quart

¼ cup olive oil

½ teaspoon salt

¼ teaspoon celery seed

¼ teaspoon freshly ground black pepper

¼ teaspoon dried tarragon

⅛ teaspoon dried thyme

1. Blanch the asparagus in boiling water,
4 pounds at a time, for about 5 minutes,
then drain.

2. Bring the vinegar, water, and sugar to
a boil.

3. Fill the hot, clean jars with the oil
and herbs.

4. Evenly divide the asparagus into the
jars and pour the hot vinegar mixture into
each, leaving 1 inch of headspace. Wipe any
traces of oil from the rim and adjust the lids.

5. Process in a boiling-water-bath canner
for 30 minutes. Adjust for altitude (page
40), if necessary.

*If your asparagus are mature and fibrous, peel
from the stem end to make them more tender.*

**Yield: 14 quarts (one hundred twelve
½-cup servings)**
Nutrition per Serving

Calories	79	Total fat	7g
% from fat	72	Saturated	<1g
Carbohydrates	5g	Cholesterol	0mg
Fiber	1g	Sodium	135mg

Pungent Green Beans

*Serve these surprising beans as a garnish for your favorite salad
or as a side dish for pork.*

Boiling-water-bath canner; five 1-pint jars

- 3 pounds green beans, washed and trimmed
- ⅓ cup olive oil
- 1 large onion, minced
- 3 cloves garlic, minced
- 4 cups water
- 3 cups white wine vinegar
- ¾ cup sugar
- 1 tablespoon celery salt
- 2 teaspoons salt
- 1 teaspoon pepper

1. Cut the beans to a uniform size. I like to cut them into pieces about 2½ inches long, but the length is a matter of personal preference.

2. Cook the beans in boiling salted water until tender, about 5–6 minutes.

3. In a large saucepan, heat the oil and sauté the onion and garlic until soft.

4. Add the water, vinegar, sugar, celery salt, salt, and pepper to the onion mixture and boil until the sugar has dissolved.

5. Add the beans and boil in the vinegar mixture for 2 minutes.

6. Ladle into hot, clean jars, leaving ½ inch of headspace.

7. Seal and process in a boiling-water-bath canner for 15 minutes. Adjust for altitude (page 40), if necessary.

YIELD: 5 PINTS (TWENTY ½-CUP SERVINGS)
NUTRITION PER SERVING

Calories 89		Total fat 4g	
% from fat	34	Saturated	<1g
Carbohydrates	15g	Cholesterol	0mg
Fiber 2g		Sodium 457mg	

Carrots in Honey and Vinegar

Tender but crunchy, these carrots will be hard to resist as a side dish or as an hors d'oeuvre. Leaving a few inches of green tops makes a lovely presentation in the jar.

Boiling-water-bath canner; two 1-pint jars

1 pound small carrots

1 cup white wine vinegar

1 cup water

2 tablespoons plus 2 teaspoons honey

2 teaspoons pickling salt

¼ teaspoon pepper

4 sprigs fresh dill

1. Scrub the carrots and trim their green tops, leaving about 3 inches, if desired. Remove the root end. Blanch in boiling water for 2 minutes and drain well.

2. Combine the vinegar, water, honey, salt, and pepper in a nonreactive saucepan and boil until the honey has dissolved.

3. Evenly divide the carrots into hot, clean jars, wedging the carrots in and stacking some upside down.

4. Fill the jars with the hot liquid, leaving ½ inch of headspace.

5. Add 2 sprigs of dill to each jar. Cap and seal.

6. Process for 30 minutes in a boiling-water-bath canner. Let the flavors marry for 2 weeks before using. Adjust for altitude (page 40), if necessary.

Note: Widemouthed jars work well for this recipe.

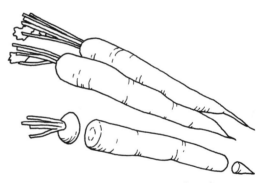

You can cut off both the root end and the green tops of the carrots or leave about 3 inches of green tops for show.

YIELD: 2 PINTS (EIGHT ½-CUP SERVINGS)
NUTRITION PER SERVING

Calories 48		Total fat <1g	
% from fat	2	Saturated	0g
Carbohydrates	13g	Cholesterol	0mg
Fiber	2g	Sodium	552mg

Stewed Tomatoes

Use these tomatoes as a soup or sauce base, or serve them alone thickened with cornstarch and an added tablespoon of butter for richness.

Pressure canner; seven 1-pint jars

- 24 large ripe tomatoes, cored and quartered
- 2 stalks celery, chopped
- 1 medium onion, chopped
- ¼ cup chopped green pepper (about ½ pepper)
- 1 tablespoon sugar
- 2 teaspoons salt

1. Combine all the ingredients in a large saucepan.

2. Cover and simmer for 10 minutes, stirring frequently.

3. Uncover the pan and, using a fork, fish out the tomato skins.

4. Ladle the mixture into hot, clean jars, leaving ½ inch of headspace. Cap and seal.

5. Process in a pressure canner for 20 minutes at 10 pounds of pressure. Adjust for altitude (page 40), if necessary.

YIELD: 7 PINTS (TWENTY-EIGHT ½-CUP SERVINGS)
NUTRITION PER SERVING

Calories	29	Total fat	<1g
% from fat	10	Saturated	0g
Carbohydrates	7g	Cholesterol	0mg
Fiber	1g	Sodium	165mg

Marinated Mushrooms

Serve this spicy side dish, adapted from a USDA recipe, with chicken, beef, or pork or as an hors d'oeuvre.

Boiling-water-bath canner; nine ½-pint jars

7 pounds small, whole, very fresh white mushrooms

½ cup bottled lemon juice, or the juice of about 4 medium lemons

2½ cups white wine vinegar

2 cups olive oil

1 tablespoon dried oregano

1 tablespoon canning or pickling salt

½ cup finely chopped onions

25 whole black peppercorns

2 cloves garlic, quartered

1. Wash the mushrooms and cut the stems short. Place in a saucepan and add the lemon juice and enough water to cover.

2. Bring to a boil and simmer for 5 minutes. Drain well.

3. Mix the vinegar, olive oil, oregano, and salt in a saucepan.

4. Add the onions and heat to boiling.

5. Divide the peppercorns and garlic quarters among the jars.

6. Fill the jars with mushrooms. Add the hot oil-and-vinegar solution to each jar, leaving ½ inch of headspace. Wipe any traces of oil from the rim. Cap and seal.

7. Process in a boiling-water-bath canner for 20 minutes. Adjust for altitude (page 40), if necessary.

YIELD: NINE ½-PINTS (EIGHTEEN ½-CUP SERVINGS)
NUTRITION PER SERVING

Calories 289		Total fat 25g	
% from fat	72	Saturated	3g
Carbohydrates	17g	Cholesterol	0mg
Fiber 5g		Sodium 368 mg	

Mixed Vegetables

. . . .

These vegetables are not just pretty to look at — they're also versatile and tasty.

Pressure canner; seven 1-quart jars

- 6 cups sliced carrots (2 pounds, or 12–14 medium carrots)
- 6 cups cut green beans (3½ pounds)
- 6 cups shelled lima beans (6 pounds)
- 6 cups sliced okra (2 pounds)
- 4 cups crushed tomatoes (2⅓ pounds)
- 4 cups diced zucchini (2 pounds)

PER QUART

- 1 slice onion
- 1 teaspoon salt

1. Wash and prepare the vegetables. Place them in a large pot and cover with water. Boil for 5 minutes.

2. Place an onion slice and the salt in each jar.

3. Ladle the hot vegetables and liquid into the jars, leaving 1 inch of headspace. Cap and seal.

4. Process in a pressure canner for 90 minutes. If you're using a dial gauge canner, process at 11 pounds of pressure. If you're using a weighted gauge canner, process at 10 pounds of pressure. Adjust for altitude (page 40), if necessary.

. . . .

YIELD: **7** QUARTS (FIFTY-SIX ½-CUP SERVINGS)
NUTRITION PER SERVING

Calories 88		Total fat <1g	
% from fat	2	Saturated	0g
Carbohydrates	17g	Cholesterol	0mg
Fiber 5g		Sodium 277mg	

. . . .

Pineapple Spears

Packed in a special honey syrup, these pineapple spears are a treat you won't find in the supermarket. Use them to garnish your next pork roast, serve as a dessert, or give as a gift.

Boiling-water-bath canner; three 1-pint jars

2 pineapples, peeled, cored, and quartered

2 cups thin Honey Syrup Blend (see recipe on page 126)

1. Cut the pineapple pieces about 1 inch shorter than the pint jars, or about 5 inches long.

2. Combine the pineapple and the syrup in a heavy saucepan or a Dutch oven.

3. Boil for 7 minutes.

4. Divide the fruit evenly, pack in the jars, and cover with syrup, leaving ½ inch of headspace. Cap and seal.

5. Process in a boiling-water-bath canner for 30 minutes. Adjust for altitude (page 40), if necessary.

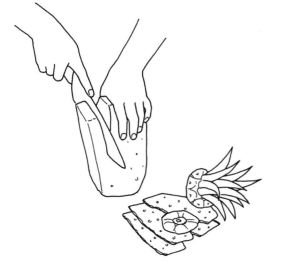

Core the pineapple by making the indicated cuts. Then slice the pineapple into spears.

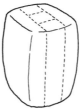

YIELD: 3 PINTS (TWELVE ½-CUP SERVINGS)
NUTRITION PER SERVING

Calories 100		Total fat <1g	
% from fat	5	Saturated	0g
Carbohydrates	26g	Cholesterol	0mg
Fiber 2g		Sodium 3mg	

Orange Syrup

Use this over buttermilk pancakes. Sprinkle fresh blueberries on top for Sunday brunch. Or drizzle the syrup over an angel food cake and decorate it with the blueberries or orange slices for a nonfat dessert.

Boiling-water-bath canner; four 1-pint jars

Zest of 6 oranges, such as Valencia, cut into strips

4⅓ cups water

4 cups sugar

2½ cups fresh orange juice from oranges above, strained

2 tablespoons citric acid

1. Cook the orange zest, water, and sugar until the sugar dissolves, stirring constantly. Boil for 3 minutes.

2. Remove from the heat and cool. Strain through several layers of cheesecloth lining a strainer.

3. Add the strained orange juice and citric acid. Mix well.

4. Reheat the syrup and pour into hot, clean 1-pint jars, leaving ½ inch of headspace. Clean the jar rims, cap, and seal.

5. Process in a boiling-water-bath canner for 30 minutes. Adjust for altitude (page 40), if necessary.

Note: Syrup will keep for 10 days unprocessed in the refrigerator.

YIELD: 4 PINTS (SIXTEEN ½-CUP SERVINGS)
NUTRITION PER SERVING

Calories	213	Total fat	<1g	
% from fat	<1	Saturated	0g	
Carbohydrates	55g	Cholesterol	0mg	
Fiber	<1g	Sodium	3mg	

Apple Pie Filling

When apples are abundant, this adapted USDA recipe fills a real need. You'll be glad you planned ahead the first time you open a jar of this filling. This recipe makes enough filling for seven pies.

Boiling-water-bath canner; seven 1-quart jars

- 6 quarts fresh tart apples (use firm, crisp apples)
- 1 teaspoon ascorbic acid, or six 500 mg vitamin C tablets
- 5½ cups sugar
- 1½ cups ClearJel (see page 16)
- 1 tablespoon cinnamon
- 1 teaspoon nutmeg
- 5 cups apple juice
- 2½ cups cold water
- ¾ cup bottled lemon juice, or the juice of 6 medium lemons

1. Wash, peel, and core the apples. Cut slices ½ inch thick. Bring to a boil 1 gallon of water containing the ascorbic acid to prevent browning.

2. Place 6 cups of fruit at a time in the boiling water.

3. Cook each batch 1 minute after the water returns to a boil. Drain, but keep fruit heated in a covered bowl or pot.

4. Combine the sugar, ClearJel, cinnamon, and nutmeg in a large kettle; stir in the apple juice and water. Stir and cook over medium-high heat until the mixture thickens and begins to bubble.

5. Add the lemon juice and boil for 1 minute, stirring constantly.

6. Fold in the drained apple slices and fill the jars immediately, leaving 1 inch of headspace. Cap and seal.

7. Process in a boiling-water-bath canner for 25 minutes. Adjust for altitude (page 40), if necessary.

TIP

Pie fillings may be canned without ClearJel. To use, drain fruit in a colander set over a measuring cup. Place fruit in pie shell. Stir 2 tablespoons of corn starch per cup of liquid into the collected liquid and pour over the fruit. Finish and bake the pie.

YIELD: 7 QUARTS (FIFTY-SIX ½-CUP SERVINGS)
NUTRITION PER SERVING

Calories 131		Total fat <1g	
% from fat	1	Saturated	0g
Carbohydrates	33g	Cholesterol	0mg
Fiber 1g		Sodium 3mg	

Peach Pie Filling

This version of a USDA favorite can't be beat.

Boiling-water-bath canner; seven 1-quart jars

6   quarts fresh peaches (44–48 medium peaches, about 11 pounds), peeled and sliced

1   teaspoon ascorbic acid

7   cups sugar

2   cups plus 3 tablespoons ClearJel (see page 16)

1   teaspoon cinnamon

5¼ cups cold water

1   teaspoon almond extract

1¾ cups bottled lemon juice, or the juice of about 14 medium lemons

1. Place the peaches in 1 gallon of water containing the ascorbic acid to prevent browning.

2. Place 6 cups of fruit at a time in the boiling water.

3. Boil each batch for 1 minute after the water returns to a boil. Drain, but keep fruit hot in a covered bowl or pot.

4. Combine the sugar, ClearJel, and cinnamon in a large kettle. Stir in the water and almond extract. Stir and cook over medium-high heat until the mixture thickens and begins to bubble.

5. Add the lemon juice and boil for 1 minute, stirring constantly.

6. Fold in drained peach slices and continue to heat the mixture for 3 minutes.

7. Fill the jars immediately, leaving 1 inch of headspace. Cap and seal.

8. Process in a boiling-water-bath canner for 30 minutes. Adjust for altitude (page 40), if necessary.

Note: This recipe makes enough filling for seven pies.

YIELD: 7 QUARTS (FIFTY-SIX ½-CUP SERVINGS)

NUTRITION PER SERVING

Calories 155		Total fat <1g	
% from fat	<1	Saturated	0g
Carbohydrates	39g	Cholesterol	0mg
Fiber 1g		Sodium 3mg	

Peeling Peaches

To peel peaches easily, submerge them in boiling water for 30–60 seconds. Immediately plunge them in cold water for 20 seconds. Slip off the skins with a knife and your fingers. This also works with apricots.

Cherry Pie Filling

*A tried-and-true favorite, this recipe continues to be good
as well as dependable. It is adapted from the USDA.*

**Boiling-water-bath canner; two 1-pint jars
or one 1-quart jar**

3⅓ cups fresh sour cherries or
unsweetened frozen sour cherries

1 teaspoon ascorbic acid

1 cup sugar

¼ cup plus 1 tablespoon ClearJel (see
page 16)

1⅓ cups cold water

¼ teaspoon almond extract

⅛ teaspoon cinnamon

6 drops all-natural red food coloring
(optional)

1 tablespoon plus 1 teaspoon fresh
lemon juice

1. Wash and pit the cherries and place in
1 gallon of water containing the ascorbic
acid to prevent darkening. If using frozen
sweetened cherries, wash off the syrup.

2. Place the cherries in boiling water. Boil
for 1 minute after the water returns to a
boil. Drain, but keep the fruit hot and
covered.

3. Combine the sugar and ClearJel in a
large saucepan; stir in the water.

4. Add the almond extract, cinnamon,
and food coloring, if using. Stir over
medium heat until the mixture thickens.

5. Add the lemon juice and boil the
mixture for 1 minute, stirring constantly.

6. Fold in the cherries.

7. Fill jars with the hot fruit mixture,
leaving 1 inch of headspace. Cap and seal.

8. Process in a boiling-water-bath canner
for 30 minutes. Adjust for altitude (page
40), if necessary.

Note: This recipe makes enough filling for one pie.

YIELD: 1 QUART (EIGHT ½-CUP SERVINGS)
NUTRITION PER SERVING

Calories 158		Total fat <1g	
% from fat	2	Saturated	<1g
Carbohydrates	38g	Cholesterol	0mg
Fiber 1g		Sodium 4mg	

CHAPTER 3

Drying

WHILE CANNED FOODS SHINE with vivid colors that are beautiful to look at, dried foods are less glamorous but no less edible. Dried foods do have advantages. The reconstituted product can be quite tasty and convenient to use, and it contains more nutrients than canned foods.

Drying was one of the earliest methods of food preservation humans found to save food from times of bounty to use when food was scarce. As far back as prebiblical times, fishermen dried and smoked fish, and farmers dried olives and dates in the hot, dry climate of the Middle East.

Drying is by far the simplest and most natural way of preserving food. Little equipment is needed, but climate is everything. If you are fortunate enough to live in a warm, dry region, all you need is fresh food and a little time. The faster food can dry without actually cooking, the better its flavor will be when it's reconstituted. If you live in a relatively moist climate, you will want to learn to use one of the more active drying methods — a dehydrator, your oven, or, in some cases, the sun. As always, the finished product can be only as good as the original, so start with the very best fresh food.

The concept of drying food is quite simple. When all the moisture is removed from food, the growth of organisms that spoil food is stopped. Bacteria, molds, and yeasts can be supported only in an environment that has adequate water in which to grow. Properly dried fruits have about 80 percent of the water removed, and properly dried vegetables have about 90 percent of the water removed. Thus, you can count on keeping your home-dried foods for about six months to two years, depending on the storage temperature. (See charts on page 86.) Remember that cooler storage temperatures are better. Food kept at 70°F does not keep as long as food stored at 52°F.

Food Preparation for Drying

Use only blemish-free perfect fruits and vegetables. Fruit should be *fully* ripe but not *overly* ripe. Save overly ripe fruit for sauces or for making fruit leathers (see pages 88–89). The smaller the piece of food, the less time it will take to dry properly. Try to keep all the pieces about the same size so each piece will dry at the same rate.

Blanching

Proper blanching, which heats the food without actually cooking it, inactivates the enzymes that cause food spoilage. For use in the drying process, steam blanching is the only method recommended for vegetables.

The method of dipping produce in boiling water, used in many areas of the world, is not recommended because it adds more water to the produce and therefore increases drying time. Because the food is heated longer and hotter, it also robs the food of nutrients and does not fully protect the produce from spoilage organisms. If you must boil fruits or vegetables, use about 3 gallons of water for every 1 quart of food, then drain and chill the pieces in ice water to stop the cooking and pat dry.

To blanch using the steam method, use a steamer, a large Dutch oven, or a canner with the lid. Use a wire basket with legs, a basket that fits in the top of

TIP

• • • • • • • •

Never use a microwave for drying food. However, you *can* use the microwave for blanching before drying. If you try to use a microwave oven to dry your food, you'll find that your food will be cooked before it can dry.

TIP

• • • • • • • •

A pretreatment, such as steam blanching, is optional for fruits that are to be dried; for vegetables, it is absolutely necessary.

Steam blanch produce before drying.

Cool blanched produce in ice water.

Dry blanched produce on towels.

the pot, or a colander that will allow 2 or more inches of water to boil without touching the produce. Steam 1 minute longer than the time given if you live 5,000 feet or more above sea level. (See chart on page 86 for steaming times.) After blanching, drain the food, then chill in ice water to stop the cooking. Drain again and dry on towels.

Blanching can be done in a microwave oven, but only in small quantities. Wattages vary, so consult the manufacturer's instructions.

OTHER PREPARATIONS FOR DRYING

To improve the chances of good color retention, dip the fruit slices in a prepared solution (see the dipping chart on the next page). This is, however, only partially effective. Steam blanching for both fruits and vegetables is still the best way to preserve color.

For decades, many people used sulfur to pretreat dried fruit to preserve color. Fruit pretreated with sulfur must be dried by the sun method. Sulfuring of fruits is not a good practice for use with a home dehydrator.

While sulfuring preserves the color and vitamin C of many fruits, it may cause serious problems for people with allergies or asthma. Sulfur is now banned as a preservative for produce in supermarkets and salad bars in restaurants.

FOUR TYPES OF DRYING

Drying meat and produce involves the simple process of exposing the food to mild heat and moving air. This can be done by placing food in the open air, in the sun, in a dehydrator, or in an oven.

AIR-DRYING

The process of air-drying is very similar to that of sun drying. Puffs of dry air circulate around the food and

Dipping

Dip/Use On	Ingredients	Time
Ascorbic acid/ all fruits	2 tablespoons ascorbic acid or five 1-gram crushed vitamin C tabs and 1 quart water	Dip for 5 minutes, drain well, pat dry
Honey/bananas peaches, pineapples	3 cups water, 1 cup sugar; heat, then add 1 cup honey; stir well	Dip and remove immediately in batches; drain well, pat dry
Juice/apples, bananas, peaches	1 quart pineapple juice, 1 quart lukewarm water, ¼ cup bottled lemon juice	Soak no longer than 5–10 minutes; drain well, pat dry
Pectin/berries, cherries, peaches	1 box powdered pectin, 1 cup water; boil together 1 minute, add ½ cup sugar and enough cold water to make 2 cups	Glaze fruit slices with thin coating; drain well, pat dry
Salt/all fruits	6 tablespoons pickling salt, 1 gallon water	Soak no longer than 5 minutes; drain, pat dry

absorb the moisture and carry it away. Keep the food out of direct sun to prevent loss of color.

Try air-drying steam-blanched green beans by stringing them on cotton thread and hanging them under the eaves of the house or porch or in a well-ventilated attic. Depending on conditions, in two or three days you will have dried, pliable "leather britches," which are great for adding to soups. Bring the beans inside at night to prevent dew from collecting on them. Keep them out of direct sun; it will make them lose all color.

To dry mushrooms, wipe them clean, string them with a needle and cotton thread, and hang in an airy location. Or place clean mushrooms on several thicknesses of paper towels. Turn them several times as the day progresses, and change the paper towels as moisture is absorbed. Place the mushrooms in a dry, airy spot (in the direct sun if you wish, but don't forget to bring them in at night). In one or two days the mushrooms will be almost brittle.

After the drying process, both green beans and mushrooms must be heated in a 175°F oven for 30 minutes to

String the mushrooms on cotton thread.

destroy insect eggs. Condition the produce (see Post-Drying Methods, page 84) and then store in a cool, dry place for up to 6 months.

Sun Drying

Because sun drying takes more time, pretreating the produce by blanching or other methods is much more important. The ideal temperature is about 100°F with low humidity — below 60 percent. If you have a climate like that, do try sun drying. In other climates, use caution. Low temperature and high humidity is the perfect combination for spoilage to occur before drying can be accomplished.

Sun-Drying Equipment

To make sun-drying equipment, I like to use old picture frames purchased from flea markets. First, clean the frames with a cloth dampened with soap and water. Then seal the frames with mineral oil. Stretch a clean, 100 percent cotton sheet or cheesecloth over the frames and secure with a staple gun. Some people use screens from their windows. This is fine, but don't use screens with galvanized wire, as it can impart "off" flavors to the food. Arrange the prepared produce on the cloth, then place the frames in direct sun, bracing them so that air can circulate on all sides. (Bring them in at night to prevent dew from collecting on them.)

Covering the food with a second screen or cheesecloth protects it from birds and insects. Turn the produce over halfway through the drying process (after about two days). Solar dryers improve on sun drying by using reflectants and air vents to increase temperature and circulation around the food. Things dry faster, reducing the possibility of mold or spoilage.

To destroy any pest eggs that may still be lurking in your homegrown foods, remove the produce from the frames and freeze it for 2 to 4 days at below 0°F, or heat it on a tray in your oven for 10 to 15 minutes at 175°F. (See Post-Drying Methods, page 84.) Whether you freeze or heat the produce,

Sun dry produce on a screen stretched over an old picture frame.

bring it to room temperature and then store it in airtight jars for up to 6 months.

DEHYDRATOR

Using a food dehydrator is simple: You fill the trays with prepared produce, set the timer, turn on the dehydrator, and go about your business. Although a commercial dehydrator can be expensive, it can pay for itself over several seasons. Comparison shopping is easiest on the Internet, since most commercial dehydrators are sold through mail order. Many of these companies have Web sites that can be accessed by searching "dehydrator" or "food drying." Request information before ordering. There are several features to consider before you buy.

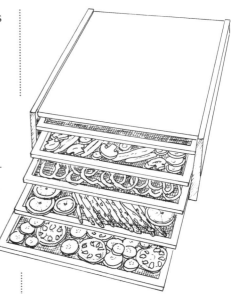

Commercial food dehydrators come in a variety of styles.

- The dehydrator should be approved for safety by Underwriters Laboratories (UL).
- Be sure you order a size that you can easily accommodate in your house and that will allow you to dry the right amount of produce or meat at a time.
- Trays should be lightweight and sturdy. Plastic screens are easier to clean and are better than metal. Metal screens can corrode, tend to retain the heat longer, and can scorch food.
- If your model has a door, make sure that it opens easily and can be completely removed.
- The controls should be easy to read. Control settings that adjust vents for airflow and regulate the heat are both important, and an automatice built-in timer is useful.
- The materials used on the outside cabinets vary greatly. Consider how easily you can move, clean, and store the cabinet.
- Look for a deydrator with double-walled insulation.
- Look for dehydrators that use less electricity.
- Check to see that consumer advice and repair service are easily available for the dehydrator you choose.

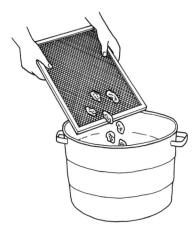

Pour sun-dried tomatoes into a large, open, nonreactive container.

Oven Drying

The most labor intensive of all the methods, oven drying is an effective (although possibly more expensive) process. In this method, place food directly on oven racks or cover the racks with clean, 100 percent cotton sheeting or cheesecloth.

Preheat your oven to 145°F. Using an oven thermometer, check the temperature periodically. Ovens vary, so you may need to experiment with a setting between 120 and 145°F. My gas oven dried produce best at 145°F. Use a wooden spoon to prop the door open to let the moisture escape. Be sure not to fill your oven too full, or the drying time will become quite long. Allow 4 to 12 hours, depending on the items and quantities being dried. Food should be dry but pliable when cool. (Test one or two pieces.)

While some authorities claim that it's possible to dry food in the microwave oven, I don't recommend it, because the microwave oven will cook your produce before it dries it. However, you can easily dry herbs in the microwave with good results.

Post-Drying Methods

After the food is dried, condition it by pouring it into a large open container, such as a big enameled canner pot. Don't use a container that is aluminum or that is porous because it might affect the flavor or consistency of the dried food. Put the pot in a warm but dry and airy place. For the next 10 to 14 days, stir it once or twice a day. Don't add newly dried food to the batch in the pot, as you want it all to finish drying at the same time.

Pasteurizing

Pasteurizing is the partial sterilization of food. Since outdoor drying and oven drying are less precise, pasteurizing dried food is recommended.

The longer you wish to keep the dried food, the more the need for pasteurizing increases. Pasteurizing ensures that insect eggs and the organisms that cause spoilage are destroyed, allowing food to be stored for longer periods.

There are two ways to pasteurize:

Heat. Spread the dried produce on trays in a thin layer and leave in a 175°F oven for 10 to 15 minutes. Cool.

Freeze. Using plastic storage bags, place dried produce in a 0°F freezer for 2 to 4 days. This destroys fewer vitamins than the oven method. The freezer *must* be at 0°F. A freezer compartment of a refrigerator will not do.

Packaging and Storing

Dried food should be packed promptly in a "user-friendly" quantity ready for meal preparation. Since light, moisture, and air are bad for dried foods, a cool, *dry,* dark place is best. (This does not necessarily mean the refrigerator, which is *moist* and dark.) Completely fill an airtight, clean glass container or a clean resealable plastic bag with all the air squeezed out. Put the jars or plastic bags inside a brown paper grocery bag to protect them from the light. Label the dried food carefully, making sure you date it properly. Always use the oldest package first. If summer's heat becomes a problem, switch to the refrigerator but make certain the packaging is absolutely airtight to guard against moisture.

Rehydrating

To rehydrate dried produce, just cover it with boiling water. Let the produce stand for several hours to absorb the water, then cook the produce in the soaking liquid that is left. Vegetables take longer to rehydrate than fruits because they lose more water to dehydration. The cooking time will be much shorter than that of produce not rehydrated before cooking. In the case of dried beans, drain the rehydrated beans and cook them in fresh water because the nitrogen released by the beans in the soaking water is difficult to digest. Cook until tender.

TIP
. . . .
Rehydrate produce early in the morning. When your day is over and it's time to cook dinner, your reconstituted produce will be ready to go.

Squeeze the air out of a packed resealable plastic bag from the bottom up.

Place the filled jars or plastic bags in a brown paper bag to protect the dried food from the light.

DRYING VEGETABLES AND FRUITS

BEST VEGETABLES/ FRUITS FOR DRYING	PREPARATION	PREFERRED PRETREATMENT METHOD
Vegetables		
Beans (green, wax, yellow)	trim or shell, string to air-dry	steam blanch 4–6 minutes
Beans (all others)	shell, pick over mature beans	steam blanch 5 minutes
Corn	shuck, cut kernels off after blanching	steam blanch whole 10–15 minutes
Mushrooms	wipe clean, string to air-dry or air-dry on paper	ascorbic dip or steam blanch for 3 minutes if not air-dry
Okra	slice	steam blanch 5 minutes
Peas	shell	steam blanch 3 minutes
Peppers (bell)	slice or chop	not necessary
Peppers (chile)	string whole, air-dry	not necessary
Tomatoes, Italian	slice in half lengthwise and remove seeds, air-dry	not necessary
Fruits*		
Apples	peel, core, slice	juice or ascorbic dip, or steam blanch 5 minutes
Apricots	slice, pit	juice or ascorbic dip, or steam blanch 5 minutes
Bananas	peel, slice	honey, juice, pectin, or ascorbic dip, or steam blanch 5 minutes
Berries: blackberry, blueberry, cranberry	drop in boiling water to burst	honey or pectin dip
Cherries	pit	pectin, juice, or ascorbic dip
Figs	remove stems	not necessary
Grapes	remove from stem	break skin
Peaches	peel, pit, slice, or halve	honey, pectin, juice, or ascorbic dip
Pears	peel, slice, or halve	ascorbic dip, or steam blanch 2 minutes
Plums/prunes	pit, halve, or leave whole	break skin
Strawberries	halve	honey dip

*All can be pretreated by blanching or dipping as indicated.

Oven or Electric Dehydrator (Hours)	Sun/Air (Days)	Final Consistency	1 Cup Dry=Cups When Cooked	Cooking Time (Minutes)	Storage Time at 52°F (Months)
12–14	2–3	leathery	2½	45	8–12
48	4–5	hard		120–180	8–12
8–12	1–2	dry, brittle	2	50	8–12
8–12	1–2	leathery	1¼	20–30	4–6
8–12	1–2	dry, brittle	1½	30–45	9–12
12–18	2–3	shriveled	2	40–45	8–12
12–18	1–2	leathery	1½	30–45	
not recomm.	2–3	shriveled	1½	use directly	16–24
6–8	1–2	pliable, leathery	1½	30	6–9
6–8	2–3	pliable, leathery	1¼	30	18–24
8–12	2–3	pliable, leathery	1½	30–45	24–32
6–8	2	brittle		not recommended	12–16
12–24	2–4	hard		not recommended	18–24
12–24	2–4	hard	1½	30–45	36–48
36–48	5–6	shriveled		not recommended	18–24
24–48	3–6	shriveled		not recommended	18–24
10–12	2–6	leathery	1¼	20–30	18–24
12–18	2–3	leathery	1½	20–30	18–24
12–18	4–5	shriveled	1½	20–30	24–32
8–12	1–2	hard		not recommended	18–24

TIP
. . . .

Making fruit leather is the perfect way to use up overly ripe fruit.

The Squeezo Strainer removes small seeds.

Spread the purée evenly over a lined cookie sheet.

FRUIT LEATHERS

Apples, bananas, peaches, and berries are perfect for fruit leathers. Many adventuresome people enjoy vegetable leathers as well. But the children's favorite, "fruit rolls" or "fruit taffy," as leathers are often called, have an incredible amount of concentrated natural sugar that frequently sticks to teeth. For that reason, dental health professionals suggest that teeth be cleaned soon after you eat this tasty treat. Leathers from cooked fruits have a very vibrant color.

Purée

The first step in making fruit leather is to pare and pit washed, ripe, raw fruit and process it through a food mill. I like the Squeezo Strainer and the VillaWare Strainer because they separate the small seeds and skins and leave you with a thick, rich purée. A blender or food processor can also be used for this. It may be necessary to add a small amount of liquid (juice or water will do) to reach a pouring consistency. There's no need to strain the fruit if a blender or processor is used. However, this is largely a matter of personal choice.

Another puréeing method, in which you cook the fruit, is to simmer clean, pared, and pitted fruit in a little water or juice for 10 to 15 minutes, or until the mixture is broken down. Make sure you've added enough liquid to prevent it from burning. Then process as described above in a food mill.

If you're using a food dehydrator to make your fruit leathers, follow the manufacturer's directions. To dehydrate your purée in the oven, use 10½-inch by 15½-inch standard cookie sheets with sides. Line each cookie sheet with plastic wrap or freezer paper and then pour about 2 to 2¼ cups of purée onto each one. You'll want the purée to be about ⅛ to ¼ inch thick. Place the cookie sheets in a 135°F oven for 8 to 10 hours. Use an oven thermometer and set the door ajar with a spoon handle to maintain low heat and let the moisture

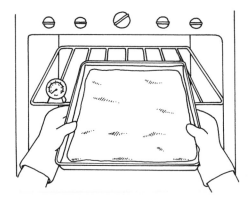

Use an oven thermometer to monitor the heat while dehydrating the purée.

Turn over the fruit leather and remove the old wrap.

escape. When the leather easily pulls away from the wrap after about 6 to 8 hours, turn over the leather onto another prepared sheet, peel off the old wrap, and continue drying in the oven for another 6 to 8 hours.

When it's done, remove the wrap and allow the leather to cool for several hours on a cake rack. Dust with cornstarch before rolling to prevent sticking. Roll the leather into a flute shape. Some people like to stack the layers, and with this method cornstarch dusting is a must. Store in an airtight container.

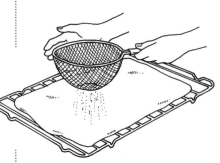

Dust the cooled leather with cornstarch to prevent sticking.

DRYING HERBS

Dried herbs have been used since ancient times as medicines to remedy common ailments, to improve the aroma of rooms, and to elevate the simplest dish to a masterpiece. New research suggests that many herbs may be useful in treating physical and psychological maladies. While the Food and Drug Administration prohibits manufacturers from unsubstantiated medical claims, more people are looking to herbs as a natural alternative to prescription medicine. Herbs are also being used more frequently for cosmetic purposes.

Cut herbs 6 to 8 inches from the base of the plant.

But by far the most common use of herbs is in the kitchen. Low in fat and calories, they enhance almost any part of the meal and can be used in all kinds of foods — even desserts. With health-conscious people looking for ways to perk up flavor without using salt or fat, herbs have come into their own. Because many herbs are so easy to grow, either in a kitchen garden or on a windowsill, cooks are relying on them to add zest to our diets.

Preserving herbs and using them in combination with other foods makes sense, and the process of preserving herbs by drying is simple. While they do not exactly impart the same flavor as fresh herbs, dried herbs are a staple on any kitchen shelf and can be relied upon to spark the flavor of any dish.

Be careful when substituting dried herbs in a recipe that calls for fresh herbs. Adjust the amounts accordingly. A good rule is that 1 teaspoon of chopped fresh herbs is equivalent to ¼ teaspoon of powdered dried herbs or ½ teaspoon of crushed dried herb leaves.

For other methods of herb preservation, see chapter 4 on freezing and chapter 7 on vinegars.

HARVESTING AND AIR-DRYING HERBS

Herbs should be harvested when their essential oils are at the highest level, usually right before flowering or bolting time when they form seeds. The best time of day to harvest them is *before* the hot sun wilts them but *after* the dew has evaporated. Cut them within 6 to 8 inches of the base of the plant. Some herbalists recommend not washing the leaves unless they are filled with grit or beaten down from rain, as washing depletes some of their essence.

To dry the cut herbs, tie small bunches of them together with garden twine and hang them with leaves pointed downward in an airy, warm, dry place that's not in direct sunlight. Gravity will force the essential oils down into the leaves.

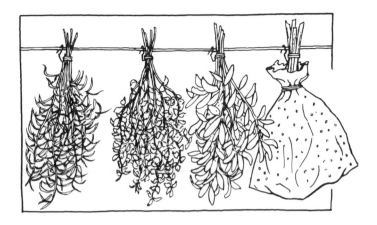

Hang herbs upside down to dry, which draws the essential oils down into the leaves.

Never hang herbs over the stove, refrigerator, or freezer. Heat from these appliances causes deterioration. Also, don't store your purchased herbs and spices in cabinets above these appliances. If you plan to use a dehydrator, consult the manufacturer's directions for drying herbs.

Before storing, test for remaining moisture. Put dried herbs, stems and all, in airtight containers in a warm place for a day or two. If there is moisture present on the *inside* of the container, it is better to return the herbs to the drying process. When the herb leaves are completely dry, put them on a tray in a warm oven for 2 to 3 minutes to further dry them. Strip the leaves from the stems. Store the leaves undisturbed in a cool place with no direct sun, ideally in a dark glass container and/or inside your kitchen cabinet. Crush the leaves between your hands for cooking as needed; the crushing releases the pungent flavors and aroma. A mortar and pestle can be used to grind the leaves into powder. Either way, deterioration sets in within 6 to 12 months, so plan on starting over with new batches the next season.

TIP

· · · · · · · · · ·

Try suspending the fresh herb bunch inside a brown paper bag — either the lunch bag size or the grocery bag size. Prepare the bag by using a hole punch in a decorative pattern to allow air to circulate through the bag. Gather and tie off the top of the bag, securing the herbs suspended upside down in the center. This method keeps dust off the drying herbs. Use colorful yarn for tying the bags, and stand them upright on a shelf in a warm, airy place. After a week or two, give the herbs as a gift, still in their brown bag, or use them yourself.

Crush the herbs between your hands for cooking.

DRYING 91

Oven-Dried Herbs

Start with herbs that are clean and, if washed, have been patted dry. Use a cookie sheet to spread the herbs in a single layer. Set the oven to about 140°F and heat the herbs for about 45 minutes. (This will not be exact, much like heating a room with a woodstove is not exact.) To allow the moisture to escape, prop the oven door ajar with a wooden spoon handle. Keep the temperature even by not opening the door farther to peek in too often. Better yet, use an oven thermometer to help you regulate the temperature. After 45 minutes, remove the herbs from the oven and let them cool and then stand for about 12 hours (or overnight). To check for moisture, try the prestorage method of closing the dried, cooked herbs in a glass jar for 24 hours (see page 91). If moisture appears on the inside of the glass, return the herbs to the oven briefly. When they are completely dry, store in a cool, dark place in an airtight container.

Store dried herbs in airtight containers.

TIP

• • • • • • • • •

Try hosing off the plants the night before you plan to pick them. Give them a good shake and make certain they are upright and not weighted with water. The next day they will be grit-free and won't require washing after harvesting.

Bouquet Garni
• • • • • • • • •

A classic French herb collection, bouquet garni is a combination of parsley, thyme, bay leaf, and lovage or celery leaves for soups, stews, sauces, and braised meat and vegetables. If you are using dried herbs, crumble them between your hands, then tie them in a wet cheesecloth pouch. (Wetting the cheesecloth prevents the oils in the herbs from being absorbed by the fibers of the cloth.) The cheesecloth pouch can easily be removed from the liquid after cooking. A tea ball also works well.

Drying Herbs in the Microwave

Microwave-dried herbs are labor-intensive, but the drying takes less time overall. All the herbs and seeds mentioned at the beginning of this section can be dried this way. Make sure you start with clean herbs. If necessary, rinse them until clean and pat them dry with a paper towel. Just use leaves from the stems or pinch off small clusters of leaves to dry. There's no need to waste energy microwaving the stems, especially since they are thicker and would take longer to dry than the leaves. Work in small batches.

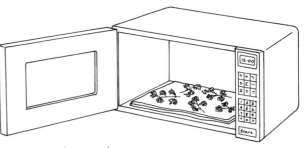

Spread the leaves over several thicknesses of paper towels in the microwave.

First, layer several thicknesses of paper towels in the microwave. Then spread the leaves or clusters in a single layer. Heat on high for 1 to 2 minutes, depending on your oven. Then rotate the towels 180 degrees and repeat the 1- to 2-minute heating time. Times will vary for different ovens and herbs. By the end of the second round you should have noticeably dryer leaves. Be careful here. You don't want to overdo it. Continue processing but only for about 30 seconds at a time. Test by removing one or two leaves and letting them cool completely to see whether they're brittle. When they are, cool the entire batch on a wire rack and store them in dark airtight containers, giving them the moisture test described on page 91. If the container remains completely moisture-free, you are ready to store your herbs. They should retain their flavor for 6 to 12 months.

Drying Meats

Meats are dried in much the same way as fruits and vegetables, except that the drying temperature must be held at 140 to 150°F to prevent spoilage. USDA advises that all meats be cooked to an internal temperature of 160°F before drying. To obtain the longest possible storage time

TIP
• • • • • • • •

Dry meats at 140 to 150°F. If the meat dries too slowly — at a lower temperature — there is a risk it will spoil before it can actually dry.

You'll get maximum flavor by drying meat over a longer time period at a lower temperature, but the oven should not be lower than 140°F.

Meat Jerky
. . . .

The oldest method of preserving meat is to dry it in the sun and then store it on the shelf. This is, however, far from the safest method. For improved safety of dried meat jerky, store it in plastic bags in the refrigerator or freezer. Use frozen meat jerky within 6 months; refrigerated within 2 months.

Cut beef into cubes.

(1 year), use only the freshest lean beef and store the finished product in resealable bags in the freezer. Dried meats will keep for 2 months in the refrigerator.

Meat jerky, which can be marinated before drying, has a much shorter shelf life. It will keep 2 to 6 months, but it is easy to prepare and very convenient to use. I store jerky in the freezer in resealable bags.

Pork does not perform well because it contains more fat than lean cuts of beef, and the fat can turn rancid. Chicken should not be used either, because it also contains too much fat for successful drying, and it may present a health hazard. As stated, lean beef is the most reliable choice for dried meat.

DRYING BEEF

Cut 2 pounds of lean beef (lean lamb may be used as well) into 1-inch cubes. Put in a heavy saucepan and add enough water to cover. Cover the saucepan and boil for 1 hour. Spread the pieces in a single layer on trays or cookie sheets and dry them in the oven at 140 to 150°F for 4 to 6 hours. Prop open the oven door with the handle of a wooden spoon to let moisture escape. To test, cool a cube and cut it open to check for moisture in the center. After 4 to 6 hours, continue drying the meat but lower the temperature to 130°F; dry until there is no moisture in the center of the cubes. An oven thermometer will help you maintain a stable low temperature. Store in the freezer.

To rehydrate, pour 1 cup of boiling water over 1 cup of meat. Let stand for 3 to 4 hours. Use in stews, casseroles, or soups. Plan to marinate for flavor, if necessary.

You can speed the rehydrating process by simmering the meat and water, in the same 1-to-1 ratio, in a covered saucepan for 40 to 50 minutes.

RECIPES FOR MAKING AND USING DRIED FOODS

Barbecued Beef Jerky

This is adapted from a recipe in the Ball Blue Book. Once you've tasted homemade jerky, you'll never want the store-bought variety again.

3 pounds lean beef (flank or round), trimmed of all fat and steamed or roasted to 160°F

1 cup ketchup

½ cup red wine vinegar

¼ cup firmly packed brown sugar

2 tablespoons Worcestershire sauce

2 teaspoons dry mustard

1 teaspoon onion powder

1 teaspoon salt

¼ teaspoon freshly ground black pepper

Dash of hot pepper sauce

1. To make cutting easier, freeze the beef, uncovered, in a bowl until ice crystals form, about 1–2 hours. Cut into thin strips against the grain (an electric knife is good for this).

2. Combine the remaining ingredients in a large nonporous bowl.

3. Add the beef strips, cover the bowl tightly, and refrigerate overnight.

4. To dry the beef strips using a dehydrator, follow the manufacturer's directions.

5. To use your oven for drying jerky, set the temperature at 145°F.

6. Drain the meat and pat dry. Lay the meat strips on oven racks and prop the oven door open with a wooden spoon handle to allow moisture to escape. Dry the meat for 4–6 hours, then let it cool. Test one piece by bending it. If it doesn't break, it's ready. (If it does, it's overcooked.) If moisture is present, dry a little longer.

7. Place in a clean freezer container and freeze for 3 days.

8. Store in an airtight container for 2 months in the refrigerator or up to 6 months in the freezer.

Note: Instead of cooking the meat before marinating, you may cook it in the marinating liquid after step 3 until the liquid reaches 160°F on a food thermometer.

YIELD: ¾ POUND (TWENTY-FOUR ½-OUNCE SERVINGS)

NUTRITION PER SERVING

Calories	143	Total fat	8g
% from fat	52	Saturated	3g
Carbohydrates	6g	Cholesterol	35mg
Fiber	<1g	Sodium	248mg

Oriental Turkey Jerky

Low fat and delicious, this turkey jerky will spice up your next picnic.

1 pound boned, skinned turkey breast, trimmed of all fat and steamed or roasted to 160°F

½ cup water

¼ cup soy sauce

2 tablespoons firmly packed brown sugar

2 teaspoons Worcestershire sauce

1 teaspoon freshly ground black pepper

¼ teaspoon garlic powder

¼ teaspoon onion powder

1. To make slicing easier, freeze the turkey until ice crystals form and then slice it thinly against the grain (an electric knife is good for this).

2. Combine the remaining ingredients in a nonporous bowl, stirring well. Add the turkey slices. Cover tightly and refrigerate overnight.

3. To dry using a dehydrator, follow the manufacturer's directions.

4. To use the oven, preheat the temperature control to 150°F.

5. Place the drained, patted-dry meat strips on oven racks. Prop oven door open with a wooden spoon handle to allow moisture to escape, and dry meat for 18–24 hours. Let cool. Test one piece by bending. If it doesn't break, it's ready. (If it does, it's overcooked.) If moisture is present, dry a little longer.

6. Place in clean freezer container and freeze 3 days.

7. Store in an airtight container for 2 months in the refrigerator or up to 6 months in the freezer.

Note: Instead of cooking the meat before marinating, you may cook it in the marinating liquid after step 3 until the liquid reaches 160°F on a food thermometer.

YIELD: ½ POUND (SIXTEEN ½-OUNCE SERVINGS)
NUTRITION PER SERVING

Calories	50	Total fat	2g
% from fat	33	Saturated	<1g
Carbohydrates	2g	Cholesterol	17mg
Fiber	<1g	Sodium	279mg

Tomato Leather

This is one vegetable leather worth trying.

4–5 medium tomatoes, chopped (2 cups)

1 medium onion, chopped

½ large stalk celery, chopped (¼ cup)

½ teaspoon salt

¼ teaspoon freshly ground black pepper

1. Mix all the ingredients in a 2-quart saucepan and simmer, covered, for 15 minutes.

2. Cool slightly and purée in a food processor. Drape a wet cloth over the lid to prevent the hot liquid from spattering out of the bowl.

3. Return the purée to the pan and cook 15 minutes longer, until thickened, being careful not to burn the purée.

4. Spread the mixture on a cookie sheet covered in plastic wrap and tilt the cookie sheet until it is evenly distributed.

5. Dry in a 120°F oven for 6–8 hours, until the mixture can be pulled away from the plastic wrap easily.

6. Invert on another plastic wrap sheet, remove the plastic wrap from the bottom, and dry about 6 hours longer.

7. Remove the wrap and let cool to room temperature.

8. Wrap carefully in foil or plastic wrap. Roll and store in an airtight container away from heat and light for up to 1 year. Some people prefer dusting the roll with cornstarch to keep it from sticking before storing and rolling. To use, cut off portions of the roll for a nutritious snack.

YIELD: 1 ROLL (EIGHT 1½-OUNCE SERVINGS)
NUTRITION PER SERVING

Calories	21	Total fat	<1g
% from fat	4	Saturated	0g
Carbohydrates	5g	Cholesterol	0mg
Fiber	<1g	Sodium	140mg

Herb Butter Blend

· · · · · · · · · · · ·

This blend makes a great herb butter with an Italian accent!

¼ cup dried basil

¼ cup dried minced garlic

¼ cup dried parsley

¼ cup garlic powder

1 tablespoon paprika

1 teaspoon freshly ground black pepper

1. Combine all the ingredients and store in an airtight jar away from heat and light.

2. When ready to use, mix 2 tablespoons of the herb mixture with 1 softened stick of butter or margarine.

3. Spread the mixture on top of or between slices of bread and warm in the oven.

TIP

· · · · · · · · ·

If you are rushed, roll the stick of butter in the herb mixture and let guests spread it on their own bread at the table.

· ·

YIELD: 1 CUP (SIXTEEN 1-TABLESPOON SERVINGS)
NUTRITION PER SERVING

Calories	15	Total fat	<1g
% from fat	7	Saturated	0g
Carbohydrates	3g	Cholesterol	0mg
Fiber	<1g	Sodium	2mg

· ·

Herbed Rice Mix

* * * * * * * * * * * * *

*In this blend, your dried herbs keep on giving. Pour it into a handsome, reclaimed jar,
add a bow of raffia or ribbon, and plain rice becomes a festive gift.
My friend Ann Herman shared this method of cooking perfect rice with me.*

1 cup long-grain converted white rice, uncooked

2 beef or all-natural vegetable bouillon cubes

1 teaspoon dried chives

½ teaspoon dried marjoram

½ teaspoon dried thyme

¼ teaspoon salt

1. Mix all the ingredients and store in an airtight container away from heat and light.

2. To cook, combine the mixture with 2 cups of water in a heavy covered 1-quart saucepan. Add 1 tablespoon of oil or butter. Bring to a boil and cover. Reduce the heat to medium. Do not lift the lid. Simmer the rice for exactly 30 minutes.

3. Leaving the lid snugly in place, turn off the heat and let the rice stand for 30 minutes. Uncover and fluff with a fork. Serve immediately. Leftovers can be frozen for later use.

YIELD: 1 CUP UNCOOKED, 2½ CUPS COOKED
(FIVE ½-CUP SERVINGS)
NUTRITION PER SERVING

Calories	160	Total fat	3g
% from fat	15	Saturated	2g
Carbohydrates	30g	Cholesterol	6mg
Fiber	<1g	Sodium	376mg

Mushroom Barley Soup

*This great recipe answers the question, "What on earth can I have for Saturday lunch?"
If you have a jar of this homemade soup mix on the shelf, a quick meal is no problem.*

Air-Dried Mushrooms

*Most vegetables are preserved most success-
fully when blanched first, but mushrooms are
the exception and require little advance
preparation.*

*To dry mushrooms, remove their stems and
wipe (don't wash) the cups with a damp
cloth. String them on a strong thread, using a
sewing needle. Don't choose a needle that is
so large in diameter that it will split the mushroom when pierced.*

*Hang the strings of mushrooms in the sun
for several days, until dry and almost brittle.
Remember to bring them in at night to avoid
exposure to the morning dew.*

*Another drying method is to use several
thicknesses of newspaper covered with a layer
of paper towels. Spread cleaned mushrooms
on the paper towel. Turn them occasionally
and change the paper if it becomes damp
until all the mushrooms are uniformly dry.
Once again, it may take more than one day.
A good breeze helps.*

*Heat the dried mushrooms in a 175°F oven
on a cookie sheet for 15 minutes to pasteurize.*

*Cool on wire racks for several hours. Store
in a cool, dry place in clean, covered glass jars.
They should keep for 6 to 12 months.*

½ cup dried medium-sized barley

¼ cup dried mushroom slices of your
choice

2 tablespoons dried minced onions

2 tablespoons dried parsley

2 tablespoons dried thyme

2 bay leaves

2 chicken (or vegetable) bouillon cubes

1. Combine all the ingredients in a clean
1-pint canning jar. Store in a dark, dry
place until needed.

2. Make the soup by adding the dried
ingredients to 1 quart of boiling water in a
2-quart saucepan.

3. Cover and reduce the heat to a simmer
until the barley and mushrooms are tender,
about 45 minutes.

YIELD: 6 CUPS (FOUR 1½-CUP SERVINGS)
NUTRITION PER SERVING

Calories	147	Total fat	1g
% from fat	6	Saturated	<1g
Carbohydrates	32g	Cholesterol	0mg
Fiber	6g	Sodium	584mg

Quiet Spirit Tea Blend

Delicious hot or cold, this tea blend of dried herbs and cloves has a wonderfully calming effect on the nerves and the digestive tract.

½ cup dried lavender flowers

½ cup dried mint leaves

½ cup dried rosemary leaves

¼ cup dried chamomile

¼ cup dried cloves

1. Combine all the ingredients and store in an airtight container away from heat, moisture, and light.

2. Use 1 teaspoon of the mix per 6 ounces of boiling water, using a tea ball or a teapot and strainer. Let steep for 5–8 minutes.

YIELD: 2 CUPS TEA MIX

(NINETY-SIX 1-TEASPOON SERVINGS)

High-Calcium Tonic

A great morning ritual or afternoon tea break, this concoction has more calcium than other herbal teas thanks to the chamomile and oatstraw.

2 ounces (4 tablespoons) dried chamomile flowers

2 ounces (3 tablespoons) dried mint leaves

2 ounces (3 tablespoons) dried oatstraw (available at health food stores)

1 ounce (3 tablespoons) dried alfalfa

1 ounce (3 tablespoons) dried red-raspberry leaves

1. Mix all the ingredients and store in an airtight container in a cool, dark place.

2. To brew, use 1 teaspoon per 6 ounces of boiling water. Infuse for 10 minutes. Use a tea ball or strain from the pot.

YIELD: 1½ CUPS TEA MIX (SEVENTY-TWO 1-TEASPOON SERVINGS)

Apple Coffee Cake

. . . .

*Dried apples make this a great winter treat. Double this recipe if you wish,
and eat one warm out of the oven and save the other one. This cake may be frozen.*

2 cups dried apples

1 teaspoon lemon juice

½ cup (1 stick) butter or margarine

¼ cup sugar

2 eggs

1½ cups all-purpose flour

2 teaspoons baking powder

½ teaspoon salt

½ cup milk

1 teaspoon vanilla extract

SUGAR TOPPING

½ cup sugar

2 teaspoons ground cinnamon

1. In a nonreactive saucepan, combine the apples, lemon juice, and enough boiling water to cover. Cook until completely reconstituted. Drain.

2. Cream the butter and sugar. Add the eggs one at a time, beating well after each addition.

3. Sift the dry ingredients. Alternate adding the dry ingredients and the milk to the butter mixture.

4. Add the vanilla; beat well.

5. Grease and flour a 9-inch-square pan or glass casserole.

6. Pour the batter into the pan and top with the rehydrated apple slices.

7. Mix together the sugar and cinnamon and sprinkle on top.

8. Bake at 325°F for 30–45 minutes.

. . . .

YIELD: ONE 9-INCH-SQUARE CAKE
(NINE 3½-OUNCE SERVINGS)

NUTRITION PER SERVING

Calories	302	Total fat	12g
% from fat	32	Saturated	7g
Carbohydrates	52g	Cholesterol	70mg
Fiber	3g	Sodium	338mg

. . . .

Blueberry Waffles

Dried blueberries bring a bit of summer to a winter's weekend brunch menu.
Substitute dried raspberries for a flavor change.

1¾ cups all-purpose flour

3 teaspoons baking powder

¼ teaspoon salt

2 eggs

1¼ cups milk

6 tablespoons vegetable oil

1 cup dried blueberries

1. In a medium-sized bowl, combine the dry ingredients.

2. In a large mixing bowl, beat the eggs until they are light colored and foamy.

3. Add the milk and oil. Mix well and set aside.

4. Gradually add the dry ingredients to the egg mixture. Beat just until smooth.

5. Fold in the dried blueberries.

6. Pour the batter onto a hot waffle iron, following the manufacturer's directions for baking.

YIELD: 4 CUPS (FOUR 1-CUP SERVINGS)
NUTRITION PER SERVING

Calories	480	Total fat	26g
% from fat	48	Saturated	5g
Carbohydrates	51g	Cholesterol	102mg
Fiber	3g	Sodium	473mg

Cranberry Bread

Dried cranberries also make good additions to muffins, waffles, and cookies.

1 cup dried cranberries with sweetener added

¾ cup orange juice, heated in 2-cup saucepan just to boiling

1 cup all-purpose flour

1 cup whole-wheat flour

½ cup wheat germ

2 teaspoons baking powder

½ teaspoon baking soda

¼ teaspoon salt

¾ cup honey

1 egg

2 tablespoons oil

Zest of 1 orange, grated

1. Combine the cranberries with the orange juice to reconstitute them. Let sit for 30 minutes.

2. Grease a loaf pan and line it with waxed paper; grease the waxed paper.

3. Combine the dry ingredients in a separate 4-cup bowl.

4. Preheat the oven to 350°F. Mix together the honey, egg, oil, orange zest, and reconstituted cranberries with any remaining juices.

5. Slowly add the dry ingredients to the cranberry mixture, stirring after each addition. Stir until smooth but do not overmix.

6. Pour the batter into the prepared loaf pan and bake for 50 minutes, or until a toothpick inserted in the center tests clean.

7. Cool for 15 minutes in the pan, then turn onto a cake rack to cool completely.

YIELD: 1 LOAF (TWELVE SERVINGS)
NUTRITION PER SERVING

Calories	191	Total fat	3g
% from fat	15	Saturated	<1g
Carbohydrates	38g	Cholesterol	15mg
Fiber	3g	Sodium	164mg

Dried-Mushroom Ragout

. . . .

Your dried mushrooms contribute concentrated flavor year-round. This recipe will make a Sunday-night supper a real treat.

1 cup boiling water

1 cup dried mushrooms of your choice

2 tablespoons butter or margarine

2 tablespoons all-purpose flour

1 cup milk

½ teaspoon salt

⅛ teaspoon white pepper

¼ cup freshly grated Parmesan cheese

1. Combine the water and mushrooms in a 1-quart saucepan. Simmer, covered, for 20–30 minutes, or until completely reconstituted.

2. Drain, reserving the liquid for other uses, such as soups.

3. Preheat the oven to 350°F.

4. Melt the butter in a 1-quart flameproof casserole.

5. Stir in the flour and gradually add the milk. Stir constantly until the white sauce is smooth and thick.

6. Add the mushrooms, salt, and pepper. Top with the cheese.

7. Bake for 25–35 minutes.

8. Serve over toast triangles.

YIELD: 2 CUPS (FOUR ½-CUP SERVINGS)
NUTRITION PER SERVING

Calories	111	Total fat	3g
% from fat	23	Saturated	<1g
Carbohydrates	18g	Cholesterol	2mg
Fiber	3g	Sodium	2,003mg

Eight-Bean Soup

· · · · · · · · · · ·

This is a great gift idea given to me by my friend Corinne. Layer the dried beans to create contrasting colors in a jar, or mix them up in a plastic bag, and include the recipe on a card.

¼ cup each (all are dried): red kidney beans, green split peas, yellow split peas, lentils, black-eyed peas, navy beans, lima beans, and pinto beans, picked over

1 tablespoon chili powder

1 teaspoon garlic powder

1 teaspoon dried savory

½ teaspoon dried thyme leaves

1 bay leaf

2 quarts water

1 can (28 ounces) tomatoes, mashed

1 beef or ham bone

2 tablespoons fine pearl barley

2 tablespoons fresh or bottled lemon juice

1. Place the beans in a 2-cup container and package the herbs in a separate smaller container. Store in a cool, dark place away from heat and light.

2. To prepare, rinse the beans and place them in a large pot or bowl; cover with water. Soak the beans overnight. Pour off the water.

3. In a large soup pot, combine the beans, water, tomatoes, bone, barley, and spices. Simmer for 2½–3 hours in a covered pot, until the beans are tender.

4. Add the lemon juice and cook 15 minutes longer. Remove the bone.

· ·

YIELD: 2 CUPS DRY, 8 CUPS PREPARED

(EIGHT 1-CUP SERVINGS)

NUTRITION PER SERVING

Calories	233	Total fat	3g
% from fat	12	Saturated	<1g
Carbohydrates	38g	Cholesterol	13mg
Fiber	12g	Sodium	39mg

· ·

Herb Cheese Appetizer

Summer's dried herbs help make this cheese appetizer a great gift when packed in a ceramic crock with a lid. My friends Ruth and Allie Blue shared this recipe with me years ago. Freezing makes this a ready solution for impromptu entertaining. Try substituting low-fat cream cheese.

2 packages (8 ounces each) cream cheese, softened

½ cup (1 stick) butter or margarine, softened

2 tablespoons milk

2 teaspoons garlic powder

1 teaspoon dried parsley

¾ teaspoon salt

½ teaspoon dried basil leaves

½ teaspoon caraway seeds

½ teaspoon dried sage

¼ teaspoon dried chives

¼ teaspoon dried tarragon

¼ teaspoon dried thyme

Freshly ground black pepper

1. Combine all the ingredients in a food processor and blend until smooth.

2. Spoon into ceramic crocks or ramekins.

3. Store, well wrapped, in the refrigerator for 1 week or the freezer for up to 2 months.

YIELD: 2½ CUPS (TWENTY 1-OUNCE SERVINGS)
NUTRITION PER SERVING

Calories	122	Total fat	13g
% from fat	91	Saturated	8g
Carbohydrates	<1g	Cholesterol	37mg
Fiber	0g	Sodium	194mg

Hummus with Dried Tomatoes

. . . .

This favorite dip, borrowed from the Middle East, brings a bit of summer heat when you use your own dried tomatoes and spicy dried red pepper flakes.

1 can (15 ounces) chickpeas, rinsed and drained

1 cup dried tomatoes

½ cup mayonnaise (regular or low fat)

¼ cup freshly grated Parmesan cheese

2 cloves garlic, minced

1. Purée the chickpeas in a food processor.

2. Add the tomatoes and process again.

3. Add the mayonnaise, cheese, and garlic. Process the mixture until smooth.

4. Serve immediately with crackers, flat bread, or vegetable sticks.

5. To freeze: Pour into a clean freezer container. Label and freeze. When you're ready to use it, let the hummus thaw in the refrigerator.

. . . .

YIELD: 2 CUPS (EIGHT 2-OUNCE SERVINGS)
NUTRITION PER SERVING

Calories	325	Total fat	16g
% from fat	42	Saturated	3g
Carbohydrates	36g	Cholesterol	7mg
Fiber	10g	Sodium	291mg

. . . .

Mexican Salad Terra Noble

Dried banana chips lend a tropical note to this cool, satisfying salad.

1 large head shredded lettuce (4 cups)

2 cups shredded red cabbage

2–3 medium carrots (1½ cups), shredded

2 cucumbers, cleaned and diced

1 cup dried banana chips

1 fresh pear, diced

½ cup dry-roasted, salted peanuts, chopped

1 tablespoon sesame seeds, toasted

DRESSING

⅔ cup olive oil

¼ cup freshly squeezed lime juice (2 medium limes)

1. Combine the oil and lime juice and mix until smooth.

2. In a large salad bowl, combine all the salad ingredients and toss well.

3. Add the dressing ¼ cup at a time until the salad fixings are coated according to taste.

YIELD: 7 CUPS (SEVEN 1-CUP SERVINGS)
NUTRITION PER SERVING

Calories	491	Total fat	38g
% from fat	67	Saturated	14g
Carbohydrates	37g	Cholesterol	0mg
Fiber	8g	Sodium	106mg

Shiitake Mushroom Soup

* * * * * * * * * * *

Never underestimate the potency of dried shiitake mushrooms.
This richly flavored soup will be one of your most memorable.

3 ounces dried shiitake mushrooms

1½ quarts chicken broth

1 medium unpeeled potato, washed and cut into ½-inch cubes

2 bunches scallions, including tops, coarsely chopped

2 tablespoons butter

4 tablespoons frozen apple juice concentrate

½ teaspoon salt

⅛ teaspoon freshly ground black pepper

1 cup half-and-half

1. Reconstitute the mushrooms by pouring boiling water over them to cover. Let stand for 30 minutes.

2. Drain the mushrooms on paper towels, reserving the liquid for added flavor in other soups or sauces.

3. In a 4-quart pot, heat the broth to a simmer. Add the cubed potato and cook until tender, about 10 minutes.

4. In a large skillet, sauté the mushrooms and scallions in the butter until the scallions are soft.

5. Add the mushroom mixture to the simmering stock. Increase the heat to medium high and cook for approximately 15 minutes.

6. Add the juice concentrate, salt, and pepper.

7. Spoon out the solids and purée them in a blender or food processor.

8. Return the purée to the pot, stir in the half-and-half, and reheat slightly. Serve immediately.

* *

YIELD: 8 CUPS (EIGHT 1-CUP SERVINGS)
NUTRITION PER SERVING

Calories	155	Total fat	7g
% from fat	39	Saturated	4g
Carbohydrates	20g	Cholesterol	19mg
Fiber	2g	Sodium	1791mg

* *

Split-Pea Soup

Here is an old favorite to warm your winter chills.

6 cups chicken or vegetable stock

1 pound (about 2¼ cups) dried green split peas, rinsed and picked over

2 medium carrots, chopped

1 medium unpeeled potato, cubed

1 medium onion, chopped

1 celery stalk with leaves, chopped

2 tablespoons butter

1 clove garlic, minced

½ teaspoon salt

1 cup diced ham or turkey sausage, cooked (optional)

1. Combine all the ingredients except the ham in a heavy 6-quart covered saucepan.

2. Bring to a boil, then reduce the heat and simmer for 2½ hours. A slow-cooker may be used on low for 6–8 hours. Stir occasionally.

3. Add the meat, if using, for the last 5 minutes and heat thoroughly.

YIELD: 9 CUPS (SIX 1½-CUP SERVINGS)
NUTRITION PER SERVING

Calories	539	Total fat	15g
% from fat	25	Saturated	6g
Carbohydrates	62g	Cholesterol	63mg
Fiber	21g	Sodium	3620mg

Vegetable Rice Beef Soup

This is a great way to use your home-dried vegetables. The ones listed are just suggestions — use them or any combination from your stock of dried goods.

2 cups dried vegetables:
    1 cup chopped carrots
    ½ cup chopped green beans
    ½ cup chopped onions

2 cups boiling water

1 large meaty beef soup bone

6 cups cold water or beef broth

1½ cups tomato purée, sauce, or whole tomatoes, chopped

¼ cup uncooked long-grain white rice

1 clove garlic, minced

2 tablespoons dried parsley

1 bay leaf

½ teaspoon salt

¼ teaspoon freshly ground black pepper

1. Rehydrate the vegetables in the boiling water, about 1–2 hours.

2. In a heavy soup pot, cover the bone with the cold water or broth and simmer, covered, for 1 hour. Remove the bone and reserve.

3. Add the tomatoes, rice, garlic, and seasonings to the broth. Simmer, covered, for 20–30 minutes.

4. Cut the meat from the bone and add it to the pot.

5. Add the rehydrated vegetables and simmer, covered, for 45–60 minutes.

YIELD: 12 CUPS (SIX 2-CUP SERVINGS)
NUTRITION PER SERVING

Calories	87	Total fat	1g
% from fat	13	Saturated	<1g
Carbohydrates	17g	Cholesterol	1mg
Fiber	3g	Sodium	1066mg

S INCE THE ADVENT of electricity, food preservation has changed dramatically. The freezer equipment available today is far superior in ability and efficiency to that of even a decade ago. Although freezing does not stop the clock, cold temperatures considerably slow the deterioration of foodstuffs and postpone spoilage by temporarily stopping the growth of organisms. While an initial investment in a good freezer can be expensive, along with the ongoing electric bills for operating it, freezing food is superior to other preserving methods. More nutrients are preserved by freezing, and the texture, color, and flavor of frozen foodstuffs are better than in food preserved by other methods.

CONTAINERS AND WRAPPERS

Air (oxygen) and moisture loss are the main enemies of frozen products. For that reason, it's important to use airtight packaging. Moisture loss occurs when ice crystals evaporate from the surface of frozen food, and the result is freezer burn. Though freezer burn is not harmful, it dries out and toughens the food and can cause off flavors. Using moisture- and vapor-proof wrapping prevents this. Warped and cracked plastic containers or storage containers designed for the refrigerator should never be used for freezing. Clean glass jars can be recycled for use in the freezer as long as you leave plenty of headspace for expansion when you fill the jars. You'll want to make your freezer containers as uniform in size and shape as possible to maximize the freezer's

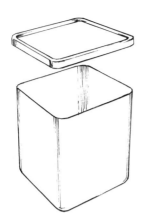

This plastic container is appropriate for freezer storage.

Always squeeze out any air in the freezer bag before you seal it.

interior space and avoid empty gaps on freezer shelves. Keeping air at freezing temperatures takes more energy than keeping food at freezing temperatures, since frozen food retains cold much better than air does. How-ever, you need to allow for some air circulation within the freezer. Paper freezer boxes in handy 1- and 2-cup sizes do solve the uniform space problem, but I don't recommend them because they are not completely airtight and can't be recycled.

The wrapping used to package meat and poultry in the supermarket allows air to penetrate and moisture to evaporate and is not adequate for long-term storage in the freezer. In addition to freezer burn, any fat on meat will turn rancid within a few weeks if not properly packaged. You can re-package these foods in moisture- and vapor-proof containers or wrapping, or you can overwrap the entire unopened package.

My favorite container is a zip-seal bag of thick plastic specially designed for the freezer. These bags can be reused if they are of good quality and have not been damaged or permeated by strong odors of previously frozen contents.

Square milk cartons are good for freezing some items. I especially like to freeze fish, shrimp, and other seafoods in them (fins and tails can puncture a plastic bag). Put loosely packed seafood in the clean carton, then add water to 1 inch from the top, allowing for expansion. Flatten the carton top by pushing it down. Seal it with sturdy freezer tape. Don't forget to label your package.

Freezing in Zip-Seal Bags

Never place plastic storage bags full of semiliquid foodstuffs directly on a freezer shelf. They will bulge around the shelf rungs, freezing to the shelf. Even if you can get the bag off the shelf when frozen, you will still have the problem of uneven packaging, which wastes interior freezer space. Instead, lay the filled freezer bags side by side on a tray that fits on the freezer shelf, allowing the packaged food to take on the flat, square shape of the freezer bag. When the bags are frozen solid, simply remove them from the tray, label them, and stack them right on the freezer shelf.

Selecting a Freezer

Freezers come in a wide variety of sizes and styles. In choosing one, consider the space you have available for it, how much food you plan to store, its energy efficiency, and how accessible you need the freezer to be. The more often you intend to go to the freezer, the more convenient it should be. Don't put your freezer in the basement if you have trouble going up and down stairs. Spend some time comparing models that fit your requirements to find the best brand.

Freezers must be kept at 0°F to prevent spoilage. Separate, freestanding freezers require less energy to do this than combination refrigerator-freezers, although combination models with separate doors are much better than single-door combination models. Larger freezers use more energy than smaller ones, so don't buy a freezer that's larger than you need. Since it takes more energy to cool air than it does solid matter, a half-full freezer uses more electricity than a full one. Buying the right size freezer for your needs can save you money.

A self-defrosting freezer costs more to operate than the older manual models — as much as 60 percent more. If you have a manual-defrosting freezer, be sure to check it frequently for ice buildup, and defrost it once the frost is ¼ inch thick to keep it running efficiently.

To further cut energy costs, choose a well-insulated freezer, place it away from heat sources, and freeze food in small batches. No more than 3 pounds of food should be added at one time to prevent an increase in energy.

Maintain your freezer by cleaning the motor housing and the condenser coils every three or four months, following the manufacturer's guidelines. Also, check the tightness of the rubber gaskets that seal the door by placing a sheet of paper between them to see whether it will stay there.

Allow enough space between the freezer and the wall for ventilation. For a longer-lasting piece of equipment, keep the coils and grill free of dust and dirt.

TIP

When adding a batch of food to the freezer, set your freezer's control to sustain -10°F so the freezer will remain below 0°, ensuring proper temperature storage for the foods already there. A large batch of room-temperature food added to a freezer will raise the air temperature and possibly affect the foods that are already frozen.

Keep your freezer well
stocked. A full freezer
actually requires less
electricity to maintain
than one that is half full.

LABELING, INVENTORY, AND STORAGE

Do you have mystery meat frozen in trapezoid-shaped lumps? Do you have huge jars of chicken stock that are longing to be soup? All of this recycling is economical and creative, as long as you don't lose track of what you have and how long it's been in the freezer. If you don't use the food you've preserved, your planning and effort will be wasted.

Clearly label each package with its contents and date, using a marker designed for freezer use. Every cook has defrosted what was supposed to be soup only to discover, to her horror, defrosted turkey gravy. Labels can fall off in the freezer, so write on the package of frozen food itself.

Start an inventory list and make a habit of adding and subtracting items from your list *every time* you open the freezer door. Train your family to do the same. I once cleaned out a sick neighbor's freezer at her request. In 1989, that freezer had two roasts from 1962 and a casserole from 1978! I post my inventory list on the freezer door or inside a nearby cupboard door. The list is organized by shelf. I keep a pencil on a string next to the list so it will be easy for everyone to strike through an item when it is removed or jot a note when food is added.

What to Do If the Freezer Stops Working

If the electricity is cut off, or if your freezer just stops working, don't open the door. You have approximately two days before a fairly full freezer begins to heat up, especially if it contains lots of meat rather than produce and bread, which are less dense. You can prolong the survival time by wrapping the whole exterior of the freezer in insulation material or, in a pinch, several quilts or multiple layers of newspaper.

Never refreeze completely defrosted, low-acid foods, such as vegetables, shellfish, or prepared casseroles that have reached room temperature. Very high-acid fruits can be refrozen if they're still cold. When in doubt, throw it out! Most foods that still have ice crystals and are cold can be cooked and refrozen or eaten immediately. There will, however, be a loss in taste, texture, and food quality.

Be sure to re-mark refrozen foods accordingly and use them quickly after refreezing. Refrozen foods do not have the shelf life of one-time frozen foods.

Thawing Frozen Foods

Freezing stops or slows the deterioration clock for food, but some microorganisms remain, though they may be inactive or at least considerably sluggish. Bacteria are not destroyed by freezing, and once food is thawed, the bacteria will begin to multiply again. That's why the best way to thaw food is to do it slowly at cold temperatures. Thawing at room temperature or in hot water will not only cause bacteria to grow again, but heat will cause them to grow faster. Because of that hazard, thaw frozen foods at the lower temperatures in your refrigerator — certainly not on your kitchen counter at room temperature, where warmth can stimulate the breeding of microorganisms.

Freezing also slows the growth of the enzymes that are present in plants and animals, though it doesn't stop it altogether. Enzymes speed the growth and ripening process of live foods and continue to cause these chemical reactions even after harvesting. The changes in color, texture, and flavor of food that occur as food ages and moves toward spoiling are caused by these enzyme reactions. To halt enzyme activity altogether, two methods — blanching and adding chemical compounds, such as ascorbic acid — are used to treat food before freezing.

Pretreating Vegetables for Freezing

Vegetables that are blanched and then frozen turn out better than those that are frozen raw. While blanching is a must for vegetables to retain color, taste, and texture, it is optional for fruits. Although blanched vegetables win on taste, color, and texture, blanching is likely to reduce the content of heat-sensitive, water-soluble vitamins.

TIP

Freeze water in clear plastic containers with tight lids. Submerge in soups, stews, and sauces to cool without diluting.

Steam blanching is the most effective method for retaining taste, texture, and nutrients.

There are several ways to blanch food. For both steam and boil blanching, heat 1 minute longer than the time given if you live 5,000 feet or more above sea level.

Steam blanching. This method produces the very best taste after freezing and provides the most protection against vitamin loss. You may use a steamer pot especially designed for steaming or a steamer basket inserted into a pot with a lid. Bring 4 to 5 inches of water to a boil under the steamer basket. Place the vegetables in the basket in a thin layer. Begin timing when you put the lid on the steamer. (See the chart at right for timing different vegetables.)

Boil blanching. This is an easy method, but the outcome is not as good as that of steam blanching because the high temperature and immersion in water tend to diminish flavor. Bring 4 quarts of water to a rapid boil and then add 1 pound of clean, pared vegetables. Allow the water to return to a boil and begin clocking the specified amount of time. (See the chart at right for timing different vegetables.)

Microwave blanching. Follow the manufacturer's directions. This method seems attractive, but experts disagree in their recommendations, and only one plastic pint- or quart-size bag of produce can be processed at a time.

The final step. Regardless of which blanching method you use, stop the cooking by plunging vegetables into ice-cold water.

Equipment for Freezing

8- to 10-quart pot

Wire mesh basket, preferably with handles, that fits in the top of the pot

Large strainer

Clean, dry tea towels

Blocks of ice made in recycled milk cartons, or two resealable plastic bags filled with ice cubes, or a clean dishpan of ice water. Do this part in your sink to avoid messy cleanups.

Freezing Vegetables

With the exception of pumpkin, which can be stored for about only 2–3 months, these vegetables will keep for 1 year at 0°F if properly prepared and packaged.

Item	Harvest	Preparation	Blanch Time in Minutes	
			Boil	Steam
Artichokes	Small is best	Cut tops and thorns; trim stems; wash.	8	8–10
Asparagus	Young, very green	Cut even-size pieces; wash.	2	3
Beans (green)	Young, tender	Wash; cut desired lengths; remove stem end.	3	4
Beans (lima)	Bright green, slightly filled-out pods	Wash; blanch; shell.	2	4
Beans (yellow)	Small beans inside pods	Wash; cut desired lengths; remove stem end.	3	4
Broccoli and Brussels sprouts	No yellow heads or pithy stalks	Wash; trim into uniform sizes. Check for worms. Soak in cold salt water 10–15 minutes.	2–4	3–6
Cabbage	Tender green heads	Wash; shred or wedge.	1½–2	2–3
Cauliflower	Well-formed heads; no brown spots	Wash; cut into florets. Check for worms. Soak in cold salt water 10–15 minutes.	3	5
Corn	Young, ripe, small ears*	Husk; remove silk; wash. Blanch 3 ears/batch; cool; then cut from cob.	4	6
Eggplant	Small and tender skinned	Wash, peel, slice, or cube. Blanch using 1 T. lemon juice to 1 qt. water.	4	6
Okra	Tender, small pods	Wash; cut stem; and slice, if desired.	2–3	5
Peas (green)	Filled out, green, and tender*	Shell but do not wash.	2	3
Peas (snow or sugar)	Green, not filled out	Wash.	2	3
Peppers, bell (sweet)	Shining skin, deep color	Wash and halve; remove seeds. Does not require blanching, but blanched is easier to pack.	1	2
Pumpkins and squash	Deep color, hard shell; best frozen in cooked form	Wash; cut into uniform pieces. Bake in 350°F oven until soft; remove skins from cooked mixture.		
Summer squash	Tender skins, small	Wash; shred, slice, or cube.	2–3	2–3
Tomatoes	Deep color, firm	See page 124.		
Zucchini	Deep green, tender skins, small	Wash and shred, slice, or cube.	2–3	2–3

Work quickly after harvesting so that the sugar does not turn to starch.

Freezing Fresh Vegetables

1. I like to organize my equipment and supplies the night before. This saves valuable time the next morning, when time is of the essence. Line up your equipment in the order needed.

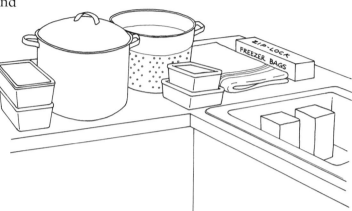

2. As always, choose fresh and tender produce. Freezing can never improve inferior-quality food. Early in the day, harvest or buy slightly underripe vegetables, avoiding those with blemishes or bruises. When you come in from the garden or farmer's market, you'll be ready to begin. Remember that you'll want to work quickly and carefully, using only small batches of food, if at all possible.

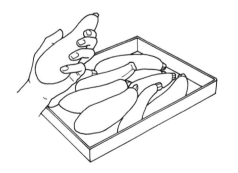

3. Wash the vegetables and cut them into uniform-size pieces where practicable.

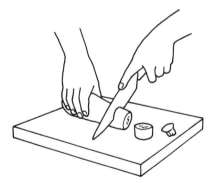

4. To steam blanch the vegetables, fill the wire mesh basket of the steamer with 1 pound of prepared produce. Set it over 1 or 2 inches of boiling water and cover the pot. Begin timing. See chart on page 121 for exact times.

5. To cool the vegetables quickly, plunge them into ice water, basket and all. Set the basket on blocks of ice and cover it with ice cubes, or place the basket on prepared resealable bags filled with ice and cover the top of the

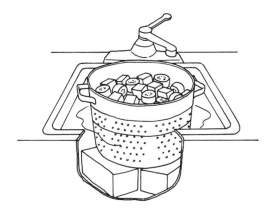

vegetables with a second prepared bag. (This method keeps extra water to a minimum.)

6. Pour the cooled vegetables from the basket onto a clean tea towel. Gently roll up the towel to remove excess moisture, but don't squeeze.

7. Pack in freezer containers at once, seal, label, and freeze. Vegetables that pack with air spaces around each piece (such as broccoli, asparagus, and artichokes) need no expansion (head) space.

Freezing Tomatoes

Tomatoes can easily be frozen in a variety of ways — stewed or cooked down in the oven, slow-cooker, or saucepan; frozen whole, peeled or unpeeled. (Add other clean, blemish-free vegetable scraps from other freezing projects and you've got a hearty soup in the making.)

It is a remarkable convenience, late in the season when the harvest is rolling in, to freeze tomatoes whole, even though it takes extra space in the freezer. My favorite way to freeze tomatoes is to wash 12 to 24 firm ones of uniform size, then core and place them on a cookie sheet in the freezer. When they're solid, I place them in a plastic freezer bag to use as needed. Skins will slide off as they thaw. To thaw, spray a little shower of warm water over the frozen tomatoes to speed the process.

It is possible to skin fresh tomatoes by first plunging them into boiling water for 30 to 60 seconds. Then lift off the skins before freezing them whole on trays; or remove skins from the pot as the tomatoes simmer.

For sauces or stewed tomatoes, wash, core, and quarter the tomatoes. Simmer, covered, in a heavy saucepan until soft, then remove the lid. For stewed tomatoes, cook 15 to 30 minutes longer. Cook sauces several hours, being careful not to burn them. Using a slow-cooker or your oven makes burning less likely than cooking on the stovetop. Cook 4 to 6 hours, stirring every 30 mintues to prevent sticking.

Freezing Fruits

Fruits are the ultimate food for freezing. Freezing them involves less labor overall because no blanching is needed. Fruits retain a good portion of their nutrients while frozen, and their color, texture, and flavor are superior to what they are after canning. They do, however, suffer some softening in the process of being frozen. Freezing converts the water contained in any food from a liquid to a solid. Because water expands when it freezes, the structure of the cells is altered, breaking down the cell walls. Consequently, all food will be softer once it has thawed. The more water in a food, the greater this change will be, and that's why some fruits and vegetables don't fare as well as others after freezing.

Fruit can be frozen two ways: using the dry-pack method or the wet-pack method. As always, use mature, ripe, fresh fruits free of blemishes.

Dry Pack

The dry-pack method is the easiest way to freeze fruit. It involves freezing fruit without added liquids or other ingredients. All that's required to dry pack is washing the fruit and drying it on clean towels. Handle the fruit carefully to avoid bruising and quickly to prevent it from darkening from exposure to air.

Spread the clean, dry fruit in single layers on cookie sheets and place in the freezer. When the fruit is solid, package it loosely in clean containers. While this way of dry packing fruit is extremely convenient and helps maintain the shape of the fruit, it may cause more texture, flavor, and color loss than freezing in sealed containers. To prevent any loss of flavor or color, pack the fruit directly in a carton or other container, bypassing the cookie-sheet step. The dry-pack method results in fewer calories than the wet-pack method and is wonderful for those with health issues that relate to sugar consumption. Allow ½ inch of headspace in your packages.

Wet Pack

As the name implies, freezing food using the wet-pack method involves adding liquid to the fruit before freezing. The liquid can be syrup, juice, or water.

Sugar syrup pack. To pack fruit in sugar syrup, add ⅓ to ½ cup of the cold sugar syrup of your choice (see chart on page 126) to 2-cup containers packed with clean

TIP
· · · · · · · · ·
Because of cellular changes, frozen fruits that will be eaten raw are at their best texture and taste when they still contain ice crystals and have not completely defrosted.

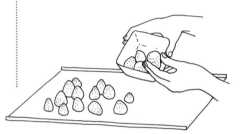

Freezing the fruit before packing is one method of dry packing.

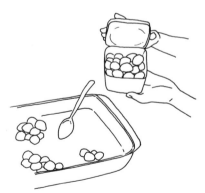

Packing the fruit before freezing is another method of dry packing.

Honey Syrup Blend

• • • • • • • • • • • • • • • •

Thin honey:
 1 cup mild honey
 4 cups water

Medium honey:
 2 cups mild honey
 3 cups water

Heat water to warm; stir in honey to blend. Cool to room temperature.

fruit. Mix them gently, label, and freeze. Allow ½ inch of headspace for pints and 1 inch of headspace for quarts.

The day before freezing the fruit, make a syrup using one of the recipes below. Bring it to a boil to dissolve the sugar and then chill it.

Syrups for Freezing Fruit

Consistency	Amount of Sugar	Amount of Water	Finished Amount
Thin	2 cups	4 cups	5 cups
Medium	3 cups	4 cups	5½ cups
Heavy	8¾ cups	4 cups	8⅔ cups

Juice pack or water pack. To pack fruit in juice or water, use the same proportions as those packed in sugar syrups. If you can't use sugar and wish to use an artificial sweetener, add it when you serve the fruit. Allow ½ inch of headspace for pint jars and 1 inch of headspace for quarts.

Sugar pack. Packing frozen fruit with sugar requires the sprinkling of sugar to taste over fresh fruit. Mix the fruit and sugar carefully or mash the mixture slightly to allow the juices to be drawn from the fruit. Stir to dissolve all of the sugar. Pack the sweetened fruit into clean containers, label, and freeze. Allow ½ inch of headspace for pints and 1 inch of headspace for quarts.

Honey pack. The easiest, lightest method of wet packing fruit, honey pack also has the fewest calories without resorting to articificial sweeteners. To substitute honey for sugar syrup, use exactly half the amount as called for in the sugar recipes. Working with honey is easiest when it is at room temperature. Add ½ cup of Honey Syrup Blend (see the recipe at left) in the consistency of your choice to 1-pint containers of fruit and 1 cup of Honey Syrup Blend to 1-quart containers. Allow ½ inch of headspace for pints and 1 inch of headspace for quarts.

FREEZING FRUITS

FRUIT	HARVEST	PREPARATION
Apples	Firm; crisp but ripe	Wash, peel, core, and slice. Pretreat fruit to prevent darkening or use wet pack method of your choice. Blanch slices or cook as for purée (page 88), then freeze.
Apricots	Soft; ripe but firm	Dip in boiling water 15–30 seconds then in cold water. Slip off skins, halve, remove pit. Wet pack with nondarkening agent.
Avocados	Soft but not overly ripe	Peel, pit, and purée. Add nondarkening agent; best frozen unflavored for versatility's sake when thawed.
Bananas	Ripe but not overly ripe	Peel, cut into chunks.* Or peel, freeze, and mash when thawed for banana bread. Use nondarkening agent dip.
Berries: blue, elder, huckle	Fresh, firm, sweet, but soft	Wash; dry pack loosely. Or mash, purée, and wet pack.
Cherries: sour and sweet	Soft, fresh; plump with glossy skin	Wash, halve, and pit. Dry pack with nondarkening agent dip.
Cranberries	Soft; ripe but firm; plump with glossy skin	Wash; dry pack. Or crush fruit, simmer 1 cup water with 1 pint (2 cups) fruit until skins burst, then wet pack.
Figs	Soft; ripe but firm	Wash, cut off stems. Dry pack or wet pack with liquid of your choice. Use nondarkening agent with both methods.
Grapes: seedless	Soft; sweet; firm but ripe	Wash, stem, and dry pack.*
Kiwi	Soft but firm and ripe	Peel and slice. Wet pack only.
Melon	Sweet, ripe	Cube, slice, or ball melon flesh. Dry pack.*
Nectarines	Ripe; unblemished; soft but firm	Wash, peel, pit. Slice or halve. Wet pack with nondarkening agent.
Peaches	Ripe; unblemished; soft but firm	Wash, peel, pit. Slice or halve. Wet pack with nondarkening agent.
Pineapple	Sweet; ripe but firm**	Peel, core, slice, or cube. Wet pack.
Plums	Sweet; ripe but firm	Wash, halve, and pit. Wet pack with nondarkening agent.
Raspberries	Firm, sweet, and ripe	Gently wash and pick over. Dry pack. Or wet pack with very light syrup.
Rhubarb	Firm, tender red stalks	Wash and cut into small pieces. Remove tough stalks. Blanch 1½ minutes in steam or boiling water; dry pack. Or wet pack with syrup without blanching.
Strawberries	Ripe; soft, unblemished	Gently wash, slice, halve, or freeze whole for dry pack. Or wet pack in light syrup.

*Half thawed, makes a delicious snack.
**Pineapple is ripe if a spiky leaf is easily pulled.

PRETREATING THE FRUIT BEFORE FREEZING

Some fruits will darken after being pared for freezing. Apples, apricots, peaches, and nectarines all have this tendency. To prevent darkening, dip the cut-up fruit in ascorbic acid, citric acid, lemon juice, or concentrated fruit juice before freezing. Be aware that fruit juice, citric acid, and lemon juice may change the flavor of the fruit, sometimes for the better. Steam blanching for 3 to 5 minutes eliminates the darkening without altering the taste.

Concentrated frozen fruit juice, such as cranberry or orange, can be thawed and used as a dip for fruits. A 12-ounce can should be enough for several quarts of fruit. Fold the fruit very gently in the concentrate, coating well. Use a mesh basket to drain excess juice.

Citric acid in crystalline (powder) or bulk (chunked) form is available from drugstores and health food stores. Use 3 tablespoons of water for dissolving the required amount. Follow package directions.

Lemon juice contains citric and ascorbic acid. While it may impart its flavor to the fruit, it is easy to use. Add 1 or 2 tablespoons of lemon juice to the freezing liquid of your choice — honey or sugar syrup, juice, or water.

Ascorbic acid in tablet or crystalline form is more commonly known as vitamin C. It can be found in drug- or health food stores. Use ½ teaspoon of the crushed tablets or crystalline powder dissolved in 1 quart of water as a dip for the fruit before you pack it in containers.

FREEZING HERBS

Drying herbs may seem like the easiest method, but freezing wins the taste test by far for some herbs.

Choose herbs that are still in season and at the peak of their essence. Harvest them before the hot sun wilts the plants, cutting them in 3- to 6-inch stalks. Holding the cut herbs by their stalks, swish them in water to remove all grit.

Freezing Herbs
. . . .

The herbs listed below freeze particularly well.

Basil

Chervil

Chives

Cilantro (coriander)

Comfrey

Dill

Lovage

Mint (most kinds)

Parsley

Savory

Sweet fennel

Thyme (a few kinds)

1. To blanch the herbs, fill a pot with water and bring to a boil. Hold the stalks with tongs and dip in boiling water until the color brightens. This will take only a few seconds per stalk. Because herbs are so tender, there's no need to blanch for long periods of time. Immediately plunge into an ice-water bath to stop the cooking.

2. Place the blanched stalks on layers of paper or tea towels to blot dry and cool.

3. Here you have choices: Remove the stem and keep the leaves whole or chop them, or leave the herbs whole on the stem. I like to keep the leaves whole on the stalk for versatility and ease of handling later. Place the prepared herbs in single layers on waxed paper. Make a flattened "roll" about 4 inches wide. Store the roll in an airtight plastic resealable freezer bag; press gently to remove all air from the bag.

4. Label and freeze your herbs for enjoyment all winter long. Use them as needed or thaw the entire roll (which will keep for 5 to 7 days in the refrigerator).

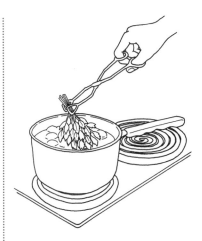

Blanch herbs by dipping them in boiling water.

Herbs can also be frozen in clean ice cube trays. Wash and chop fresh herbs and place a portion in each cube compartment. Add sufficient boiling water to cover the herbs and freeze. No need to blanch, as the boiling water takes care of that. When the cubes are solid, pop them out of the trays, then bag and label accordingly. Herb cubes are a great item to toss into sauces or soups. Another great way to freeze fresh herbs is in a prepared butter or paste.

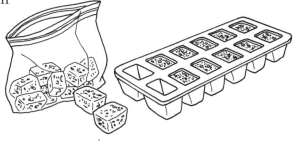

Freeze fresh chopped herbs in ice cube trays filled with water.

Grape Leaves

• • • • • • • • • • •

Grape leaves fare well when frozen by the method above. (Spring leaves are the most tender.) Note that they require a 2-minute blanching and that their color will then darken rather than lighten. Plunge several leaves at one time into cold water. Place them on layers of paper towels and gently blot dry. Place in single layers on waxed paper. Make a flattened "roll" about 4 inches wide. Store the roll in a resealable freezer bag. Use for stuffed grape leaves later.

FREEZING MEATS AND POULTRY

Fresh meats and poultry freeze very successfully and, when properly packaged, can be stored for many months. The same is not true of cured meats. Meats with a high salt content, such as bacon and cured ham, will keep for only a month or two in the freezer. That's because salt increases the rate at which rancidity develops in fat, and freezing does not prevent fat from becoming rancid. Added spices or seasonings limit the freezer life of ground meats and sausages, and hot dogs and luncheon meats are not suitable for freezing at all.

Freshly butchered meats, such as beef, lamb, and veal, can chill for up to 48 hours in the refrigerator at 40°F before freezing without loss of flavor. (This also takes a big load off your freezer if, for instance, you have a whole lamb to process because the meat is prechilled before freezing.) Chilling first allows the natural enzymes to age the meat as well as tenderize it. Fresh-killed poultry can prechill at 40°F for no longer than 12 hours before it starts to lose flavor. Meats and poultry purchased at a supermarket, however, should be rewrapped and frozen immediately after purchase.

PACKAGING MEAT AND POULTRY

The meat and poultry inside will be only as good as the wrap on the outside. Using regular plastic wrap, aluminum foil, or waxed paper is a false economy. Don't do it. Freezer wrap should be strong and pliable, moisture-proof, and impervious to air (oxygen). Heavy-duty plastic, aluminum foil, and freezer paper are recommended. For longer storage times, it's a good idea to prewrap meat and poultry in heavy plastic and then again in one of the recommended wraps or freezer bags. To prevent freezer burn, make sure all the air pockets are squeezed out of the final packaging, paying special attention to irregular shapes and sizes.

Freeze meat and poultry in the quantity that you intend to use it, and trim excess fat, which will become rancid over time and give food an "off" odor. If you plan to remove bones before you cook the food, remove them before you freeze it. They take up space in your freezer. When freezing cut pieces of poultry, put freezer paper between them to help you separate them as they thaw. Package giblets separately; they don't keep in the freezer as long as the rest of the bird.

Label well, providing the exact contents, weight, and date. Then freeze. When you're freezing large quantities of anything, it's a good idea to turn down your freezer temperature control to the coldest position. A large batch of room-temperature food added to a freezer will raise the air temperature and possibly affect the foods that are already frozen. Remember to reset your temperature control back to 0°F after 24 to 48 hours.

Note

· · · ·

Double-plastic freezer bags have been specially designed to reduce freezer burn.

THAWING POULTRY IN THE REFRIGERATOR

Chicken	4 or more pounds	1–1½ days
Duck	3–7 pounds	1–1½ days
Goose	6–12 pounds	1–2 days
Turkey	4–12 pounds	1–2 days
	12–20 pounds	2–3 days
	20–24 pounds	3–4 days
	Pieces of large turkey (half, quarter, half breast)	1–2 days
	Cut-up pieces	3–9 hours
	Boneless roasts	12–18 hours

Courtesy of the University of Missouri Extension Publications Library

FREEZING FISH

Freeze fish immediately after catching or purchasing. To improve the quality, fish should be treated before freezing. Fish containing fat — salmon, tuna, mackerel, mullet, and trout, for instance — can become rancid and should be dipped for 20 seconds in an ascorbic acid solution made from 2 teaspoons of crystalline ascorbic acid to 1 quart of cold water. Flounder, cod, whiting, redfish, snapper, grouper, and other lean fish should be dipped for 20 seconds in a brine of ¼ cup salt to 1 quart of cold water.

PACKAGING FISH

Wrap fish in heavy plastic wrap, aluminum foil, freezer paper, or other moisture- and vapor-proof wrapping. Place freezer paper between pieces for ease of separation during thawing, then freeze.

Another method involves placing the fish in a shallow pan, covering with water, and freezing. Remove the ice block from the container and wrap with moisture- and vapor-proof wrapping.

Glazing is another method that preserves the flavor of fresh fish. Place the unwrapped fish in the freezer. As soon as it freezes, remove it and dip in ice water. Again place the fish in the freezer to harden the glaze. Repeat until the fish is covered in ice, then wrap in moisture- and vapor-proof wrapping or place in a freezer bag.

Freezing Dairy Products

Most dairy products can be frozen if the proper procedure is followed. Dairy products that have been frozen should be thawed in the refrigerator and consumed within a few days.

Whole eggs. Stir to mix whites with yolks, but don't whip in air. For each cup of whole eggs, add 1½ teaspoons of sugar (for use in sweet foods) or ½ teaspoon of salt (for use in salty foods or for scrambling) to prevent gumminess. Pour into a container, leave headspace, then seal, label, and freeze.

Egg yolks. Separate eggs and stir the yolks together. For each cup of egg yolks, add 2 teaspoons of sugar (for use in sweet foods) or 1 teaspoon of salt (for use in salty foods). Pour into a container, allowing for headspace, then seal, label, and freeze.

Egg whites. Separate eggs and strain egg whites through a sieve. Do not stir or add sugar or salt. Pour into a container, allowing for headspace, then seal, label, and freeze.

Butter and cheeses. Wrapped in vapor- and moisture-proof wrapping, butter and cheeses freeze well. Like most foods, they should be thawed in the refrigerator. The texture of cheese that has been frozen changes slightly and it crumbles more easily, but when used in cooking, there is no discernible difference. Freeze in small blocks or portions that are 1 pound or less and no more than 1 inch thick.

Cream. Pasteurized cream that is at least 40 percent butterfat may be frozen whipped or unwhipped, though unwhipped cream that has been frozen and thawed will not whip well. To freeze liquid cream, heat it to 170°F for 10 to 15 minutes. For each quart, add ⅓ cup of sugar, pour into containers, leave headspace, then seal, label, and freeze.

TIP

Don't freeze eggs in their shells. The shells will break because of expansion. Instead, break the eggs into a bowl and freeze in the quantities you will use. An alternative is to suspend whole egg yolks in water and then freeze. An ice cube tray may be used.

TIP

Do not freeze whipped butter, buttermilk, cream cheese, cottage cheese, or sour cream, all of which either separate or become mushy when thawed.

SHELF LIFE FOR BEST-QUALITY HOME-FROZEN FOODS

Food	Storage Period at 0°F	Food	Storage Period at 0°F
Butter	6–7 months	Roasts	
Margarine	12 months	beef	6–12 months
Cheese		lamb, veal	6–9 months
natural	6–8 months	pork	3–6 months
processed	4 months	Steaks, chops	
Cream (all kinds)	2 months	beef	6–12 months
whipped	1 month	lamb	6–9 months
Eggs (whole, whites, yolks)	9–12 months	veal	3–4 months
Fish		Poultry (chicken, turkey, duck)	
fatty (perch, salmon, mackerel)	2–3 months	Whole: chicken or turkey	12 months
lean (cod, flounder, haddock, sole)	3–6 months	duck or goose	6 months
Fruit and fruit juice		Cut up: chicken	9 months
(except citrus)	8–12 months	turkey	6 months
citrus fruit and juice	4–6 months	Giblets	3 months
Ice cream or sherbet	2 months	Home-prepared foods	
Meat		bread	3 months
bacon	1 month	cake	3 months
frankfurters and luncheon meat	not recommended	casseroles (meat, fish, poultry)	3 months
ground beef, lamb, veal	2–3 months	cookies (baked and unbaked)	3 months
ground pork	1–2 months	pies (unbaked fruit)	3 months
ham	1 month	Vegetables	
Milk, fresh	1 month	home frozen	10 months
		purchased	8 months
		Yogurt	
		plain	1 month
		flavored	5 months

Courtesy of the University of Missouri Extension Publications Library

Recipes for Freezing

Croustade Appetizer Cups

. . . .

With very little labor, you can make these little bread cups and produce them from the freezer as an elegant appetizer whenever company stops in to visit. Once you see how easy they are, you'll make sure to keep your freezer stocked.

2 tablespoons butter or margarine

24 thin slices fresh white bread

1. Preheat the oven to 400°F.

2. Use your clean fingers or a paper towel to coat with butter the inside of two mini-muffin tins of 12 cups each.

3. Cut each bread slice into a 3-inch round; reserve the crusts for another use (I make toast points for serving appetizer spreads).

4. Push the bread rounds into the muffin tins similar to a pie crust in a pie plate.

5. Toast the croustades in the oven for about 10 minutes, or until browned.

6. Cool, pack into a plastic freezer bag, label, and freeze for up to 4 months.

. . . .

YIELD: 24 MUSHROOM CROUSTADES (ONE FILLED CROUSTADE PER SERVING)

NUTRITION PER SERVING

Calories	79	Total fat	3g
% from fat	37	Saturated	2g
Carbohydrates	10g	Cholesterol	7mg
Fiber	<1g	Sodium	167mg

. . . .

FILLING FOR CROUSTADES: MUSHROOM
Yield: 2 cups filling (about thirty-two 1-tablespoon servings)

½ pound fresh mushrooms, finely chopped

3 tablespoons chopped scallions, with tops

4 tablespoons butter or margarine

2 tablespoons flour

1 cup whole milk

½ teaspoon salt

1 tablespoon finely chopped fresh parsley

½ teaspoon lemon juice (bottled may be used)

⅛ teaspoon cayenne pepper

2 tablespoons grated Parmesan cheese

1. Sauté the mushrooms and scallions in the butter in a heavy skillet. Do not let them brown, but make sure all moisture from the mushrooms has evaporated.

2. Sprinkle the flour over the mushrooms and stir constantly to mix. Remove from the heat and add the milk and salt. Mix well.

3. Return to the heat and cook, stirring constantly, until the sauce thickens. Season with parsley, lemon juice, and pepper. Cool.

4. Mushroom filling may be frozen at this point or refrigerated, covered, until ready to use, up to 2 days later.

FILLING FOR CROUSTADES: QUICK WHITE SAUCE
Yield: 2 cups filling (about thirty-two 1-tablespoon servings)

6 tablespoons butter or margarine

½ cup flour

2 cups whole milk

2 tablespoons grated Parmesan cheese

1. Melt the butter over low heat in a heavy 1-quart saucepan. Add the flour and stir evenly and carefully until the mixture begins to bubble.

2. Remove from the heat and add the milk, stirring constantly.

3. Return to the heat. Stir carefully to keep from burning and continue until mixture is thickened.

TO ASSEMBLE

Preheat the oven to 350°F. Remove the croustades from the freezer and insert back into the muffin tins. Let them thaw slightly. Fill each bread cup with filling and top with Parmesan cheese.

Bake for about 10 minutes, until the filling is hot and the cheese is golden brown. Serve immediately.

Filling Suggestions
• • • • • • • • • • • • • •

Croustades are a great invention — as long as the filling is a thick, cream-type sauce. Custards or thin sauces will make your croustades soggy. Vary the Quick White Sauce with these options and enjoy!

Shrimp and cheese. *Add ½ cup each of finely chopped shrimp and Swiss cheese to taste.*

Cheese and ham. *Add cayenne pepper, ½ cup ham bits, and ½ cup Swiss cheese.*

Bacon and cheese. *Add 4 slices of sautéed bacon, finely chopped, and ¼ cup Swiss cheese.*

Spinach and bacon. *Add sautéed bacon bits and chopped, cooked, squeezed, and drained frozen spinach to taste.*

Note: Include 1 teaspoon of garlic or your favorite prepared mustard to add zip to any of the sauce suggestions. Reheat any leftover filling the next day and enjoy over toast.

• •
YIELD: 24 CROUSTADES WITH QUICK WHITE SAUCE (ONE FILLED CROUSTADE PER SERVING)
NUTRITION PER SERVING

Calories	93	Total fat	4g
% from fat	40	Saturated	2g
Carbohydrates	12	Cholesterol	10mg
Fiber	1g	Sodium	143mg

• •

Spiced Pear Butter

Biscuits, waffles, pancakes, and English muffins will never be the same again after you've tasted them spread with this pear butter.

5 ripe pears, peeled, cored, and chopped

2 tablespoons honey

2 tablespoons lemon juice

1 tablespoon cider vinegar

1 tablespoon finely minced fresh ginger root

½ teaspoon ground cinnamon

¼ teaspoon ground allspice

¼ teaspoon ground nutmeg

1. Combine the pears, honey, lemon juice, vinegar, ginger, cinnamon, allspice, and nutmeg in a heavy 2-quart saucepan.

2. Cook over low heat, uncovered, for 30 minutes, or until the mixture is very soft and relatively thick. Stir occasionally and mash with a spoon.

3. Ladle into two clean, 1-cup freezer containers. Cool in the refrigerator.

4. Label and freeze one; keep the other for immediate use.

5. To use the frozen pear butter, thaw it in the refrigerator. Refrigerated, it will keep for 10 to 14 days.

YIELD: 2 CUPS (SIXTEEN 1-OUNCE SERVINGS)
NUTRITION PER SERVING

Calories	37	Total fat	<1g
% from fat	4	Saturated	0g
Carbohydrates	10g	Cholesterol	0mg
Fiber	1g	Sodium	0mg

Eggplant Caviar

This flavorful recipe is perfect for entertaining. Serve it on toast points or melba toast.

1 large eggplant, halved lengthwise

1 tablespoon olive oil

1 medium red bell pepper, seeded and finely diced

1 small onion, minced

3 cloves garlic, minced

1 large tomato, diced

3 tablespoons fresh lemon juice

2 tablespoons minced chives

1 tablespoon fresh basil, minced

1. Preheat the oven to 350°F.

2. Brush the eggplant well with 1 teaspoon of the olive oil and place the halves, cut side down, on a cookie sheet lightly coated with vegetable cooking spray. Bake for about 1 hour, or until tender.

3. Let cool, then scoop out the meat and discard the skin. Chop.

4. Heat the remaining olive oil in a heavy skillet and sauté the red pepper, onion, and garlic until soft, about 5 minutes.

5. Stir in the eggplant, tomato, lemon juice, chives, and basil. Sauté 1 minute longer to heat the mixture through and to dry up some of the tomato juice.

6. Put in a 1-quart container, label, and freeze for up to 1 month. This may also be refrigerated and consumed the next day.

7. To use the frozen eggplant caviar, thaw in the refrigerator and serve at room temperature.

YIELD: 4 CUPS (SIXTEEN 2-OUNCE SERVINGS)
NUTRITION PER SERVING

Calories	22	Total fat	1g
% from fat	36	Saturated	<1g
Carbohydrates	3g	Cholesterol	0mg
Fiber	1g	Sodium	2mg

Pungent Eggplant Chutney

This rich and elegant appetizer is perfect for a summer buffet or picnic.

¾ cup olive oil

2 medium eggplants, peeled and cubed

1 clove elephant garlic, chopped

1¼ cups finely chopped celery

2 medium onions, finely chopped

½ cup finely chopped green olives (with or without pimiento)

1 can (8 ounces) Italian tomato sauce (or 1 cup homemade)

¼ cup capers, drained

¼ cup white wine vinegar

1 tablespoon red wine vinegar

1 tablespoon sugar

Freshly ground black pepper

1. Heat the oil in a skillet. Add the eggplant cubes and garlic and cook over moderately high heat for 8–10 minutes, until lightly browned. Stir often.

2. Using a slotted spoon, remove the eggplant from the oil and set aside.

3. Add the celery, onions, and olives to the oil, cooking until tender. Add the tomato sauce and simmer the mixture for 5 minutes.

4. Add the capers, vinegars, sugar, and pepper. Return the eggplant to the pan; cook over low heat 5 minutes longer.

5. Cool, ladle into freezer containers, and freeze for up to 1 month.

6. To serve, defrost and serve cold or at room temperature with toast or crackers.

YIELD: 4 CUPS (SIXTEEN ¼-CUP SERVINGS)
NUTRITION PER SERVING

Calories	124	Total fat	11g
% from fat	75	Saturated	2g
Carbohydrates	7g	Cholesterol	0mg
Fiber	2g	Sodium	225mg

Pâté of Chicken Livers

This American version of Strasbourg pâté de foie gras is made with chicken liver and is a very successful appetizer for freezing.

1 medium onion, finely chopped (about ½ cup)

1 small tart apple, peeled, cored, and chopped

1 garlic clove, chopped

1 pound chicken livers

6 tablespoons butter

¼ cup cream or whole milk

½ cup (1 stick) butter, softened

1½ teaspoons salt

1 teaspoon fresh lemon juice

¼ teaspoon freshly ground black pepper

1. In a heavy 2-quart skillet, sauté the onion, apple, and garlic in 3 tablespoons of the butter until soft but not browned. Remove from the skillet and reserve.

2. Sauté the chicken livers in the remaining butter for about 10 minutes over medium heat. Livers can be pink in the center.

3. Pour the livers and butter from the skillet into a blender or food processor. Add the cream and purée.

4. In a large mixing bowl, combine the two mixtures and let cool until barely warm.

5. Beat in the softened butter, salt, lemon juice, and pepper.

6. Pour the smooth mixture into three 8-ounce ceramic crocks.

7. Wrap, label, and freeze for up to 1 month.

8. To use, thaw overnight in the refrigerator. Serve at room temperature with toast points or melba toast.

YIELD: 3 CUPS (TWENTY-FOUR ⅛-CUP SERVINGS)
NUTRITION PER SERVING

Calories	64	Total fat	5g
% from fat	65	Saturated	3g
Carbohydrates	2g	Cholesterol	94mg
Fiber	<1g	Sodium	183mg

Picnic Chicken Roll

* * * * * * * * * *

Lean and delicious, try this American version of a French pâté at your next picnic.

2 pounds boned, skinned chicken breast, cubed

3 tablespoons dried onion flakes

2 tablespoons grated Parmesan cheese

1 tablespoon firmly packed brown sugar

2 teapoons dried basil

2 teaspoons dried marjoram

2 teaspoons dried oregano

1½ teaspoons salt

1. Finely grind the chicken in a food processor or meat grinder.

2. Add the seasonings and mix well.

3. Preheat the oven to 225°F.

4. Spray two 12-inch by 18-inch sheets of heavy aluminum foil with cooking oil. Divide the meat mixture in half and place on the prepared foil. Shape the chicken mixture into two logs, each about 8 inches long. Roll them in the foil and secure the ends tightly. Prick the foil logs with a fork several evenly spaced times to allow steam and juices to escape while cooking.

5. Bake in a 9-inch square pan for 3 hours, or until the logs are firm when pressed.

6. Peel off the foil while the meat is still warm and gently roll the logs on several layers of paper towels to drain the fat.

7. Wrap the logs in freezer wrap and chill in the refrigerator.

8. Label and freeze for up to 3–4 weeks.

9. To use, thaw overnight in the refrigerator. Slice very thin and serve cold.

* * * * * * * * * * * * * * * * *

YIELD: TWO 12-OUNCE LOGS (EIGHT 3-OUNCE SERVINGS)
NUTRITION PER SERVING

Calories	156	Total fat	4g
% from fat	21	Saturated	1g
Carbohydrates	4g	Cholesterol	70mg
Fiber	<1g	Sodium	491mg

* * * * * * * * * * * * * * * * *

Rosemary Paste for Angel-Hair Pasta

*My friend Silvano, who lives in Tuscany, has a rosemary hedge that is 4 feet wide
by 15 feet long. Imagine what could be done with all that rosemary!
This sauce is also wonderful over a grilled, butterflied leg of lamb.*

¼ cup chopped fresh parsley

2 tablespoons fresh oregano leaves

2 tablespoons fresh rosemary leaves

1 tablespoon grated orange zest

2 cloves garlic, peeled

1 cup chopped scallions, with green tops

¼ cup olive oil

2 teaspoons lemon juice

1. Combine the parsley, oregano, rosemary, orange zest, and garlic in the bowl of a food processor. Pulse the machine to coarsely chop the mixture. Scrape down the sides of the bowl and add the scallions, pulsing again to chop.

2. With the motor running, add the oil in droplets until the mixture forms a paste.

3. Add the lemon juice and mix well, scraping the bowl.

4. Pour into three ½-cup freezer containers, leaving ½ inch of headspace. Label and freeze for up to 3 months.

5. To serve, thaw the paste in the refrigerator, bring to room temperature, and pour over ½ pound of cooked angel-hair pasta. Do not heat the paste, as it may cause the oil to separate. The heated, cooked pasta is just right for combining with the room-temperature paste.

YIELD: 1½ CUPS (SIX ¼-CUP SERVINGS)
NUTRITION PER SERVING

Calories	90	Total fat	9g
% from fat	88	Saturated	1g
Carbohydrates	2g	Cholesterol	0mg
Fiber	<1g	Sodium	4mg

Pesto with Green Bell Peppers

* * * * * * * * * * *

The garnish for this recipe can be prepared and frozen separately,
or you can simply add the garnish when you serve the dish.

2 green bell peppers, seeded and coarsely chopped

1 cup fresh basil

½ cup grated Parmesan cheese

¼ cup olive oil

4 cloves garlic, chopped

⅔ cup salted and roasted pumpkin seeds

1. Steam blanch the green peppers over boiling water for 3 minutes. Drain, then transfer to the bowl of a food processor.

2. Add the basil, cheese, oil, and garlic and process until smooth.

3. Freeze in two portions of 3–4 servings each for ease of use. Freeze the pesto for up to 3 months.

4. To use, thaw overnight in the refrigerator.

5. Spoon the pesto over hot, cooked pasta and top each serving with some of the pumpkin seeds.

* *

YIELD: 2 CUPS (EIGHT ¼-CUP SERVINGS)
NUTRITION PER SERVING

Calories	119	Total fat	10g
% from fat	72	Saturated	2g
Carbohydrates	5g	Cholesterol	5mg
Fiber	3g	Sodium	119mg

* *

Garden Tomato Sauce

•••••••••••

Try this as an alternative to canning those abundant tomatoes.
Serve with pasta, chicken, or veal.

2 dozen Italian tomatoes, or 12 cups chopped tomatoes

1 tablespoon olive oil

1 medium onion, chopped

2 cloves garlic, crushed

2 tablespoons chopped green bell pepper

2 tablespoons chopped carrot

2 tablespoons chopped celery

2 tablespoons chopped fresh parsley

1 teaspoon chopped fresh oregano

1. Wash, core, and coarsely chop the tomatoes.

2. Purée in the bowl of a food processor.

3. Heat the olive oil in a heavy saucepan or an ovenproof, flameproof casserole and sauté the onion until soft, about 5 minutes.

4. Add the garlic, pepper, carrot, celery, and herbs.

5. Add the tomato purée to the mixture and simmer, uncovered, for about 2 hours. Be careful not to let it burn. Stir the sauce occasionally as it thickens. (This process can also be completed in an uncovered ovenproof, flameproof casserole at 350°F.)

6. Cool slightly and pour the sauce into 1-cup freezer containers, leaving ½ inch of headspace. Label and freeze the sauce for up to 3 months.

7. To use, thaw in the refrigerator.

YIELD: 4½ PINTS (EIGHTEEN ½-CUP SERVINGS)
NUTRITION PER SERVING

Calories	14	Total fat	1g
% from fat	48	Saturated	<1g
Carbohydrates	2g	Cholesterol	0mg
Fiber	<1g	Sodium	3mg

Apple Beet Purée

*The best of autumn combined in one dish — and it tastes great
as a side dish with pork.*

5 medium beets, scrubbed, with tops
   removed

2 tablespoons plus ½ teaspoon salt

2 onions, minced

½ cup (1 stick) butter

4 tart apples, peeled, cored, and sliced

¼ cup red wine vinegar

1 tablespoon sugar

1. In a saucepan, combine the beets and
2 tablespoons of the salt and cover with
water. Cover with a lid and simmer for
30–40 minutes, or until fork-tender.

2. Drain and cool the beets, then remove
their skins and roots. Set aside.

3. In a covered saucepan over low heat,
sauté the onions in the butter for about 20
mintues, or until soft.

4. Add the apples to the pan and toss
them in the butter mixture. Add the
vinegar, sugar, and remaining salt.

5. Uncover and continue to cook over
medium heat for 15 minutes, until the
onions and apples are very tender.

6. Let cool slightly and transfer the apple
mixture and the beets to the bowl of a food
processor. Process until smooth.

7. Cool, chill, and freeze in a 1-quart
freezer container for up to 3 months.

8. To serve, thaw overnight in the
refrigerator. Serve chilled.

YIELD: 3 CUPS (SIX ½-CUP SERVINGS)
NUTRITION PER SERVING

Calories	122	Total fat	2g
% from fat	15	Saturated	1g
Carbohydrates	25g	Cholesterol	5mg
Fiber	5g	Sodium	2,397mg

Tomato Salsa

This salsa is not just for chips; try it over scrambled eggs. Lovers of spicy salsa should add a dash of bottled hot sauce when serving.

2 tablespoons olive oil

1 medium onion, finely chopped

1½ stalks celery, minced

2 tablespoons serrano chiles, seeded and chopped (wear rubber gloves)

1 clove garlic

4 medium tomatoes, seeded and quartered

3 tablespoons chopped fresh cilantro

2 tablespoons lime juice

1 teaspoon mild honey

1 teaspoon chopped fresh basil (½ teaspoon dried)

¼ teaspoon ground cumin

¼ teaspoon chili powder

1. Heat the oil in a heavy skillet. Add the onion, celery, chiles, and garlic.

2. Sauté for about 5 minutes, or until soft. Add the tomatoes, cilantro, lime juice, honey, basil, cumin, and chili powder. Bring to a boil, cover, and reduce the heat. Simmer for 15 minutes. (Fish out the tomato skins as the mixture cools.)

3. Ladle into two 1-cup freezer containers and let cool. Cover and chill overnight in the refrigerator. Label the containers; freeze for up to 3 months.

4. To use, thaw in the refrigerator. The salsa will be thin but delicious.

YIELD: 2 CUPS (FOUR ½-CUP SERVINGS)
NUTRITION PER SERVING

Calories	119	Total fat	7g
% from fat	51	Saturated	1g
Carbohydrates	14g	Cholesterol	0mg
Fiber	3g	Sodium	30mg

Gazpacho

Guests always ask for this recipe and can't believe it came from the freezer.
Serve it in teacups with saucers as a buffet selection or in mugs
on the patio if bowls aren't available.

6 medium tomatoes, peeled, cored, and chopped

5 cups vegetable juice, or 40 ounces canned

2 medium cucumbers, peeled, seeded, and chopped

1 large onion, chopped

1 large green bell pepper, seeded and chopped

1 stalk celery, chopped

⅓ cup red wine vinegar

2 tablespoons olive oil

1 tablespoon fresh dill, chopped

1 clove garlic, minced

1 teaspoon salt

½ teaspoon hot pepper sauce

¼ teaspoon coarsely ground black pepper

1. Combine all ingredients and toss until the vegetables are evenly coated with oil, vinegar, and herbs.

2. Pour into two 1½-quart freezer containers. Seal, label well, and freeze for up to 3 months.

3. To serve, thaw in the refrigerator overnight and store chilled. It will keep for 3 days thawed in the refrigerator.

YIELD: 2½ QUARTS (TEN 1-CUP SERVINGS)

NUTRITION PER SERVING

Calories	93	Total fat	3g
% from fat	27	Saturated	<1g
Carbohydrates	16g	Cholesterol	0mg
Fiber	3g	Sodium	668mg

Tomato-Basil Soup

Tomatoes and basil are natural companions in the kitchen. Fresh from the garden, they make this soup more than an introduction to a meal.

½ cup (1 stick) butter

6 medium onions, thinly sliced (about 3 cups)

2 cloves garlic, minced

3 pounds plum tomatoes, chopped

2 quarts (8 cups) chicken stock

1 tablespoon lime juice

Pinch of sugar

¾ cup chopped fresh basil leaves

Zest of 1 small orange

1. In a heavy saucepan, melt the butter over low heat. Add the onions, cover, and cook until soft, about 15 minutes. Add the garlic and cook 2–3 minutes longer.

2. Add the tomatoes, stock, lime juice, and sugar. Bring to a boil, reduce the heat, and simmer, covered, for 15 minutes.

3. Add the basil and orange zest.

4. Transfer the soup to the bowl of a food processor and purée.

5. Cool. Ladle into two 10-cup freezer containers. Allow 1 inch of headspace.

6. Chill in the refrigerator, label, and freeze for up to 3 months.

7. To use, thaw in the refrigerator overnight. Serve cold or hot.

YIELD: 5 QUARTS (TWENTY 1-CUP SERVINGS)
NUTRITION PER SERVING

Calories	46	Total fat	1g
% from fat	19	Saturated	<1g
Carbohydrates	8g	Cholesterol	2mg
Fiber	2g	Sodium	872 mg

Winter Onion Soup

* * * * * * * * * *

A plain yellow onion develops a deep, rich flavor during the long, slow cooking in this recipe. After initial organization, the soup pot can simmer away almost unattended.

3 tablespoons butter

1 tablespoon vegetable oil

1½ pounds (about 5 cups) yellow onions, peeled and thinly sliced

1 teaspoon salt

¼ teaspoon sugar

3 tablespoons flour

2 quarts beef broth

1 bay leaf

Salt and freshly ground black pepper

1½ cups prepared garlic croutons

2 cups grated Swiss cheese

1. Melt the butter with the oil in a heavy 4-quart saucepan.

2. Add the onions, cover, and cook slowly over low heat until soft.

3. Raise the heat to medium high, uncover, and stir in the salt and sugar. This step requires some watching to avoid burning the contents. Continue cooking 20–40 minutes, stirring frequently. The onions will caramelize, turning a deep, rich brown, thanks to the sugar. They will also develop a rich, nutty flavor, thanks to the slow cooking.

4. Sprinkle the flour over the onion mixture and stir for 2–3 minutes, then remove from the heat.

5. Add the broth and bay leaf. Partially cover and simmer for 45 minutes. Season to taste.

6. Let cool, discard the bay leaf, then pour the soup into an 8-cup freezer container, allowing ½ inch of headspace.

7. Chill, label, and freeze the soup for up to 2 months.

8. To use, thaw in the refrigerator, then heat in the microwave until piping hot.

9. Prepare six soup bowls, each with ¼ cup of croutons and ⅓ cup of Swiss cheese.

10. Gently pour the hot soup over the cheese and croutons and serve.

* *

YIELD: 6 CUPS (SIX 1-CUP SERVINGS)
NUTRITION PER SERVING

Calories	366	Total fat	24g
% from fat	59	Saturated	12g
Carbohydrates	22g	Cholesterol	54mg
Fiber	3g	Sodium	2,725mg

* *

Butternut Squash Soup Base

This soup works well with apple juice or milk. Either way, it will make an October brunch very special.

2 large butternut squash
(about 2 pounds each)

2 tablespoons olive oil

2 large carrots, peeled and sliced

2 medium onions, chopped

1 clove garlic, chopped

1 tablespoon minced fresh ginger

2 teaspoons curry powder

¼ teaspoon ground cinnamon

⅛ teaspoon ground nutmeg

3 cups apple juice or milk*

1. Preheat the oven to 350°F. Bake the whole squash on a baking sheet for about 45 minutes. Remove from the oven and let cool.

2. Open the squash and discard the seeds. Spoon out the meat and place it in the bowl of a food processor. (You can speed this process by cubing and seeding the raw squash, boiling it for 15 minutes, and then slipping off the skins before placing it in the food processor.)

* *Only 1 cup is used before freezing.*

3. Heat the oil in a heavy saucepan. Sauté the carrots, onions, and garlic until soft, about 5 minutes. Add the ginger, curry, cinnamon, and nutmeg and continue cooking until the spices are evenly distributed.

4. Add this mixture to the squash in the food processor. Add 1 cup of the apple juice or milk and process until smooth.

5. Ladle the soup into two 2-pint containers. Cool, chill, label, and freeze for up to 2 months.

6. To use, thaw the soup overnight in the refrigerator, then add 1 cup of the remaining apple juice or milk to each container.

YIELD: 4 PINTS (EIGHT 1-CUP SERVINGS)
NUTRITION PER SERVING

Calories	162	Total fat	4g
% from fat	20	Saturated	<1g
Carbohydrates	33g	Cholesterol	0mg
Fiber	4g	Sodium	16mg

Pumpkin Soup

. . . .

*This recipe is so thick and creamy that guests will think it is high in calories, but
instead of coming from rich cream, the texture is achieved by adding puréed pumpkin.*

2 pounds pumpkin, cut into chunks

3 large baking potatoes, cut into chunks

1 large onion, coarsely chopped

3 cups chicken stock

2 cups water

½ teaspoon dried rosemary

½ cup grated Parmesan cheese

½ teaspoon salt

¼ teaspoon ground nutmeg

¼ teaspoon ground white pepper

1. In a heavy, 2-quart saucepan combine the pumpkin, potatoes, onion, stock, water, and rosemary. Cover and simmer for about 30 minutes, or until the pumpkin is tender.

2. When cooled, peel the skin from the pumpkin pieces and return to the broth. Purée the mixture in batches in a blender or food processor. Add the cheese, salt, nutmeg, and pepper. Adjust the seasonings.

3. Ladle into a 10-cup freezer container, label, and freeze for up to 2 months.

4. To serve, thaw in the refrigerator. Heat and serve with additional Parmesan cheese, if desired.

. . . .

YIELD: 10 CUPS (TEN 1-CUP SERVINGS)
NUTRITION PER SERVING

Calories	79	Total fat	2g
% from fat	20	Saturated	1g
Carbohydrates	12g	Cholesterol	4mg
Fiber	2g	Sodium	849mg

. . . .

Black Bean Soup

*Serve it with a salad and bread, and this rich bean soup
becomes a complete, hearty meal.*

1 cup dried black beans, rinsed and picked over

4 cups water

2 large onions, chopped

1 large green bell pepper, seeded and chopped

3 bay leaves

2 cloves garlic, minced

⅛ cup olive oil

⅛ cup red wine vinegar

1. Soak the dried beans overnight in a large pot of water.

2. Discard the soaking water and cover the beans with the 4 cups of fresh water. Add the onions, pepper, bay leaves, and garlic and cook until the beans are tender, about 1–1½ hours.

3. Remove 1 cup of beans and broth and purée in a blender or food processor. Return to the pot to thicken the liquid.

4. Cool, chill, and freeze in a 6-cup freezer container for up to 2 months.

5. To serve, thaw in the refrigerator overnight.

6. Add the olive oil and vinegar; mix well. Heat until bubbly. Garnish with a dollop of low-fat sour cream and serve.

YIELD: 5 CUPS (FIVE 1-CUP SERVINGS)
NUTRITION PER SERVING

Calories	212	Total fat	6g
% from fat	25	Saturated	<1g
Carbohydrates	32g	Cholesterol	0mg
Fiber	7g	Sodium	10mg

Lentil and Sausage Soup

*My friend Lane, who is an excellent cook, gave this recipe to me.
It has been a family favorite ever since. I use green lentils for this recipe.
If you use brown lentils, reduce the cooking time as noted.*

2 cups green (or brown) lentils,
rinsed and picked over

7 cups water

1½ teaspoons fresh thyme, minced

1 bay leaf

½ teaspoon freshly ground black pepper

½ teaspoon salt

⅛ teaspoon dried rosemary

⅛ teaspoon dried tarragon

1 pound bulk sausage

1 pound hot Italian sausage, casings
removed

2 carrots, sliced

2 stalks celery, sliced

2 medium onions, sliced

2 cups chopped fresh plum tomatoes

1 package (1.8 ounces) oxtail soup mix,
or 4 tablespoons beef bouillon granules

½ cup dried angel-hair pasta, broken into
2-inch pieces

1. In a 3-quart kettle, cover the lentils
with the water, add the seasonings, and
simmer for 30–40 minutes. If you are using
brown lentils, simmer for 20 minutes.

2. Sauté the sausage in a large skillet.
Remove from the skillet with a slotted
spoon and drain on paper towels.

3. Sauté the carrots, celery, and onions in
the sausage skillet.

4. Add the tomatoes, sautéed vegetables,
and sausage to the lentil mixture.

5. Add the soup mix and simmer for
1 hour, stirring frequently. Add the pasta
for the last 10 minutes.

6. Cool. Discard the bay leaf and ladle
into one 10-cup freezer container, or into
individual serving-size freezer containers
according to your family's needs.

7. Label and freeze for up to 2 months.

YIELD: 10 CUPS (EIGHT 1¼-CUP SERVINGS)
NUTRITION PER SERVING

Calories	676	Total fat	42g
% from fat	56	Saturated	15g
Carbohydrates	44g	Cholesterol	83mg
Fiber	17g	Sodium	1,343mg

Vegetarian Chili

Serve this hearty soup with or without rice for a filling, satisfying meal.

1 cup dried brown lentils, rinsed and picked over

6 cups water

2 medium onions, chopped

2 tablespoons vegetable oil

2 inches fresh ginger root, peeled and minced

1 serrano chile, seeded and chopped (wear rubber gloves)

1 teaspoon chili powder

1 tablespoon ground coriander

1 tablespoon curry powder

1. In a heavy saucepan, simmer the lentils in the water until tender, about 20 minues.

2. Sauté the onions in the oil until soft, about 10 minutes.

3. Add the ginger, chile, and seasonings to the onions and cook for 5 minutes, stirring to mix the flavors.

4. Add the onions to the lentils. Cook, covered, for about 15 minutes.

5. Cool. Ladle the chili into freezer containers. Chill, label, and freeze for up to 2 months.

6. To serve, thaw in the refrigerator overnight. Heat in the microwave or on the stovetop.

YIELD: 8 CUPS (FOUR 2-CUP SERVINGS)
NUTRITION PER SERVING

Calories	264	Total fat	8g
% from fat	25	Saturated	<1g
Carbohydrates	36g	Cholesterol	0mg
Fiber	17g	Sodium	26mg

Ratatouille

· · · · · · · · · · · ·

This old favorite adapts to the freezer. Serve this dish with eggs, over pasta, or with lamb or beef. Whatever the time of year, your kitchen will be perfumed with the essence of the summer's garden.

4 small zucchini, sliced

2 yellow onions, sliced

2 green bell peppers, seeded and chopped

3 cloves garlic, minced

6 tablespoons olive oil

3 medium tomatoes, peeled, seeded, and chopped

3 small eggplants, cubed

½ teaspoon salt

2 tablespoons chopped fresh parsley

1 tablespoon chopped fresh basil

1 teaspoon dried oregano

1. In a heavy 2-quart skillet, sauté the zucchini, onions, peppers, and garlic in 4 tablespoons of the oil until soft. Add the tomatoes and heat thoroughly to help evaporate the liquid.

2. Meanwhile "sweat" the eggplants by tossing the eggplant cubes with the salt in a large bowl. Let rest for 30 minutes. Drain the cubes well.

3. Sauté the eggplant cubes in the remaining oil.

4. Add the eggplant cubes to the onion mixture and stir well.

5. Add the herbs and stir to distribute evenly. Cool.

6. Pour into a 3-quart casserole or divide into two portions and store in plastic freezer bags. Chill, label, and freeze for up to 3 months.

· ·

YIELD: 7½ CUPS (FIFTEEN ½-CUP SERVINGS)
NUTRITION PER SERVING

Calories	87	Total fat	6g
% from fat	55	Saturated	<1g
Carbohydrates	9g	Cholesterol	0mg
Fiber	3g	Sodium	78mg

· ·

Oriental Pork Roll

. . . .

*Rich in flavors but low in calories, this homemade sausage roll will be a
winner at your next party or picnic.*

2 pounds pork tenderloin, trimmed
  and cubed

4 teaspoons firmly packed brown sugar

1 tablespoon soy sauce

2 teaspoons crushed, dried, hot chiles
  (wear rubber gloves)

1½ teaspoons ground ginger

½ teaspoon garlic powder

½ teaspoon salt

1. Preheat the oven to 225°F. Spray two
12- by 18-inch sheets of heavy-duty
aluminum foil with cooking oil.

2. Finely grind the meat in a food
processor.

3. Add the remaining ingredients to the
processor bowl and mix well.

4. Divide the meat mixture in half and
place each on its own sheet of prepared foil.

5. Roll each meat mixture into a log
about 8 inches long. Wrap each tightly
in its foil blanket, securing the ends.
Use a fork to prick the foil, which will
allow steam and juices to escape as the
pork roll cooks.

6. Bake in a 9-inch square pan for
3 hours, or until the logs seem firm
when pressed.

7. When the logs are done but still warm,
peel off the foil and blot the meat on
several layers of paper towels to degrease.
Wrap in freezer paper and chill.

8. Label and freeze for up to 4 weeks.

9. To serve, thaw overnight in the
refrigerator. Slice very thin and serve cold
on crackers or melba toast. Add a dollop of
spicy mustard to each cracker, if desired.

. . . .

**YIELD: TWO 16-OUNCE LOGS (THIRTY-TWO
1-OUNCE SERVINGS)**

NUTRITION PER SERVING

Calories	37	Total fat	1g
% from fat	25	Saturated	<1g
Carbohydrates	<1g	Cholesterol	18mg
Fiber	0g	Sodium	80mg

. . . .

Marinated Italian Pork

· · · · · · · · · · ·

This dish is easy, delicious, and a perfectly presentable leftover.

1 medium onion, sliced

¼ cup cider vinegar

2 cloves garlic, chopped

⅔ cup balsamic vinegar

½ cup plus 2 tablespoons olive oil

Juice of ½ lemon

3 tablespoons fresh rosemary
(1½ tablespoons dried)

2 tablespoons minced fresh sage leaves
(1 tablespoon dried)

1 tablespoon chopped fresh parsley

1 tablespoon whole peppercorns

1½ pounds boneless pork tenderloin

½ teaspoon salt

½ teaspoon freshly ground black pepper

½ cup water

⅓ cup unsweetened apple juice

· ·

YIELD: 24 OUNCES (FOUR 6-OUNCE SERVINGS)
NUTRITION PER SERVING

Calories	542	Total fat	40g
% from fat	65	Saturated	7g
Carbohydrates	11g	Cholesterol	111mg
Fiber	<1g	Sodium	356mg

· ·

1. To prepare the marinade, simmer the onion, cider vinegar, and garlic for 5 minutes in a heavy, nonreactive saucepan. Add the balsamic vinegar, ½ cup of the oil, lemon juice, rosemary, sage, parsley, and peppercorns. Stir and set aside to cool.

2. Preheat the oven to 375°F. Pat the meat dry, rub it with 1 tablespoon of the remaining olive oil, and sprinkle with salt and pepper.

3. Brown the meat in the remaining oil in an ovenproof skillet over medium-high heat. Turn the meat to be sure it browns on all sides.

4. Add the water and apple juice, then place the skillet in the oven for 25 minutes, or until the meat is cooked internally to 160°F (check with a meat thermometer).

5. Cool the meat and marinade; transfer the meat to a heavy-duty freezer bag, then pour in the marinade. Chill in the refrigerator for 12 hours. At this point, it's ready to be served sliced and chilled or at room temperature. Or label and freeze for up to 4 weeks.

6. To serve, thaw overnight in the refrigerator, slice thinly, and serve chilled or at room temperature as a main course.

Broiled Flank Steaks Oriental

Wow your dinner guests with this easy, lean version of steak. Leftovers are wonderful for sandwiches or added to a stir-fry.

2 pounds flank steak, scored with a knife

2 tablespoons lemon juice

2 tablespoons vegetable oil

2 tablespoons water

1 tablespoon red wine vinegar

1½ teaspoons soy sauce

1½ teaspoons Worcestershire sauce

⅛ teaspoon ground ginger

Pinch of garlic powder

1. Tenderize the meat and put it in a heavy-duty resealable plastic freezer bag.

2. Combine the remaining ingredients and pour over the meat in the bag.

3. Label, chill, and then freeze the steaks for 3–4 weeks.

4. To serve, thaw in the refrigerator overnight. Remove the steak from the marinade and grill or broil for 3 minutes on each side for rare. Slice on the diagonal and serve.

Tenderizing Meat

Meat mallets, used to tenderize meat, are usually made of hardwood and have one flat end and one textured end. Pounding the meat with a mallet breaks up the tough fibers. It also flattens and compacts the meat, making it easier to roll around stuffings.

Generally, use the textured side of the mallet on tougher cuts of beef and the flat side on chicken and other tender cuts of meat. Lightly flour the mallet or spray it lightly with cooking spray to prevent sticking.

If your meat needs tenderizing and you do not have a mallet, try pounding the meat with the edge of a heavy saucer, a rolling pin, or even a large, heavy serving spoon. If you are pounding on a wooden surface, a heavy unopened can will also work.

YIELD: 32 OUNCES (EIGHT 4-OUNCE SERVINGS)
NUTRITION PER SERVING

Calories	263	Total fat	15g
% from fat	53	Saturated	5g
Carbohydrates	<1g	Cholesterol	58mg
Fiber	0g	Sodium	153mg

Baked Beans

. . . .

Adults and children love these beans.

3 pounds dried navy beans, rinsed and picked over

2¼ cups dark molasses

3 tablespoons frozen orange juice concentrate

3 teaspoons dry mustard

3 medium onions

18 whole cloves

1. In a large pot, cover the dried beans with water and soak overnight.

2. Drain the beans and cover with fresh water. Simmer, covered, in a 6-quart pot until tender, 2–3 hours. (A 4-quart slow-cooker may be used for 6–8 hours instead.)

3. Preheat the oven to 300°F.

4. For storing and serving convenience, divide the precooked beans into two 2-quart bean pots or heavy casseroles.

5. Mix together the molasses, orange juice concentrate, and mustard. Add, in equal amounts, to each pot.

6. Cut each onion in half and stud each half with 3 of the cloves. Add 3 onion halves to each pot.

7. Cover and bake for 5–6 hours, being careful not to let the beans dry out. Add water, if necessary.

8. Cool the bean pots. Chill, then wrap the entire bean pot or casserole in freezer paper or pour the baked beans into freezer bags to save space. Label and freeze for up to 2 months

9. To use, thaw overnight in the refrigerator.

10. Heat in a saucepan for 20–30 minutes until hot or, if stored in bean pots, bake in a 350°F oven until heated through.

Note: In a pinch, canned, rinsed beans can be seasoned in this manner. Omit the freezing step.

. . . .

YIELD: 4 QUARTS TOTAL; 2 QUARTS EACH POT OR PLASTIC BAG (SIXTEEN 1-CUP SERVINGS)

NUTRITION PER SERVING

Calories	445	Total fat	3g
% from fat	5	Saturated	<1g
Carbohydrates	91g	Cholesterol	0mg
Fiber	24g	Sodium	72mg

. . . .

Green and Gold Squash Casserole

Capture the harvest in late summer when the zucchini and yellow squash are at their peak. I usually double this recipe to make one for dinner and one for the freezer. It disappears fast.

1 medium onion, chopped

2 tablespoons olive oil

2 medium zucchini (about 1 pound), coarsely grated

2 medium yellow summer squash (about 1 pound), coarsely grated

3 eggs, beaten (egg substitute may be used)

1 cup Saltine crumbs

2 tablespoons fresh parsley, chopped

1½ teaspoons fresh oregano, chopped (or ½ teaspoon dried)

1¼ teaspoons freshly ground black pepper

½ teaspoon salt

1 cup grated Cheddar cheese (or use Swiss for a different flavor)

1. In a large skillet, sauté the onion in the oil until soft.

2. Add the zucchini and squash to the onion and sauté until much of the moisture disappears, about 15 minutes.

3. Remove from the heat and stir in the eggs, cracker crumbs, and seasonings. Blend well and place in a greased 9-inch casserole.

4. To prepare immediately, preheat the oven to 325°F.

5. Top with the grated cheese and bake for 45 minutes.

6. To save for future use, omit the cheese, pour into a foil-lined 9-inch casserole, chill, then freeze. When it is frozen solid, remove it from the dish, wrap, label, and store in the freezer for up to 1 month.

7. To use, remove the wrap and thaw in a casserole dish. Top with the cheese and bake at 325°F for 45 minutes. Test for doneness with a baking straw or toothpick, as you would a cake.

YIELD: 6 CUPS (SIX 1-CUP SERVINGS)
NUTRITION PER SERVING

Calories	344	Total fat	18g
% from fat	46	Saturated	6g
Carbohydrates	34g	Cholesterol	111mg
Fiber	3g	Sodium	838mg

Mashed Winter Squash

. . . .

This dish will warm you all winter long.

2 medium winter squash (about 3–4 pounds each), scrubbed, or about 6 cups cooked puréed squash

FOR EACH CUP OF PURÉE, ADD

1 tablespoon butter

1 teaspoon firmly packed brown sugar

¼ teaspoon salt

⅛ teaspoon ground ginger

Orange juice

1. Preheat the oven to 375°F.

2. Oil the squash skins, then prick them with a fork. Bake on a cookie sheet for about 1 hour. Remove the squash from the oven when soft. Split in half and remove the seeds.

3. Spoon out the pulp into a large mixing bowl and mash it.

4. Add the butter, brown sugar, salt, and ginger. Mix well, adding a little orange juice to thin the pulp, if necessary, to make the consistency of a thick purée.

5. Spoon the squash into a freezer container, packing the pulp according to your family's needs. Freeze for up to 1 month.

6. To serve, thaw in the refrigerator overnight. Heat in the oven or on top of the stove and serve.

. . . .

YIELD: 6 CUPS (SIX 1-CUP SERVINGS)

NUTRITION PER SERVING

Calories	129	Total fat	11g
% from fat	77	Saturated	7g
Carbohydrates	7g	Cholesterol	31mg
Fiber	<1g	Sodium	652mg

. . . .

Sweet Potatoes and Carrots

· · · · · · · · · · ·

*Two fall vegetables team up to make a remarkable combination. Double this recipe
so you can freeze one and have the other right away.*

4 large sweet potatoes

1 pound carrots, peeled and cut into
½-inch slices

2½ cups water

4 tablespoons unsalted butter

1 tablespoon sugar

½ cup nonfat sour cream

1 tablespoon frozen orange juice
concentrate

½ teaspoon ground nutmeg

½ teaspoon orange zest, finely grated

Salt and freshly ground black pepper

1. Preheat the oven to 350°F.

2. Scrub the sweet potatoes and bake
until done, about 1 hour. The sweet
potatoes can be cooked the day before and
refrigerated until ready to use.

3. In a large saucepan, add the carrots,
water, 2 tablespoons of the butter, and the
sugar. Cover and simmer until soft. Remove
the cover and boil until the water has
evaporated. Check after 15 minutes. Shake
the pan to coat the carrots in the butter.

4. Spoon out the sweet potato flesh and
combine with the carrots in the bowl of a
food processor.

5. Add the sour cream, orange juice
concentrate, nutmeg, orange zest, and
remaining butter to the food processor
bowl and process until smooth. Adjust the
seasonings. Pour into a foil-lined casserole
dish and freeze until solid.

6. Remove the frozen vegetables from
the dish, wrap, label, and freeze for up to
1 month.

7. When you're ready to use, remove
the foil, return the sweet potato–carrot
mixture to the original dish, and thaw the
preparation in the refrigerator overnight.

8. Bake at 350°F until very hot (about
30 minutes).

· ·

YIELD: 6 CUPS (SIX 1-CUP SERVINGS)
NUTRITION PER SERVING

Calories	187	Total fat	9g
% from fat	41	Saturated	5g
Carbohydrates	26g	Cholesterol	23mg
Fiber	4g	Sodium	41mg

· ·

Caramel Onions

· · · · · · · · · · · ·

This exceptional onion preparation will complement almost all meat dishes.

1 cup balsamic vinegar

½ cup olive oil

5 teaspoons sugar

6 large mild onions, peeled

1. Preheat the oven to 425°F and grease a covered casserole dish.

2. Mix together the vinegar, olive oil, and sugar.

3. Place the onions in the casserole dish and drizzle the vinegar mixture over them. Cover and bake for 1 hour.

4. Remove the cover, move the casserole to the bottom rack of the oven, and bake for 45 minutes longer. Check the oven often to make sure the sauce does not burn. The sauce will thicken as it turns a rich brown. Roll the onions in the thickening sauce to coat them well.

5. After cooking, cool the onions in the refrigerator, then place them in a clean freezer container, label, and freeze for up to 1 month. Easy!

6. To use, thaw overnight in the refrigerator. Transfer the onions and sauce to an uncovered casserole dish and bake in a 350°F oven for 20 minutes, or until heated through.

YIELD: 6 ONIONS (SIX SERVINGS)
NUTRITION PER SERVING

Calories	235	Total fat	18g
% from fat	67	Saturated	3g
Carbohydrates	19g	Cholesterol	0mg
Fiber	3g	Sodium	5mg

Fresh Tomato Pudding

This freezes extremely well — so well that it goes into my freezer in August for Thanksgiving dinner. A great vegetable side dish, tomato pudding goes well with poultry, pork, or turkey. This version is adapted from The Joy of Cooking.

14 very ripe medium tomatoes

1 cup fresh white breadcrumbs

5 tablespoons firmly packed light brown sugar

2 teaspoons chopped fresh basil

1 teaspoon chopped fresh chives

1 teaspoon chopped fresh parsley

¼ teaspoon salt

4 tablespoons butter or margarine, melted

1. Blanch the tomatoes by dropping them in boiling water for 1 minute. Remove the skins and seeds and purée in a blender or food processor.

2. Pour the crumbs into a foil-lined 9-inch baking dish prepared with vegetable oil cooking spray.

3. In a heavy, nonreactive saucepan, heat the tomato purée until it boils. Add the sugar, herbs, and salt; mix well. Boil gently for 3 minutes.

4. Pour the melted butter over the crumbs in the foil-lined baking dish.

5. Pour the tomato mixture over all and mix well.

6. Cool. Cover. Chill, then freeze for up to 6 months.

7. When the pudding is frozen, remove it from the dish; wrap, label, and return to the freezer.

8. When ready to thaw, return the casserole to its dish, removing the foil.

9. Place the dish on a cookie sheet on the bottom rack in the oven, cover loosely with foil, and bake for 2½–3 hours at 325°F until it cooks down to a pudding consistency. Uncover during the last hour of cooking.

YIELD: 5 CUPS (TEN ½-CUP SERVINGS)
NUTRITION PER SERVING

Calories	150	Total fat	6g
% from fat	33	Saturated	3g
Carbohydrates	24g	Cholesterol	12mg
Fiber	3g	Sodium	213mg

Colorful Freezer Slaw

· · · · · · · · · · ·

This recipe swells when shredded and then shrinks when dressed. Unique and delicious, it can be enriched by adding 3 tablespoons of olive oil.

1 pound green cabbage, shredded

1 pound red cabbage, shredded

3 large carrots, washed and grated

1 large green bell pepper, seeded and grated

1 medium onion, chopped

1 teaspoon salt

1 cup cider vinegar

1 cup sugar (or less, if desired)

½ cup water

1 teaspoon celery seed

1 teaspoon dry mustard

1. Combine the vegetables in a crockery bowl and sprinkle salt over them. Let stand for about 1 hour, then drain off the liquid that forms.

2. Combine the remaining ingredients in a heavy nonreactive saucepan and boil for 3 minutes. Let the dressing cool before you pour it over the cabbage.

3. Let the prepared slaw stand for 5 minutes. Ladle it into freezer containers.

4. Seal and label. Chill, then freeze for up to 2 months.

5. To use, thaw in the refrigerator overnight. Serve chilled.

YIELD: 5 PINTS (TWENTY ½-CUP SERVINGS)
NUTRITION PER SERVING

Calories	57	Total fat	<1g
% from fat	2	Saturated	0g
Carbohydrates	14g	Cholesterol	0mg
Fiber	1g	Sodium	116mg

Mushroom Stacks

* * * * * * * * * * *

*Use this scrumptious concoction for an elegant first course or as a complementary
side dish with beef or veal.*

2 tablespoons olive oil

6 portobello mushrooms, cleaned and
stems removed

1 small eggplant, sliced 1 inch thick
(6 slices)

12 tablespoons tomato sauce

2 tablespoons basil pesto

6 slices roasted red bell pepper

⅛ teaspoon garlic powder

¼ cup grated Parmesan cheese

1. Heat 1 tablespoon of the olive oil in a
skillet. Sauté the mushrooms until soft and
all the moisture has dried up.

2. In a large skillet, sauté the eggplant
"circles" in the remaining olive oil until
soft. Drain on paper towels.

3. On a lightly greased baking sheet,
construct six stacks of vegetables, layering
eggplant, 2 tablespoons of tomato sauce,
mushrooms, pesto, and red pepper slices.

4. Sprinkle each stack with garlic powder,
then cheese.

5. Freeze, uncovered, on a tray until
solid, about 4 hours.

6. When frozen, wrap in freezer paper,
label, and freeze for up to 6 weeks.

7. To use, thaw overnight in the refrigerator. Transfer the stacks to a greased
baking sheet and heat in a 400°F oven for
20 minutes, until they are hot and the cheese
has melted.

Fresh Frozen Shiitake Mushrooms

* * * * * * * * * * * * * * *

*Trim, stem, and wipe fresh mushrooms clean
with a damp cloth; slice in half. Place slices on
a baking sheet and place uncovered in the
freezer. When frozen solid, store in an airtight
freezer bag. Use within 2 months as you
would fresh mushrooms in sauces and soups.*

*Buy mushrooms in spring and fall, when
they are plentiful, and enjoy a fresh-tasting
supply months later.*

YIELD: 3 CUPS, 6 STACKS (SIX ½-CUP SERVINGS)
NUTRITION PER SERVING

Calories	128	Total fat	8g
% from fat	56	Saturated	2g
Carbohydrates	11g	Cholesterol	5mg
Fiber	3g	Sodium	301mg

Mediterranean Artichokes

. . . .

This presentation of intense flavors makes a savory low-calorie luncheon or side dish.

4 tablespoons plus 1 teaspoon olive oil

2 cups eggplant, peeled and cubed

1 cup chopped onion

1 cup chopped zucchini

2 cloves garlic, chopped

1 cup chopped tomatoes

6 mushrooms, cleaned and chopped

4 large artichokes, thorns, choke, and pith stem removed

1 lemon, sliced and seeds removed

4 black olives, sliced

2 tablespoons chopped fresh parsley

1 tablespoon capers

½ teaspoon chopped fresh basil

½ teaspoon chopped fresh thyme

½ teaspoon salt

Freshly ground black pepper

½ cup crumbled feta cheese

. . . .

YIELD: 4 STUFFED ARTICHOKES (FOUR SERVINGS)
NUTRITION PER SERVING

Calories	288	Total fat	19g
% from fat	53	Saturated	4g
Carbohydrates	29g	Cholesterol	13mg
Fiber	10g	Sodium	614mg

. . . .

1. In 4 tablespoons of the oil, sauté the eggplant, onion, zucchini, and garlic in a heavy skillet until tender, about 4–5 minutes. Add the tomatoes and cook 2–3 minutes longer. Add the mushrooms and cook until the vegetable moisture disappears. The mixture will be thick. You can prepare the recipe to this point a day ahead and refrigerate, or freeze in clean containers for up to 2 months until you're ready to continue.

2. In a 4-quart pot, cover the artichokes with water. Add the lemon, cover, and boil for 20–30 minutes, or until tender. This can be done up to 2 days ahead and refrigerated.

3. If you froze the eggplant mixture, thaw it in the refrigerator. Reheat the artichokes by wrapping them in plastic wrap and re-heating in the microwave oven at medium. Check at 30-second intervals until hot but not overcooked.

4. Add all the other ingredients except the feta cheese to the mushroom mixture.

5. Fill the warm artichokes by gently spreading the leaves apart and spooning in the vegetable mixture. Pour the remaining filling over the top of each artichoke.

6. Top each with cheese. Heat in a 325°F oven for 10–15 minutes, until heated through.

Avocado Frozen Yogurt
with Candied Lime Zest Garnish

*Light and refreshing, this recipe may make your guests wonder
what this surprising flavor actually is.*

2 ripe avocados

⅔ cup lime juice (about 8 medium limes)

½ cup sugar

1 quart nonfat vanilla frozen yogurt,
softened

1. Remove the skin and pit from each
avocado.

2. Blend the avocado flesh, lime juice,
and sugar in a blender or food processor.

3. In a medium-sized mixing bowl,
combine the avocado mixture and yogurt.

4. Pour into an 8-inch square pan. Cover,
chill, and freeze for up to 1 month.

5. To serve, remove the pan from the
freezer and use an ice cream scoop to fill
bowls. Sprinkle with Candied Lime Zest
Garnish.

CANDIED LIME ZEST GARNISH

¼ cup thinly sliced lime zest strips

¼ cup sugar

¼ cup water

1. In a small, heavy saucepan, cover
the zest strips with water and boil for
5 minutes. Drain well.

2. Blend the sugar and the water and boil
over medium heat. Add the lime strips and
simmer for 2 minutes. Cool, drain, then
chill the candied lime strips.

YIELD: 48 OUNCES (SIX 8-OUNCE SERVINGS)
NUTRITION PER SERVING

Calories	339	Total fat	13g
% from fat	33	Saturated	5g
Carbohydrates	55g	Cholesterol	2mg
Fiber	2g	Sodium	90mg

Laura's Banana Bread

. . . .

The best banana bread ever, this recipe freezes beautifully.

2 cups sugar

1 cup (2 sticks) butter, margarine, or shortening, softened

1 teaspoon vanilla extract

4 eggs

6 ripe bananas, mashed

2½ cups flour

2 teaspoons baking powder

½ teaspoon baking soda

½ teaspoon salt

1. Cream together the sugar, butter, and vanilla until fluffy.

2. Add the eggs one at a time and beat well after each addition.

3. Gradually stir in the bananas.

4. Sift together the dry ingredients. Add to the banana mixture, carefully folding in. Do not overmix.

5. Preheat the oven to 350°F.

6. Lightly grease two loaf pans.

7. Pour the batter into the pans and bake in the oven for 45–60 minutes.

8. Let cool for 10 minutes, then remove from the pans and place on a cooling rack.

9. When cool, wrap, label, and freeze for up to 2 months.

Note: Overripe bananas can be peeled, wrapped in a freezer bag, and frozen until needed to make this bread. When thawed, they will be soft and ready for the batter without much mashing at all. Don't be put off because they have turned dark. They will work beautifully for this bread. This is a good way to save that last banana in the bunch that is so ripe no one wants to eat it.

YIELD: 2 LOAVES (TWENTY-FOUR SERVINGS)
NUTRITION PER SERVING

Calories	207	Total fat	9g
% from fat	36	Saturated	5g
Carbohydrates	31g	Cholesterol	51mg
Fiber	<1g	Sodium	188mg

Pineapple Sherbet

This is an old-fashioned favorite my mother-in-law taught me. Both children and adults love it.

1 quart buttermilk

½ medium-sized, ripe, cored pineapple (about 1½ cups), chopped, with juice

1 cup sugar, or ½ cup honey

1. Mix all the ingredients in a clean, 6-cup freezer container, stirring until the sugar has dissolved.

2. Chill; label. Freeze for up to 1 month.

3. Thaw slightly before serving. Delicious!

YIELD: 6 CUPS (TWELVE ½-CUP SERVINGS)
NUTRITION PER SERVING

Calories	114	Total fat	<1g
% from fat	7	Saturated	<1g
Carbohydrates	25g	Cholesterol	3mg
Fiber	<1g	Sodium	86mg

Fruit Salad

This is a variation of Pineapple Sherbet.

1 quart buttermilk

2 medium ripe peaches, peeled, pitted, and sliced

½ medium-sized, ripe, cored pineapple (about 1½ cups), chopped, with juice

1 cup white (or red) seedless grapes, halved

1 cup sugar, or ½ cup honey

½ teaspoon mint flavoring

1. Combine all the ingredients in a clean, 8-cup freezer container. Stir well to dissolve the sugar.

2. Chill; label. Freeze for up to 1 month.

3. When ready to serve, remove from the freezer and thaw slightly.

Note: One serving method is to make the salad in two 4-cup loaf pans, then freeze it so it can be sliced for serving.

YIELD: 8 CUPS (SIXTEEN ½-CUP SERVINGS)
NUTRITION PER SERVING

Calories	95	Total fat	<1g
% from fat	6	Saturated	<1g
Carbohydrates	21g	Cholesterol	2mg
Fiber	<1g	Sodium	66mg

Apple Crumb Pie

* * * * * * * * * * *

An easy, delicious alternative to pie with a crust, this recipe can be made by substituting an equal quantity of peaches or a combination of peaches and blackberries for the apples.

FILLING

- 4 large tart apples, peeled and thickly sliced
- ½ cup sugar
- 1 teaspoon cinnamon

CRUMB TOPPING

- ¾ cup all-purpose flour
- ½ cup sugar
- ⅓ cup butter

1. Toss the apples, sugar, and cinnamon until the apples are well coated.

2. Mix the topping ingredients in the bowl of a food processor.

3. Line a 9-inch pie plate with foil.

4. Spoon in the apple filling and sprinkle with the crumb topping.

5. To use immediately, bake in a 400°F oven for 40–50 minutes, until the topping has browned.

6. To store, freeze the unbaked pie. When it's solid, remove the pie from the plate, wrap, label, and freeze for up to 3 months.

7. When it is time to cook the frozen pie, remove the wrapping and put it back into the pie plate.

8. Bake on a cookie sheet in the middle third of the oven for 45–60 minutes, until the crumb mixture is brown and crusty.

YIELD: ONE 9-INCH PIE (EIGHT SERVINGS)
NUTRITION PER SERVING

Calories	238	Total fat	8g
% from fat	29	Saturated	5g
Carbohydrates	42g	Cholesterol	20mg
Fiber	2g	Sodium	79mg

Nectarine Cobbler with Pecan Crunch Topping

This is so good that I usually double the recipe.

8 medium (about 2 pounds) ripe unpeeled nectarines, pitted and sliced

¼ cup sugar

1 tablespoon all-purpose flour

1 tablespoon lemon juice

TOPPING

1 cup all-purpose flour

¾ cup firmly packed light brown sugar

½ cup (1 stick) unsalted butter, cut into small pieces

½ cup coarsely chopped pecans, very lightly toasted

1 teaspoon ground cinnamon

1. If baking immediately, preheat the oven to 375°F and use the center rack.

2. In a large mixing bowl, combine the fruit, sugar, flour, and lemon juice, folding gently so as not to bruise the fruit slices.

3. Pour the fruit mixture into an 8-inch by 8-inch baking pan.

4. Combine the topping ingredients in a food processor until crumbly. Sprinkle the crumb topping over the fruit mixture.

5. If making two cobblers, freeze one at this point, wrapping well and labeling. It will keep in the freezer for up to 6 months.

6. To bake immediately, place on a cookie sheet and bake for 45–50 minutes, or until browned.

7. To bake the frozen cobbler, place on a cookie sheet in the oven and bake for 50–60 minutes, or until browned.

YIELD: 1 COBBLER (EIGHT SERVINGS)
NUTRITION PER SERVING

Calories	355	Total fat	15g
% from fat	37	Saturated	8g
Carbohydrates	55g	Cholesterol	33mg
Fiber	3g	Sodium	10mg

Herbed Water Tonic

· · · · · · · · · · ·

When hot weather makes your herbs begin to flower, pinch off the buds so that you can enjoy this refreshing tonic all winter long. The selection can vary according to the availability of herbs and your tastes.

Fresh basil flowers

Fresh chamomile flowers

Fresh lavender flowers

Fresh lemon-balm flowers

Fresh rosemary flowers

Fresh sage flowers

Fresh thyme flowers

Fresh lemon slices

1. Thoroughly wash all the flowers and place ½ to 1 teaspoon in each section of an ice cube tray. Cover with water and freeze.

2. When frozen, transfer the herb cubes to a plastic bag. Label and store in the freezer for up to 3 months.

3. Use 1 cube per glass. Cover with chilled sparkling water and garnish with a fresh lemon slice.

CHAPTER 5

AT MY HOME IN NORTH CAROLINA it would not seem like August if I weren't making jams from the bounty of seasonal fruit that bursts into and overflows from the farmer's markets. The trick is to "transform" and "transfix" the booty into beautiful rows of preserved concoctions that wait patiently to be taken from the shelf in the leaner times of winter. The comforting pleasure of a cup of herbal-blend tea accompanied by toast with homemade apple butter is an underrated joy of life. (The toast is merely the vehicle for getting as much apple butter as possible to the palate.)

The perfume of simmering raspberries wafting through the house is another memory maker. The seasonal ritual can include berry picking with the children. Go to a pick-your-own orchard, or pick wild blackberries. (I once had to throw away the clothes my children wore for blackberry picking because they were so stained. But years later, nobody remembers that part — only the fun we had together!)

The art and science of turning fresh fruits into tempting fruit spreads make for a satisfying experience. Frequently, young berry pickers like to help make the jam as well. It's never too early to learn creative, economical, environmental, and conservation-minded habits. Besides, preserving can turn your kitchen, pantry shelf, or freezer into a virtual rescue mission for the distressed cook. A half-pint jar of apple jelly can serve not only for breakfast bread but also as a basting sauce for a pork roast or a

Jams & Jellies

175

*Fresh fruit may be frozen for
future jam or jelly making.*

grilled chicken. A supply of orange marmalade can be added
by the tablespoonful to gravy or sauces for duck, pork, or
Cornish hens. Let your culinary imagination run wild.

INGREDIENTS

Making homemade fruit spreads is easy. The main ingredients are sugar, fruit (which contains acid), additional fruit
acid (for nonacidic fruits), and pectin. The ratio of these
ingredients creates the gel and preserves the flavor of a
homemade fruit spread.

Sugar. This acts as a preserving agent in the large quantities called for in fruit spread recipes.

Fruit. The distinctive flavor comes from the fruit. Also,
depending on the fruit and its ripeness, natural fruit acids
contribute to the gel quality. If the fruit is not naturally
acidic enough, the recipe will call for added acid, usually in
the form of lemon juice.

Pectin. Along with the fruit acid and sugar, pectin
makes the proper consistency for a fruit spread.

Fruit spreads are easy to make and a good project for
beginning canners. However, be sure to follow the recipe
without changing the ratio of sugar, fruit, and pectin; nor
should you change the order in which they are added in a
recipe. Your Cooperative Extension agent can help if com-
plicated changes need to be made to a recipe.

FRUIT

While each spread is slightly different, you will, as
always, want to start with the best fresh produce. I steer
away from supermarket produce unless I am sure of its origin. However, you can freeze just-picked fruit to make fruit
spreads later without losing a significant amount of flavor.

There's no need to thaw frozen fruit before cooking;
just combine it in the kettle with the other ingredients in
your recipe. For jams, mash the fruit and add a little fruit
juice, if necessary — ¼ cup for each 1 quart of fruit.

Freezing Fruit for Jams and Jellies

In my hometown, my friend Nancy is noted for her preserves and jellies. She recommends the following simple method for making fruit spreads.

Dry-packed fruits (clean, dry fruit frozen without any liquid or sweetening; see page 125) can be frozen premeasured and ready for making into your favorite fruit spreads. Label them with the quantity, the kind of unsweetened dry-packed fruit, and the date. Later, the frozen fruit may be puréed in a food processor for immediate jam making.

Preserves can be made from the frozen fruit placed in a nonreactive saucepan, heated slightly, and mashed with a little fruit juice (¼ cup of juice per 1 quart of fruit).

PECTIN

Pectin is a gelling agent found naturally in all fruits. Fruit that is underripe contains much more pectin than ripened fruit. Including some underripe fruit in the fruit portion called for in a recipe can help the final product gel. You can buy pectin in either powdered or liquid form in most supermarkets. Commercial pectins are usually made from the white material under the skin of citrus fruits, though some kinds are made from apples. Recipes that call for purchased pectins will benefit in flavor and consistency from using ripe fruit.

The fruit's ripeness, its natural pectin content, its natural acid content, and the amount of sugar added all influence the quality of the gel of the finished product. In recipes that do not call for commercial pectin, the sugar acts as a preservative and gel agent, along with the natural pectin found in the fruit.

Fruit spreads are slow cooked or fast cooked, depending on whether the pectin is added or is only derived from the fruit used. In the slow-cook method (see page 185), no pectin is added, and the ¾-to-¼ ratio of fully ripe to slightly

TIP

Stick with the original recipe. Don't change the proportions or the ratio of sugar to fruit or the order in which ingredients are added — you may end up with syrup or glue instead of jelly! Don't double a recipe, either. It is better to make one batch at a time.

ripe fruit is used to produce the gel. This slow-cooked, no-added-pectin method requires a lot of guesswork, however, and can be chancy for the less experienced cook, who may not be able to judge the fruits' ripeness accurately.

The fast-cooked method, in which purchased pectin is added, can reduce guesswork (see page 184). The recipe will tell you the exact quantity of pectin and the exact cooking time. Never cook a recipe for more than 20 minutes when pectin is added, because after that the pectin will begin to break down. Less fruit, of course, is required for recipes with added pectin.

MAKING YOUR OWN PECTIN

Underripe apples are all you need to make your own pectin. In mid-August in my area, small, immature green (underripe) apples begin appearing before the regular crop of apples starts rolling in. These little apples are loaded with natural fruit pectin and acid and can be used to contribute pectin for preserving. You can get the jump on the

PECTIN AND ACID IN FRUIT

The amount of naturally occurring pectin and acid varies from fruit to fruit and depends on the fruit's ripeness. The fruits in the lists below are given from highest pectin and acid content to lowest.

Fruits with High Natural Pectin and Acid Content	Fruits with Low Natural Pectin or Acid Content	Fruits with Both Low Natural Pectin and Acid Content
Sour apples	Apples, ripe	Apricots
Plums (Damson)	Blackberries, ripe	Peaches
Blackberries	Sour cherries	Grapes (Western Concord)
Crab apples	Grape juice (Concord,	Guavas
Cranberries	from commercial	Figs
Grapes (Eastern Concord)	concentrate)	Prunes
Quince	Strawberries	Pears
Currants		Raspberries
Citrus fruit		

apple crop by using these small apples, but if you want crystal-clear jelly, you'll be better off waiting for the mature apples to appear.

Our trees are Golden Delicious, and we don't spray them. I have found that these young apples, even with insect holes and bruises and bumps, can be used successfully for making pectin by merely cutting away the damage. No need to peel the apples, as the pectin is mostly found in or near the peelings. Do wash them carefully, however, and slice them rather thinly.

TIP

Make your own pectin the day before you make your fruit spread. Store it in the refrigerator overnight. This will save considerable time on jelly-making day.

Making Pectin

To make pectin, follow these simple instructions:

1. Combine in a large stockpot 1 pint of water for each 1 pound of apple slices. Boil for about 15 minutes, stirring occasionally.
2. Line a strainer with one thickness of cheesecloth. Pour the apple pulp and juice through the strainer into a large pot that comfortably fits the strainer. Pour the juice into a 4-cup-capacity measuring cup.
3. Pour the pulp back into the stockpot and add the same amount of water as before, depending on the number of pounds of apples you used in the beginning. Cook the mixture over medium heat this second time for about 15 minutes.
4. Remove from the heat and let stand for 10 minutes. Strain this second time through another single thickness of cheesecloth lining your strainer. Add this second round of juice to the 4-cup measuring cup.
5. When cool enough to handle, gather up the cheesecloth containing the pulp and form into a bag shape. Squeeze the bag to extract all the remaining juices. (Caution: Never squeeze the cheesecloth bag or jelly bag unless the recipe specifically directs you to do this, as I do here. Squeezing the pulp bag can sometimes cloud your finished fruit spread.) Add this last juice to the 4-cup measurer. You should have 1 quart of cooked juice for every pound of apples. This "stock" will serve as your pectin. Some folks refer to this as "jelly stock." Four cups of jelly stock equals a half bottle or 3 ounces of commercial liquid pectin.
6. I prefer to freeze my jelly stock for future use. To do this, pour it into clean 4-cup freezer containers and allow at least 1 inch of headspace for freezing expansion.

LOW-METHYL PECTIN

Low-methyl pectin, a natural product used for gelling, is derived from citrus peel and requires the addition of dicalcium phosphate, a calcium salt, in order to gel. It can be purchased in most health food stores and has the advantage of needing no sweetener (except for taste) in order to gel. Follow the package directions to combine the low-methyl pectin and the dicalcium phosphate. Recipes that call for low-methyl pectin cook much more quickly and thus result in a fruit spread with a fresher flavor.

What's the Difference?
• •

Although people use the word "preserves" to refer to all forms of sweetened jarred fruit, there are many different varieties.

Butter. This fruit spread is made from puréed fruits with sugar and sometimes spices added. The mixture is cooked down and naturally thickened and is very easy to make. Apples and pears are the favorite fruits for making butter. When cooking, be careful not to scorch it.

Conserve. At their height in popularity in Victorian England, conserves were whole or sliced fruits preserved in a syrup base. They were eaten for dessert and were much richer and more syrupy than conventional jams and jellies. Today they are often made with two or more chopped fruits, may contain nuts or raisins, and have the ingredients and consistency of jam.

Curd. A type of preserve that contains, in addition to fruit, eggs and butter. Very smooth and rich, curds are most often made with citrus, lemon being the most common. Because they contain dairy products, curds should always be refrigerated and should not be stored for longer than three months.

Jam. This is the least labor-intensive way to process spreadable fruit. It consists of washed, crushed fruit; sugar; and possibly pectin (depending on the recipe). Jams can be cooked or freezer-preserved with sugar or a sugar substitute. Jams may even be made by an uncooked method (see page 192).

Jelly. Made from strained fresh fruit juice or purchased frozen fruit juice, plus sugar, with or without pectin, jelly is clear with no fruit pieces.

Marmalade. More like jelly than jam, marmalade has small pieces of suspended fruit or peel added to the gel.

Preserves. Similar to jams, preserves have bits of one or more fruits and are made with or without pectin.

The disadvantage is that recipes made with low-methyl pectin sometimes "weep." Liquid will puddle around a spoonful of the jam on a plate, or the whole jar will have a puddled liquid. This is a natural occurrence and is caused by the calcium. Simply blot the liquid with paper towels or spoon it or drain it out of the jar. Another disadvantage to low-methyl pectin is that the absence of sugar (which is a natural preservative) means you can't store the fruit spread as long after it is opened. You must use it within 2 to 3 weeks of opening the jar and, of course, refrigerate it. Low-methyl pectin recipes are processed in a boiling-water-bath canner for 5 minutes for jellies using half-pints and for 10 minutes for jams using half-pints; correct for altitude as necessary. Follow your recipe instructions carefully.

Spreads made with low-methyl pectin sometimes "weep."

Sweeteners

Sweeteners for fruit spreads vary greatly. Following is a list of choices both natural and artificial. Most artificial sweeteners cannot be used in fruit spreads that require cooking, as the sweetener breaks down under heat. Sugar's purpose goes beyond making the fruit sweet; it is used as a preservative and gelling agent in large quantities when making fruit spreads. Never change the ratio of sugar, fruit, and pectin in your recipes.

Sugar. Besides adding flavor to fruit spreads, sugar is a key ingredient in the gelling process. (A large amount of sugar does, however, add calories.) Granulated sugar made from cane or beets or light brown sugar, which has maltose added, is appropriate for making fruit spreads.

Honey. Light and mild honey can be used instead of sugar. Because it has double the sweetening power of sugar, it adds fewer calories. Choose a recipe that specifies the use of honey. Don't switch from sugar to honey on your own. Honey will cause more foam on top of the cooked fruit mixture.

Perils of Paraffin

Those of us who remember Granny's pantry shelves lined with sparkling jars of preserves and jellies also remember the thick layer of paraffin that covered the contents. There were always sticky fingers in the house when the children tried to push it in and pry it out. While we remember those days with fondness, we must not return to that method of preserving fruit spreads. Paraffin allows mold to grow, and some forms of mold can be dangerous. Rather than paraffin, use new rubber-lined lids and clean screw rings in the recommended boiling-water-bath canner.

Equipment for Fruit Spreads

· · · · · · · · · · ·

Most of the equipment you'll need for jams and jellies is already in your kitchen if you've done some canning, but a few items are needed especially for fruit spreads.

Heavy, large, stainless steel or enamel pot (not aluminum or iron)
Regulation jars and lids (see page 24)
Cooling rack
Measuring cups and spoons
Jelly bag, or cheesecloth and kitchen twine
Potato ricer, canning strainer, or other masher
Long-handled wooden spoon
Pierced long-handled metal spoon
Clean tea towels
Candy thermometer
Colander
Soft vegetable brush
Knife
Timer
Spatula
Ladle
Widemouthed funnel
Jar lifter
Boiling-water-bath canner
Kitchen scales

Artificial sweeteners. Saccharin, aspartame, and other artificial sweeteners cannot be used in cooked products, as they break down when heated. Use artificial sweetener only in uncooked fruit spread recipes for the freezer or refrigerator. For a cooked and processed recipe, add artificial sweetener when you open the individual jar for use.

EQUIPMENT FOR MAKING FRUIT SPREADS

The method for preserving jams, jellies, conserves, preserves, and other fruit spreads is boiling-water-bath canning, the same method used for fruits and other high-acid foods. If you have canned fruits or other foods, you probably have most of the equipment you need, since the same equipment is used and the same process is followed. For a more detailed explanation of the boiling-water-bath method, refer to chapter 2 (page 27).

A food mill is useful for separating the raw fruit pulp from the seeds and skins. Several brands of food mills are available. You may also use a potato ricer, which forces the raw fruit pulp through small holes, but smaller seeds can slip through.

A candy or cooking thermometer is essential for the beginning cook. It allows a foolproof method of gelling. Treat your thermometer kindly when it's not in use and avoid mistreatment, such as dropping or bumping it.

A timer is a valuable tool for anyone who wants to master the art and science of canning. Precision is the order of the day for fruit-spread making, as well as for other forms of canning.

JELLY BAGS AND JUICING

A jelly bag is used to strain juice from the fruit pulp. It is a simple cloth bag that can be purchased or made from several layers of muslin or cheesecloth, filled with fruit pulp, and tied into a pouch with kitchen twine. Be sure to dampen it first in water to prevent juice from being wicked into the fabric instead of dripping into the bowl. The bag is then suspended by the string over a clean glass or enamel bowl. The weight of the fruit pulp allows the juice to drip into the bowl below, a process that usually takes 8 to 10 hours. I like to use an 8-cup glass mixing/measuring bowl with a handle.

TIP

. . . .

Begin straining the juice in the evening the night before and have your bowl of juice ready for jelly making early in the morning. You can also freeze fresh juice for making jelly later.

TIP

. . . .

For a less labor-intensive procedure, use frozen prepared juice concentrate and add commercial pectin.

You may have to be creative to find an effective setup for the jelly bag.

PREPARING FRUITS FOR JUICING

As always, start with ripe, blemish-free fruit. Wash the fruit well to remove all grit. Crush the fruit before adding it to the wet jelly bag. You don't need to remove the seeds or skins, since straining through the jelly bag will take care of that.

FRUIT	AMOUNT	PREPARATION	WATER	COOK TIME (MINUTES)	CONSISTENCY	FINISHED AMOUNT
Apples, crab apples, guavas	1 lb.	wash, cut up coarsely	1 cup	15–20	soft	2 cups
Berries	2½ qts.	wash, crush in kettle	none	5–10	soft	5½ cups
Grapes, cherries, currants, peaches	3 lbs.	wash, pit, cut up	½ cup	5–10	translucent	5½ cups
Plums	3 lbs.	wash, cut up, pit, mash	little or none	15	soft	5½ cups

Unless your recipe specifies it, don't squeeze the bag and force more juice out, as this may make the final product cloudy. Add a little water to the pulp and continue the straining if you come up short.

Be sure to wash the bag thoroughly after use. The pulp makes a great addition to your compost pile!

THE PROCESS OF PRESERVING FRUIT SPREADS

Making fruit spreads is relatively simple, though sometimes experience is needed to achieve the perfect taste and texture. The challenge is to combine the fruit, the sugar, and in some cases the pectin, depending on the fruit and method used, in the correct ratio and for the right amount of time to create the desired gel consistency when the fruit is cooked and then canned. The recipes included in the second part of this chapter will take the guesswork out of the process.

Cooking the Fruit and Juice for Canning

The goal of cooking the fruit is to acquire the proper gel for the final fruit spread product. Follow the recipe instructions exactly; add ingredients in the order given.

There are two ways to cook the fruit and juice for fruit spreads: the fast way, which uses added pectin, and the slow way, which relies on the pectin found naturally in the fruit being processed.

The Fast Way — Adding Pectin

Bring the mixture to a full boil that you cannot stop by stirring and maintain it for the exact amount of time called for in your recipe. If pectin is overcooked, it may break down, resulting in runny jam. Always add the liquid or powdered pectin exactly how and when the recipe indicates. Never substitute liquid pectin for powdered, or vice versa.

The Slow Way — without Adding Pectin

The less exact way, the slow or "cook-down" method of preserving fruits for spreads, worked great for Granny and it still works today as well. This method relies on the pectin found in fruit to make the spread congeal. Use fruits that have a high pectin content, such as sour apples, crab apples, blackberries, Concord grapes, lemons, oranges, Damson plums, quince, and cranberries. Place the fruit or fruit acid and the sugar in an uncovered pot and cook for the proper time to create the gel. Because the amount of pectin in fruit will vary, depending on ripeness as well as variety, there is some guesswork involved. The recipe will indicate approximate cooking times to achieve the gel, but there are other ways to determine whether the fruit mixture is ready to pour into the jars.

Some recipes may not indicate a specific cooking time but may say instead, "Cook until done," or "Cook until it reaches 220°F." In such cases, you'll need to use your candy or cooking thermometer for making jelly or marmalade. When it reaches 220°F, your jelly is ready. For jams and preserves, you know it is ready when a spoonful holds its shape or "mounds up" on a cold spoon or plate. At high altitudes, subtract 2 degrees for every 1,000 feet above sea level.

Preserves and conserves. When a spoonful of fruit mixture holds its shape or mounds up on a cold spoon or plate, it's ready for canning. Remove the fruit mixture from the heat and stir it for about 5 minutes before you fill the jars. This prevents the fruit from floating after canning.

Jams. When a spoonful of fruit dropped in a cold bowl holds its shape, it is ready for the canning jar and boiling-water-bath canner.

Butters. This is a slow, cook-down process that can work quite well in your oven at 300 to 325°F. The mixture will become a thick brown mash. Using the oven takes 4 to 5 hours and helps prevent burning and the labor intensity of watching the pot.

When making jelly or marmalade without added pectin, use a thermometer to determine when it is ready.

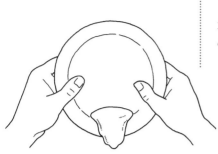

One alternative to using a thermometer to test for doneness is the sheeting method.

Jelly or marmalade. If you don't have a candy or cooking thermometer, try one of these old-fashioned methods of testing for doneness:

- *The sheeting method.* Put 1 tablespoon or so of the hot fruit mixture on a cold plate or spoon, then turn the plate or spoon on its side over the sink. If the fruit mixture falls off or "sheets off" in one large drop, the jelly is done.
- *The freezer method.* Put 1 tablespoon of the hot fruit mixture on a cold plate and place it in the freezer for 2 to 3 minutes. Remove and shake the plate. If the fruit mixture quivers, it is done.
- *The metal bowl method.* Take a metal bowl from the freezer and drop 1 teaspoon of hot fruit mixture into it. Wait 1 minute. Run your finger through it; if it separates into two parts and doesn't run back together, the mixture is ready for processing.

PREWASHING AND STERILIZING JARS AND LIDS

The jars you use for jellies and jams must fit the same standards as those you use for other canning methods. They must be free of cracks and chips and otherwise in good condition. Jars made for commercial use should never be used; they are not of the same sturdy quality as jars made specifically for canning and may not be able to withstand the lengthy exposure to the high temperatures of the boiling-water bath. Commercial jars can shatter, destroying your food and possibly causing injury to you or others.

Most recipes for fruit spreads call for half-pint jars. Each jar must have a two-piece lid that consists of a new metal vacuum lid and a new or used metal screw ring. Special jars and lids for canning fruit spreads fill this requirement.

The screw ring holds the vacuum lid in place and, unlike the vacuum lid, can be used year after year. Twenty-four hours after the canning process, when the jars have thoroughly cooled, remove the metal screw rings from the jars before storing your canned goods in the pantry. Metal screw rings that are left on jars may rust. If a screw ring is stuck or stubborn, don't force it and risk breaking the seal, but rather leave the ring in place. *Under no circumstances should you tighten the screw ring after processing.* This action could break the seal and leave the contents vulnerable to spoilage.

The USDA says it is not necessary to sterilize jars for fruit, tomatoes, or pickled foods that will be processed *longer than 10 minutes* in a boiling-water bath. Instead, before each use, wash your empty jars and rings in the dishwasher or submerge them in hot soapy water. Rinse the jars and rings thoroughly, being careful to remove all traces of soap. Keep the lids and rings hot in gently boiling water until you are ready to use them.

For boiling-water-bath processing times of less than 10 minutes, it is necessary to sterilize the containers by submerging clean, prewashed jars in a boiling-water bath. To do this, fill the jars with hot tap water and lower the water-filled jars into a canner of hot (not boiling) water, making sure the water level rises to 1 inch above the jar tops. At sea level, boil the jars for 10 minutes. At higher elevations, boil 1 additional minute for every 1,000 feet.

After the proper number of minutes has passed, use a jar lifter to remove one sterilized jar at a time and fill immediately with the prepared fruit spread. Be sure to leave appropriate headspace. Repeat until every jar is filled. Be sure to wipe any spillage from the jar rims with a clean cloth. Add the metal lid and rings by the method below, doing one jar at a time. (Save the boiling water for the canning process.)

TIP

• • • • • • • •

You can use the dishwasher to prewash jars for canning fruit spreads as long as the canning time is longer than 10 minutes. If the processing time is less than 10 minutes, you must wash and then sterilize the jars.

FILLING AND SEALING CONTAINERS

Begin filling the jars one at a time. This is where the canning funnel and ladle are invaluable.

Be careful to avoid drips when you remove the funnel from the filled jar. Not only can drips burn the cook, but they can also spoil the canning seal if they are allowed to remain on the lid or the mouth of the jar. I like to use a very clean, thin, wet dish towel pulled over my index finger to rub around the rim of the jar to get the smallest drip of food or liquid. This allows you to feel the slightest chip on the rim as well. A wet paper towel works for this cleaning job, also.

Do not overfill or leave too much headspace in the jars. Be sure to fill the fruit spread according to the headspace requirements and in the exact size jar specified in the recipe. Precision is important here. Too little headspace may cause the food to be forced out of the jar during processing when the heat causes the contents of the jar to expand. In addition to being messy, the leakage prevents the proper seal from forming. Too much headspace leaves too much air to be forced out during processing, which also prevents a seal from forming.

If bubbles appear in the liquid, tap the side of the jar with a knife handle. If your fruit spread has pieces of fruit in it, run a clean, plastic spatula along the sides of the jar to help remove bubbles between the pieces of fruit. Don't stir. That creates more bubbles.

In a saucepan, prepare the metal self-sealing lids by submerging them in boiling water for 10 minutes. Place the clean metal lids on the mouth of the jars and secure with the metal ring.

The canning lids are best kept clean and hot in the boiling-water bath mentioned above. After filling the first hot, sterile jar with fruit spread, place the hot metal lid on the jar and secure it with the metal ring. Then proceed to the next jar until all the jars are filled with fruit spread and ready to be processed.

TIP

· · · · · · · ·

Jars and metal rings may be reused if they're in good condition, but never recycle the self-sealing metal lids.

Boiling-Water-Bath Method for Fruit Spreads

Follow these steps for successful boiling-water-bath canning of jellies, jams, preserves, marmalades, and conserves:

1. Fill the canner halfway with water.

2. Preheat the water to 180°F for hot-pack fruit spreads.

3. Load the filled jars, fitted with lids, one at a time into the canner rack and use the handles to lower the rack into the hot water; or fill the canner one jar at a time with a jar lifter.

4. Add boiling water, if needed, so the water level is at least 1 to 2 inches above the jar tops.

5. Turn the heat to its highest position until the water boils vigorously.

6. Set a timer for the minutes required for processing the fruit spread.

7. Cover with the canner lid and lower the heat setting to maintain a gentle boil throughout the amount of time stated in the recipe. Adjust for altitude (page 40).

8. Add more boiling water, if needed, to keep the water level 1 to 2 inches above the jars.

9. When the jars have boiled for the recommended time, turn off the heat and remove the canner lid.

10. Using a jar lifter, remove the jars and place them on a clean towel, leaving at least 1 inch of space between the jars as they cool.

Checking the Seals

After the filled and finished jars of fruit spread have cooled, in 12 to 24 hours, use your thumbs to test the seal of the metal lids. Press hard on the center of one. If the lid does not move downward or "give," your jar is sealed. If one or two aren't sealed, you can store those faulty jars in the refrigerator to enjoy, though you must use them quickly.

Another method to ensure that your jar is properly sealed is to remove the screw ring and try lifting your newly canned jar by its lid using the weight of the jar to test the strength or weakness of the seal. (Protect yourself and the jar by doing this over the sink prepared with a towel to pad the possible fall.)

A List of Questions to Ask Yourself

1. Did I properly use the processing method called for in the recipe?
2. Did I fill the canner with the correct amount of water to cover the jars properly?
3. Did I correctly figure the altitude adjustment and headspace?
4. Did I verify that the jar rims were free of cracks and chips and use new lids?
5. Did I fill the jar to the proper density and cap it in the prescribed method?
6. Did the jars cool naturally at room temperature and in a reasonable amount of time, about 12 to 24 hours?
7. Were the metal screw rings left intact after the canning process or were they tightened before the jars were put on the pantry shelves or before being opened for eating?

Labeling and Storage

Always label fruit spreads with the contents, the processing method, and the date. You can purchase decorative glue-on labels, which are wonderful to use when you plan to make a gift of your fruit spread. You can make your own labels on the computer, as well.

Home-canned fruits require no expensive storage equipment — just a cool shelf in a dark, dry place. No matter how you label your fruit spreads and where you store them, make sure they are in a place where they won't be knocked off a shelf or exposed to high temperatures or sunlight. The many attributes of home canning, including the pleasure of enjoying and sharing quality, chemical-free food all winter long, are lost when jars fall and break the seal or your food spoils.

Homemade jams, jellies, and preserves always make wonderful hostess gifts, and they are a great way to say "thank you" to a neighbor who was kind enough to collect your mail while you were away for the weekend. They can serve as the focal point of more elaborate gifts, too. Refer to chapter 9 (page 317) for gift ideas.

Evaluating Your Jams and Jellies

Evaluating your jams and jellies can teach you as well as, if not better than, any instructions. Here are the questions to ask after preserving fruits:

1. *Did I examine each jar carefully before storing them?* This gives you a good chance to admire your work as well as time to spot problems.

2. *Are my jars sealed properly?* If the top inch of a jar of fruit spread turns dark, it can indicate an improper seal or storage in a place that's too warm. Mold is the most common indicator of spoilage from improper seals, but if the

The best storage temperature for fruit spreads is between 50 and 70°F.

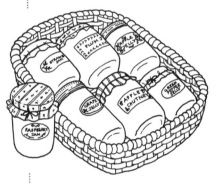

A basket of homemade jams and jellies makes a wonderful gift.

fruit spread is discolored, doesn't look the same as other jars, or has an unpleasant, "off" odor, don't take chances; throw it away. (Also, see box on page 48.) However, if you used honey instead of sugar, your spread will be darker in color. If the seal is good and no other signs of spoilage are present, the fruit spread is probably okay. Bright fruits, such as strawberries, darken naturally after processing.

3. *Has the fruit in my preserves floated to the surface?* Stirring off the heat for 5 minutes after kettle cooking and before bottling can eliminate this problem.

4. *Is the fruit spread too soft?* When the jar is tilted sideways does the fruit mixture move more like a liquid? If the consistency is too liquid and you used pectin, it may mean you boiled the mixture too long. Or perhaps you doubled the recipe, used liquid instead of powdered pectin, or used honey instead of sugar. If pectin wasn't used, it could mean you didn't cook the mixture long enough.

5. *Is the finished fruit spread too thick?* This can be caused by the pectin-fruit-sugar ratio being off. Also, overcooking a no-pectin spread can make the finished product stiff.

No-Cook Freezer and Refrigerator Fruit Spreads

• •

Today's busy world doesn't always allow time to stock a pantry the old-fashioned way. Throughout this book are recipes designed to let your refrigerator be your "pantry."

To make no-cook jelly, use fresh, uncooked fruit and juice or frozen juice concentrate. (Do not use canned commercial sweetened juices with the no-cook method. This would defeat the fresh flavor advantage.) If you dry-packed fruit and froze it earlier in the season (see page 125), this is an ideal use for it. Combine the sugar, fruit juice, and pectin according to the pectin directions. Use sterilized containers for storage and allow 1 inch of headspace for expansion during freezing. Because there is no cooking and, therefore, no sterilizing, no-cook jams keep up to only 3 weeks in the refrigerator and up to 6 months in the freezer.

6. *Is the finished product weeping?* Too-warm storage or the use of low-methyl pectin can cause weeping. Also, honey recipes tend to weep more than sugar ones because sugar is a natural gelling agent. If there are no signs of spoilage, the spread is probably still safe to eat. Before using, drain off the liquid or blot it with paper towels.

Low-Sugar, No-Cook Freezer Fruit Spreads

For those on special diets or who enjoy the sometimes-tart taste of fresh fruit, try this unconventional way of making fruit spreads.

Agar is a gelling, stabilizing agent that is used to solidify the no- or low-sugar, no-cook fruit spreads. This plant product, sometimes called Asian gelatin or agar-agar, is derived from ocean algae and is available in natural food stores and Asian markets.

Common household gelatin, which is an animal product, also can be used as a solidifying agent for low- or no-sugar cooked fruit spreads for the refrigerator or freezer.

Agar strands and flakes are used to solidify fruit spreads.

Strawberry Jelly with Liquid Pectin

1. Using a wooden spoon, crush 2½ quarts of washed, hulled, ripe strawberries.

2. Put the pulp into a damp jelly bag or cheesecloth and allow the juice to drip through. This will vary from a few hours to overnight, depending on the juiciness of the fruit. To avoid cloudy jelly, don't squeeze.

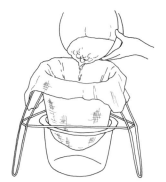

3. Measure 3¾ cups of juice into a large saucepan. Add ¼ cup of lemon juice and 7½ cups of sugar. Place over high heat and bring to a boil, stirring constantly. Stir in the liquid pectin, bring to a full rolling boil, and boil hard for 1 minute, stirring constantly. Skim off the foam with a metal spoon.

4. Remove from the heat and skim off all the foam with a metal spoon.

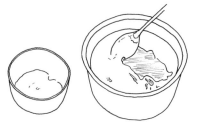

5. Pour quickly into hot, sterilized jars, leaving ¼ inch of headspace. Wipe the rims clean.

6. Adjust the lids and process in a boiling-water bath for 5 minutes to ensure a good seal. Be sure to adjust for altitude (page 40). Set the jars upright to cool.

7. Cool the jars for 12 to 24 hours. Remove the screw rings and test the seals.

Equipment
· · · · · · · · ·

The equipment you need for the recipes in this chapter is the same in each. You'll need a boiling-water-bath canner and jars of the appropriate size. For a complete list of supplies for making fruit spreads, see page 182.

RECIPES FOR JAMS, JELLIES, PRESERVES, CONSERVES, MARMALADES, AND BUTTERS

Agar Berry Jam

This no-process, low-sugar fruit jam is wonderful with strawberries, raspberries, blackberries, or blueberries. Experiment with combinations.

1 tablespoon lemon juice

3 cups washed, hulled, and finely chopped berries, at room temperature (about 1 quart whole)

1 cup cold water

2 tablespoons agar flakes

¼ cup mild-flavored honey, such as clover

1. In a mixing bowl, stir the lemon juice into the fruit. Set aside.

2. Place the water in a small saucepan and stir in the agar flakes. Wait 1 minute and then, without further stirring, bring the agar to a simmer over medium-low heat. Once it's simmering, stir for 2–5 minutes, or until the agar is completely dissolved.

3. Stir the honey into the agar. Use a heatproof rubber spatula to scrape the sides and bottom of the pot.

4. Pouring with one hand and stirring with the other, add the agar mixture to the fruit (do not add the fruit to the agar). Continue stirring until they are completely mixed. Taste at this time and add more honey, up to 3 tablespoons, if desired.

5. Pour the jam into hot, scalded half-pint jars, leaving ½ inch of headspace.

6. Cap and seal. Let cool in the refrigerator for 10–12 hours before freezing. Label and freeze the jam for up to 6 months.

7. When ready to use, thaw the jam in the refrigerator. It will keep about 3 weeks in the refrigerator.

YIELD: FOUR ½-PINTS (THIRTY-TWO 1-OUNCE SERVINGS)

NUTRITION PER SERVING

Calories	12	Total fat	<1g
% from fat	3	Saturated	0g
Carbohydrates	3g	Cholesterol	0mg
Fiber	<1g	Sodium	1mg

Fresh Strawberry Preserves

This no-sugar, no-cook jam using gelatin is adapted from Stocking Up, *Rodale Food Center.*

1 cup water

1 envelope unflavored gelatin

2 cups coarsely chopped strawberries (about 1 quart whole berries), hulls and stems removed

2 tablespoons honey

2 teaspoons lemon juice

4 packets (.035 ounce each) aspartame

1. Pour the water into a saucepan and sprinkle the gelatin on top. Let stand for 5 minutes.

2. Heat the mixture over medium heat for 1 minute, stirring constantly to dissolve the gelatin.

3. Remove the mixture from the heat and add the fruit, honey, and lemon juice. Stir well and cool slightly.

4. Add the aspartame and stir well.

5. Pour the mixture into hot, scalded containers, leaving ½ inch of headspace.

6. Cap and seal. Label and store in the refrigerator. Use within 3 weeks.

YIELD: THREE ½-PINTS (TWENTY-FOUR 1-OUNCE SERVINGS)

NUTRITION PER SERVING

Calories	16	Total fat	<1g
% from fat	2	Saturated	0g
Carbohydrates	3g	Cholesterol	0mg
Fiber	<1g	Sodium	2mg

Spiced Strawberry Jam Using Fruit Pectin

*Easy to prepare and spicier than most, this jam will
delight children and adults alike.*

5 cups crushed strawberries (about
2 quarts cleaned and stemmed)

½ teaspoon ground allspice

½ teaspoon ground cinnamon

¼ teaspoon ground cloves

1 box (1¾ ounces) powdered fruit
pectin

½ teaspoon butter or margarine

7 cups sugar

1. In an 8-quart saucepan, combine the strawberries and the spices. Add the pectin and butter to the saucepan.

2. Bring to a full boil on high heat, stirring constantly.

3. Stir in exactly 7 cups of sugar and mix well.

4. Return to a full boil and boil for 1 minute exactly, stirring constantly.

5. Remove the saucepan from the heat and skim off any foam using a metal spoon.

6. Ladle into sterilized jars, leaving ¼ inch of headspace.

7. Cap, seal, and process for 5 minutes in a boiling-water-bath canner. Adjust for altitude (page 40), if necessary.

YIELD: FIVE ½-PINTS (FORTY 1-OUNCE SERVINGS)
NUTRITION PER SERVING

Calories	145	Total fat	<1g
% from fat	<1	Saturated	0g
Carbohydrates	37g	Cholesterol	0mg
Fiber	1g	Sodium	4mg

Baked Low-Sugar Strawberry Jam

Try substituting raspberries or blackberries for the strawberries.

8 cups strawberries, washed, drained, patted dry, and halved

1 cup sugar

3 tablespoons lemon juice

1. Preheat the oven to 375°F.

2. Combine all the ingredients in a 2-quart casserole dish.

3. Bake, uncovered, for about 15 minutes.

4. Reduce the heat to 325°F. Bake for 1–1½ hours. Stir often. Let a spoonful of jam cool and test for gelling capabilities (see pages 185–86).

5. If it is too runny, return it to the oven and bake at 325°F for up to 45 minutes longer, then test again for thickening.

6. Place in clean freezer cartons. Refrigerate for up to 2 weeks or freeze for up to 6 months.

YIELD: THREE ½-PINTS (TWENTY-FOUR 1-OUNCE SERVINGS)

NUTRITION PER SERVING

Calories	47	Total fat	<1g
% from fat	3	Saturated	0g
Carbohydrates	12g	Cholesterol	0mg
Fiber	1g	Sodium	1mg

Strawberry Rhubarb Jelly

This jelly recipe, which is a southern tradition, has been adapted from the USDA.

1½ pounds red rhubarb stalks, washed and cut into 1-inch pieces

1½ quarts strawberries, washed, hulled, and crushed

6 cups sugar

6 ounces liquid fruit pectin

1. Purée the rhubarb by pulverizing it in a blender or food processor.

2. Prepare a jelly bag by pouring boiling water through it. Squeeze out the excess moisture. Line the bag with a double layer of cheesecloth.

3. Place both fruits in the bag, let drain into a bowl, and squeeze gently to remove the excess juice.

4. Measure 3½ cups of strained juice into a 3-quart saucepan. Add the sugar, mix thoroughly, and boil until the sugar dissolves.

5. Remove the pan from the heat and stir in the pectin.

6. Return to the heat and bring to a full boil. Boil for exactly 1 minute. Remove from the heat and skim off any foam with a metal spoon.

7. Ladle into sterile half-pint jars, leaving ¼ inch of headspace.

8. Seal and process for 5 minutes in a boiling-water-bath canner. Adjust for altitude (page 40), if necessary.

YIELD: SEVEN ½-PINTS (FIFTY-SIX 1-OUNCE SERVINGS)
NUTRITION PER SERVING

Calories	99	Total fat	<1g
% from fat	<1	Saturated	0g
Carbohydrates	26g	Cholesterol	0mg
Fiber	<1g	Sodium	7mg

Strawberry and Blackberry Jam

This old favorite is adapted from the Ball Blue Book.

2 cups strawberries, rinsed, hulled, halved, and crushed

1 cup firmly packed blackberries

3 tablespoons lemon juice

1 package (1¾ ounces) powdered pectin

½ cup light corn syrup

3½ cups sugar

1. Combine the berries and lemon juice in a large bowl; stir well.

2. Slowly add the pectin, stirring constantly for 2 minutes.

3. Let the mixture stand for 30 minutes, stirring occasionally.

4. Add the light corn syrup and stir well.

5. Gradually stir in the sugar, beating well. The jam is ready when the sugar has completely dissolved.

6. Pour the jam into canning or freezer jars, leaving ½ inch of headspace.

7. Cap, seal, and cool in the refrigerator. Let stand until set, about 24 hours.

8. Label and freeze.

YIELD: SIX ½-PINTS (FORTY-EIGHT 1-OUNCE SERVINGS)

NUTRITION PER SERVING

Calories	73	Total fat	<1g
% from fat	<1	Saturated	0g
Carbohydrates	19g	Cholesterol	0mg
Fiber	<1g	Sodium	5mg

Freezer Tip

Precool filled containers of no-process fruit spread in the refrigerator overnight before freezing them: It saves strain on your freezer.

Blackberry Preserves

James R. Coffee shared this recipe with me after he read my book
Preserving Fruits and Vegetables. His recipe won the 1996 Ball Canning award
at his local Pennsylvania fair.

3 quarts blackberries*

6 cups sugar

*Note: Blackberries can be frozen, then made up later as needed. Do not wash them before freezing. Just put them in containers and freeze. When you're ready to use the berries, put them in a colander and rinse them thoroughly. This washes them and starts the thawing process. Place the washed berries in a bowl and cover with plastic wrap. Store them in the refrigerator overnight, then proceed with the recipe instructions.

1. In a 4-quart saucepan, heat the berries slowly until the juice is extracted, then add the sugar. Boil the mixture, uncovered, for 20 minutes.

2. Skim off the foam with a metal spoon. Pour the preserves into sterilized jars, leaving ½ inch of headspace.

3. Wipe each sealing edge clean. Cap and seal.

4. Process in a boiling-water-bath canner for 15 minutes. Adjust for altitude (page 40), if necessary.

YIELD: 4 PINTS (SIXTY-FOUR 1-OUNCE SERVINGS)
NUTRITION PER SERVING

Calories	86	Total fat	<1g
% from fat	1	Saturated	0g
Carbohydrates	22g	Cholesterol	0mg
Fiber	1g	Sodium	0mg

Blackberry, Cranberry, and Pink Grapefruit Preserves

Present this tart but sweet spread to a neighbor and you'll have a friend for life.

1 bag (12 ounces) fresh cranberries

6 cups frozen blackberries, thawed, with their juice

1½ cups sugar

2 pink or ruby red grapefruit, juiced (about 1 cup)

1. Pick over the cranberries to remove any stems or bad berries.

2. Mix the cranberries, 4 cups of the blackberries, sugar, and grapefruit juice in a heavy nonreactive saucepan.

3. Bring to a boil over medium to high heat until the mixture sheets on the end of a spoon (see page 186), about 25 minutes. Stir frequently and be careful not to burn the mixture.

4. As the mixture cooks, gradually add the remaining blackberries and their juice to the hot mixture and return to a boil.

5. Ladle the hot mixture into clean jars, leaving ¼ inch of headspace. Cap and seal. Process in a boiling-water-bath canner for 15 minutes. Adjust for altitude (page 40), if necessary.

YIELD: 4 PINTS (SIXTY-FOUR 1-OUNCE SERVINGS)
NUTRITION PER SERVING

Calories	31	Total fat	<1g
% from fat	2	Saturated	0g
Carbohydrates	8g	Cholesterol	0mg
Fiber	<1g	Sodium	0mg

Red Raspberry Preserves

A classic — not only a favorite, but also easy to prepare.

4 cups raspberries, washed, picked over, and drained

3 cups sugar

¼ cup fresh lemon juice, strained

1. Combine all the ingredients in a ceramic 2-quart bowl, stirring occasionally to let the sugar dissolve, about 2 hours.

2. Pour the mixture into a heavy 3-quart saucepan.

3. Bring to a boil, reduce the heat, and simmer, stirring frequently, until a cooking thermometer reaches 220°F or until it passes one of the jelly tests on page 186. (Allow about 5 minutes, depending on how juicy the berries are.)

4. Remove from the heat and skim off any foam that may have formed with a metal spoon.

5. Ladle into three sterile half-pint jars, allowing ¼ inch of headspace. Cap and seal.

6. Process for 15 minutes in a boiling-water-bath canner. Adjust for altitude (page 40), if necessary.

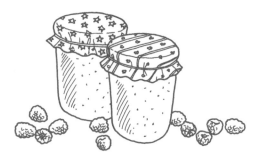

YIELD: THREE ½-PINTS (TWENTY-FOUR 1-OUNCE SERVINGS)

NUTRITION PER SERVING

Calories	107	Total fat	<1g
% from fat	<1	Saturated	0g
Carbohydrates	28g	Cholesterol	0mg
Fiber	<1g	Sodium	0mg

Lime Marmalade

* * * * * * * * * *

A trip to England produced this recipe. Try it instead of the more familiar orange marmalade.

3 pounds (about 18) large Persian limes, peeled, zest cut into thin strips 2 inches long

9 cups water

6 pounds (13½ cups) sugar

Note: My British exchange student's family advised softening citrus in a microwave for 10 seconds per fruit to make it easier to peel or juice.

1. Cut the peeled limes in half and squeeze the juice. Set the juice aside.

2. Scrape the pulp and seeds from the lime halves. Place in a cheesecloth bag.

3. Place the cheesecloth bag, zest, juice, and water in a 6-quart saucepan, then cover them and soak overnight, or for about 8 hours.

4. Bring the water mixture to a boil and cook about 2 hours, until the peels are soft.

5. Remove the cheesecloth bag.

6. Add the sugar to the pan and stir to dissolve.

7. Boil, stirring often, until a cooking thermometer reaches 220°F.

8. Ladle into clean jars, leaving ¼ inch of headspace. Cap and seal.

9. Process for 10 minutes in a boiling-water-bath canner. Adjust for altitude (page 40), if necessary.

YIELD: 10 PINTS (ONE HUNDRED-SIXTY 1-OUNCE SERVINGS)

NUTRITION PER SERVING

Calories	68	Total fat	0g
% from fat	0	Saturated	0g
Carbohydrates	18g	Cholesterol	0mg
Fiber	<1g	Sodium	1mg

Lemon Jelly

· · · · · · · · · · ·

Delicious with tea and toast, this jelly is also great on angel food cake with fresh strawberries for a nonfat dessert.

3 pounds (about 15) lemons

9 cups water

3 pounds (6¾ cups) sugar

1. Peel the lemons and cut the zest into 2-inch strips.

2. Halve the peeled lemons. Squeeze the juice into a large bowl. Set aside.

3. Scrape the pulp from the lemon halves. Set aside. Save the seeds.

4. Combine 2½ cups of the water with the seeds and zest and boil for 30 minutes in a 2-quart saucepan. Cover and let cool.

5. Place the lemon pulp, lemon juice, and remaining water in a 4-quart saucepan. Strain in the seed/zest water and simmer, uncovered, for 40 minutes.

6. Pour the pulp mixture through a wet jelly bag and let drain over a 6-quart saucepan overnight. Don't squeeze the bag.

7. Measure the juice. In a saucepan, combine 2 cups of sugar for each 2½ cups of juice.

8. Stir over low heat to dissolve the sugar.

9. Bring to a boil, stirring frequently, and boil until the mixture reaches 220°F on your cooking thermometer, about 10 minutes.

10. Ladle into clean jars, leaving ¼ inch of headspace. Cap and seal.

11. Process for 5 minutes in a boiling-water-bath canner. Adjust for altitude (page 40), if necessary.

· ·

YIELD: 5 PINTS (EIGHTY 1-OUNCE SERVINGS)
NUTRITION PER SERVING

Calories	69	Total fat	0
% from fat	0	Saturated	0g
Carbohydrates	19g	Cholesterol	0mg
Fiber	<1g	Sodium	1mg

· ·

Lemon-Pineapple Preserves

This is delicious on banana bread or toast at breakfast, or on a muffin at teatime.

3 large lemons

3 pounds (about 2 whole) fresh pineapple, cleaned, cored, and chopped

2½ cups water

3 pounds (6¾ cups) sugar

1. Squeeze the lemons of all their juice. Reserve the seeds and lemon hulls. Strain the juice.

2. In a cheesecloth bag, combine the lemon hulls and seeds.

3. Combine the strained lemon juice, pineapple, water, and cheesecloth bag in a 4-quart saucepan. Bring to a boil and simmer until the pineapple is tender, about 15–20 minutes.

4. Remove the cheesecloth bag and add the sugar to the pan, stirring to dissolve.

5. Bring to a boil and simmer, stirring frequently, until a cooking thermometer reaches 220°F, about 12–15 minutes.

6. Ladle into clean jars, leaving ¼ inch of headspace. Cap and seal.

7. Process for 20 minutes in a boiling-water-bath canner. Adjust for altitude (page 40), if necessary.

YIELD: 6 PINTS (NINETY-SIX 1-OUNCE SERVINGS)
NUTRITION PER SERVING

Calories	59	Total fat	0g
% from fat	0	Saturated	0g
Carbohydrates	15g	Cholesterol	0mg
Fiber	<1g	Sodium	0mg

Old-Fashioned Peach Preserves

What can be said about such a classic?

1 quart water

½ teaspoon ascorbic acid (crystals, powder, or crushed tablets)

3½ pounds (about 7 large) peaches, peeled, pitted, and chopped

5 cups sugar

¼ cup lemon juice

¾ teaspoon almond extract

1. Prepare an acid bath by pouring the water into a medium-sized bowl and adding the ascorbic acid.

2. Dip the peaches in the acid bath; drain well. Combine the fruit, sugar, and lemon juice in a heavy 6–8 quart saucepan. Stir over medium heat to dissolve the sugar.

3. Boil slowly, stirring constantly, until the mixture thickens, the fruit is translucent, and a cooking thermometer reaches 220°F.

4. Stir in the almond extract.

5. Remove from the heat and skim off the foam, if there is any, with a metal spoon. Ladle into sterile jars, allowing ¼ inch of headspace. Cap and seal.

6. Process for 10 minutes in a boiling-water-bath canner. Adjust for altitude (page 40), if necessary.

YIELD: 7 PINTS (ONE HUNDRED TWELVE 1-OUNCE SERVINGS)

NUTRITION PER SERVING

Calories	39	Total fat	0g
% from fat	0	Saturated	0g
Carbohydrates	10g	Cholesterol	0mg
Fiber	<1g	Sodium	0mg

Spiced Peach Jam

This is an old standby enjoyed by all who try it.

4 pounds (about 8 large) peaches, peeled, pitted, and chopped

5 cups sugar

2 tablespoons lemon juice

½ teaspoon ground nutmeg

⅛ teaspoon ground cinnamon

1. Place all the ingredients in a heavy 8-quart saucepan. Cook over medium heat, stirring constantly, to dissolve the sugar.

2. Bring to a boil, stirring constantly, and boil until the mixture reaches 220°F on a cooking thermometer. (Or use one of the methods to test for doneness found on page 186.)

3. Ladle into sterile jars, allowing ¼ inch of headspace. Cap and seal.

4. Process for 15 minutes in a boiling-water-bath canner. Adjust for altitude (page 40), if necessary.

YIELD: FIVE ½-PINTS (FORTY 1-OUNCE SERVINGS)
NUTRITION PER SERVING

Calories	112	Total fat	0g
% from fat	0	Saturated	0g
Carbohydrates	29g	Cholesterol	0mg
Fiber	<1g	Sodium	0mg

Grape Jelly

Using green grapes creates a finished product that is surprisingly pink!

3 pounds green grapes, washed, stemmed, picked over, and chopped

2 lemons, juiced

2⅓ cups water

2¼ cups sugar

1. Bring the grapes, lemon juice, and water to a boil in an 8-quart saucepan and simmer for about 30 minutes, until the fruit is very soft.

2. Meanwhile, scald a jelly bag by pouring boiling water through it. Squeeze out the excess water. Hang the bag in a convenient but out-of-the-way place with a large drip pot positioned underneath. (I use a dowel threaded through cabinet hardware for the bag, with the drip pot on the counter below.)

3. Pour the mixture into the wet jelly bag. Let drip for 24 hours or less. (Do not squeeze the pulp in the bag.)

4. Measure the strained juice. Add 2¼ cups of sugar for each 2⅓ cups of juice. Pour into a heavy 3-quart saucepan.

5. Stir the mixture over medium heat until the sugar has dissolved.

6. Boil the mixture for 10–12 minutes, or until a cooking thermometer reaches 220°F. Read about other methods of testing for doneness on page 186.

7. Skim off any foam with a metal spoon. Ladle into sterile jars, leaving ¼ inch of headspace. Cap and seal.

8. Process for 5 minutes in a boiling-water-bath canner. Adjust for altitude (page 40), if necessary.

YIELD: FOUR ½-PINTS (THIRTY-TWO 1-OUNCE SERVINGS)

NUTRITION PER SERVING

Calories	81	Total fat	<1g
% from fat	2	Saturated	0g
Carbohydrates	21g	Cholesterol	0mg
Fiber	<1g	Sodium	2mg

Spiced Grape Jelly for the Freezer

Just a touch of cinnamon and nutmeg makes this jelly a whole new flavor sensation.

2 cups lukewarm water

1 package (1¾ ounces) powdered pectin

6 ounces frozen grape juice concentrate

3½ cups sugar

⅛ teaspoon ground cinnamon

⅛ teaspoon ground nutmeg

1. Carefully combine the lukewarm water and the pectin in a 4-quart bowl, stirring constantly. Let stand for 45 minutes.

2. Thaw the grape juice concentrate and pour it into a 2-quart bowl.

3. Add 1¾ cups of the sugar to the juice bowl, stirring to dissolve it completely.

4. Add the remaining sugar to the pectin mixture, again stirring well to dissolve the sugar completely.

5. Add the juice mixture to the pectin mixture, then add the spices.

6. Ladle the jelly into freezer containers, leaving ½ inch of headspace. Cap the containers.

7. Let the containers stand until the mixture sets.

8. Label and freeze.

YIELD: FOUR ½-PINTS (THIRTY-TWO 1-OUNCE SERVINGS)

NUTRITION PER SERVING

Calories	99	Total fat	0g
% from fat	0	Saturated	0g
Carbohydrates	26g	Cholesterol	0mg
Fiber	0g	Sodium	4mg

Blueberry Marmalade

This is a new combination of flavors that is certain to please.

1 lemon

1 medium orange

¾ cup water

⅛ teaspoon baking soda

4 cups blueberries, rinsed, picked over, and crushed

5 cups sugar

6 ounces liquid pectin

1. Peel the lemon and orange and chop the zest.

2. Remove the white membranes from the citrus and chop the pulp. Set aside.

3. Combine the chopped zest, water, and baking soda in a small saucepan. Bring to a boil, reduce the heat, and simmer for about 10 minutes, stirring occasionally. Drain well and reserve the zest.

4. Combine the blueberries, citrus pulp, and sugar in an 8-quart saucepan and bring to a boil. Reduce the heat and simmer for 5 minutes.

5. Remove from the heat. Let cool for 5 minutes. Add the drained zest.

6. Add the liquid pectin and return to a boil. Boil for exactly 1 minute, stirring constantly.

7. Skim off the foam with a metal spoon.

8. Ladle into sterile jars, leaving ¼ inch of headspace. Cap and seal.

9. Process in a boiling-water-bath canner for 10 minutes. Adjust for altitude (page 40), if necessary.

YIELD: SIX ½-PINTS (FORTY-EIGHT 1-OUNCE SERVINGS)

NUTRITION PER SERVING

Calories	100	Total fat	<1g
% from fat	1	Saturated	<1g
Carbohydrates	26g	Cholesterol	0mg
Fiber	<1g	Sodium	11mg

Blueberry and Cherry Preserves

Two great taste sensations team up to make a mellow-spiced spread.

3 cups cherries, washed, pitted, and crushed

3 cups blueberries, rinsed, picked over, and crushed

4½ cups sugar

1 tablespoon thinly sliced lemon zest

½ teaspoon ground nutmeg

1. Combine all the ingredients in a heavy 4-quart saucepan. Stir over medium heat to dissolve the sugar.

2. Boil over high heat, being careful not to burn, until the mixture reaches 220°F on a cooking thermometer (or use one of the methods found on page 186).

3. Ladle into sterile jars, allowing ¼ inch of headspace. Cap and seal.

4. Process for 15 minutes in a boiling-water-bath canner. Adjust for altitude (page 40), if necessary.

YIELD: FIVE ½-PINTS (FORTY 1-OUNCE SERVINGS)
NUTRITION PER SERVING

Calories	102	Total fat	<1g
% from fat	1	Saturated	<1g
Carbohydrates	26g	Cholesterol	0mg
Fiber	<1g	Sodium	1mg

Apple Ginger Marmalade

A particular favorite of adults, this has just the right blend of flavors to delight the palate.

3 lemons

2½ cups water

3 pounds (9–10) apples, peeled, cored, and sliced, about 7½ cups (reserve the peelings)

8 cups sugar

4 ounces crystallized ginger, finely chopped

2¼ teaspoons ground ginger

1. Grate the zest from the lemons and reserve. Cut the lemons in half and squeeze, reserving the juice.

2. Make a "stock" with the water and apple peelings. Boil, covered, in an 8-quart saucepan for about 15 minutes.

3. Remove the peelings from the stock and add the apple slices. Simmer until soft, about 10 minutes.

4. Add the sugar, ginger, ground ginger, lemon zest, and lemon juice.

5. Boil, stirring occasionally, until the spread thickens or until a cooking thermometer reaches 220°F. Or you may use one of the tests for doneness found on page 186. (Remember to allow for thickening when the spread has cooled.)

6. Ladle into sterile jars, leaving ¼ inch of headspace. Cap and seal.

7. Process for 10 minutes in a boiling-water-bath canner. Adjust for altitude (page 40), if necessary.

YIELD: TEN ½-PINTS (EIGHTY 1-OUNCE SERVINGS)
NUTRITION PER SERVING

Calories	92	Total fat	<1g
% from fat	<1	Saturated	0g
Carbohydrates	23g	Cholesterol	1mg
Fiber	<1g	Sodium	1mg

Marion's Apple Butter

My friend Marion lives in the middle of an apple orchard. She makes many creative treasures out of her abundance of Rome apples. My very favorite is her recipe for apple butter. The ground spices and peelings give the mixture a deep, rich flavor and appearance.

10 large (about 5 pounds) tart apples

2 cups apple cider

3–5 cups sugar

3 teaspoons ground cinnamon

¾ teaspoon ground cloves

½ teaspoon ground allspice

½ teaspoon ground nutmeg

1. Wash, core, and quarter the apples. No need to peel them.

2. Cook the apples slowly in the cider until tender. Blend in a food processor. You should have about 12–14 cups of pulp.

3. Add 3 cups of the sugar, then more sugar, if needed, to attain the desired sweetness. Add the spices and mix thoroughly.

4. Cook in a 350°F oven or slow-cooker for 6–8 hours, stirring often. Test for desired thickness by spooning the mixture onto a cold plate. If no liquid oozes around the edges, it is thick enough.

5. Ladle into sterile jars, leaving ¼ inch of headspace.

6. Process in a boiling-water-bath canner for 10 minutes. Adjust for altitude (page 40), if necessary. This apple butter can also be frozen.

Note: The apple butter will keep for up to 2 weeks in the refrigerator after it is freshly made or thawed and opened.

YIELD: TEN ½-PINTS (EIGHTY 1-OUNCE SERVINGS)
NUTRITION PER SERVING

Calories	59	Total fat	0g
% from fat	0	Saturated	0g
Carbohydrates	15g	Cholesterol	0mg
Fiber	<1g	Sodium	1mg

Apple-Plum Butter

A variation on an old favorite, this is sure to delight your family.

2½ pounds (about 15 medium) plums, washed and pitted

1 cup water

½ cup lemon juice

2½ pounds apples, peeled, cored, and sliced

5½ cups sugar

1 teaspoon ground cinnamon

¼ teaspoon ground cloves

¼ teaspoon ground nutmeg

½ teaspoon salt

1. In a covered 3-quart saucepan, combine the plums, ½ cup of the water, and ¼ cup of the lemon juice. Cook over medium-high heat until the plums are soft, about 20 minutes.

2. Meanwhile, in another 3-quart saucepan, combine the apples, the remaining water, and the remaining lemon juice. Cook over medium-high heat until the apples are soft, about 10 minutes.

3. Let both mixtures cool slightly; combine in a blender or food processor and purée.

4. Pour the mixture into a heavy 8-quart flameproof roasting pan along with the sugar, spices, and salt.

5. Preheat the oven to 300°F.

6. Cook on top of the stove over medium heat until all the sugar dissolves.

7. Transfer the roasting pan to the oven.

8. Bake uncovered, stirring occasionally, until the mixture thickens. This will take 1–3 hours.

9. Test for doneness by spooning some onto a plate. If no liquid appears on the edges, it is ready.

10. Ladle into sterile jars, leaving ¼ inch of headspace. Cap and seal.

11. Process for 10 minutes in a boiling-water-bath canner. Adjust for altitude (page 40), if necessary.

YIELD: SIX ½-PINTS (FORTY-EIGHT 1-OUNCE SERVINGS)

NUTRITION PER SERVING

Calories	113	Total fat	<1g
% from fat	2	Saturated	0g
Carbohydrates	29g	Cholesterol	0mg
Fiber	<1g	Sodium	23mg

Apple-Zucchini Butter

This is a delicious way to use abundant zucchini in late summer.
The brown sugar gives it a rich taste.

4 pounds zucchini, peeled and chopped

5 tablespoons salt

2 pounds cooking apples, peeled, cored, and chopped

3 medium onions, chopped (2 cups)

5 cups distilled white vinegar

2⅔ cups firmly packed light brown sugar

1 piece dried ginger root (about 2 inches long)

2 tablespoons pickling spice

1. Layer the zucchini and salt in a large ceramic bowl. Cover and let stand for 12 hours or overnight.

2. Rinse and drain the zucchini and place in a 6-quart saucepan. Add the apples, onions, vinegar, and sugar.

3. Tie the whole spices in a cheesecloth bag and add to the pan.

4. Slowly bring to a boil, stirring often, until the mixture thickens, simmering uncovered for about 1–1½ hours. Be careful not to burn the mixture. Remove the spice bag.

5. Ladle into clean jars, leaving ¼ inch of headspace. Cap and seal.

6. Process for 10 minutes in a boiling-water-bath canner. Adjust for altitude (page 40), if necessary.

YIELD: 6 PINTS (NINETY-SIX 1-OUNCE SERVINGS)
NUTRITION PER SERVING

Calories	34	Total fat	<1g
% from fat	2	Saturated	0g
Carbohydrates	9g	Cholesterol	0mg
Fiber	<1g	Sodium	3mg

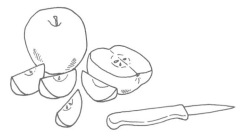

Basil-Apple Jelly

On a biscuit, with pork or chicken, or spread over pineapple cream cheese,
this herb jelly is a winner.

2 cups apple juice

⅓ cup dried basil

3½ cups sugar

3 tablespoons fresh lemon juice, strained

¼ teaspoon butter or margarine

3 ounces liquid pectin

1. In a 5-quart saucepan, bring the apple juice to a boil. Add the dried basil, remove from the heat, and let stand for 2 hours.

2. Strain the apple-basil infusion through a paper coffee filter.

3. Rinse out the saucepan and return the mixture to it. Add the sugar, lemon juice, and butter.

4. Bring the new mixture to a boil over high heat, stirring constantly.

5. Add the liquid pectin and return the mixture to a full boil. Boil for exactly 1 minute, stirring constantly. Ladle the jelly into clean jars, leaving ½ inch of headspace. Cap and seal.

6. Process in a boiling-water-bath canner for 5 minutes. Adjust for altitude (page 40), if necessary.

YIELD: 2 PINTS (THIRTY-TWO 1-OUNCE SERVINGS)
NUTRITION PER SERVING

Calories	103	Total fat	<1g
% from fat	<1	Saturated	0g
Carbohydrates	27g	Cholesterol	0mg
Fiber	<1g	Sodium	7mg

Coriander and Honey Jelly

. . . .

*Golden amber in color and subtle in flavor, this jelly stands up best
on delicate dinner rolls or breakfast breads.*

3 cups water

⅓ cup coriander seeds, bruised

3 cups sugar

¼ cup fresh lemon juice, strained

¼ cup mild honey

1 package (1¾ ounces) powdered pectin

*Note: To bruise coriander seeds, partially crush them
with the back of a spoon.*

1. Boil the water and coriander seeds for 2 minutes in a 3-quart saucepan. Let stand, covered, for 6 hours or overnight.

2. Strain the infusion through a coffee filter and return 2½ cups of the liquid to the pan.

3. Add the sugar, lemon juice, and honey. Mix well. Boil hard and add the pectin.

4. Bring to a boil again and boil for exactly 1 minute. Remove from the heat and skim off any foam with a metal spoon.

5. Pour into four half-pint sterile jars, leaving ¼ inch of headspace. Cap and seal.

6. Process for 5 minutes in a boiling-water-bath canner. Adjust for altitude (page 40), if necessary.

. . . .

YIELD: FOUR ½-PINTS (THIRTY-TWO 1-OUNCE
SERVINGS)

NUTRITION PER SERVING

Calories	89	Total fat	<1g
% from fat	2	Saturated	0g
Carbohydrates	23g	Cholesterol	0mg
Fiber	<1g	Sodium	4mg

. . . .

Nutmeg-Scented Geranium Jelly

You'll find this aristocratic concoction in specialty food stores. Now that you have the recipe, you can wow your family and friends.

4 cups apple juice

2 cups nutmeg-scented geranium leaves, washed and dried (always make sure plants have not been sprayed with insecticides)

5 cups sugar

3 tablespoons fresh lemon juice

3 ounces liquid pectin

¼ teaspoon freshly grated nutmeg

1–2 drops all-natural green food coloring (optional)

1. Boil the apple juice and geranium leaves for 2 minutes in an 8-quart saucepan. Strain. Let the mixture cool overnight. You can do this step several days ahead and refrigerate the mixture until needed.

2. Combine the juice mixture, sugar, and lemon juice in an 8-quart saucepan. Boil, stirring frequently, over high heat for 5 minutes.

3. Add the pectin. Return the mixture to a boil, timing it for exactly 1 minute.

4. Remove the pan from the heat. Skim off any foam. Add the grated nutmeg.

5. Add a drop or two of all-natural green food coloring, if using.

6. Pour the jelly into clean jars, leaving ¼ inch of headspace.

7. Process in a boiling-water-bath canner for 5 minutes. Adjust for altitude (page 40), if necessary.

8. Let the jars cool, check the seals, label, and then store them for about a week so the flavors can marry.

YIELD: SIX ½-PINTS (FORTY-EIGHT 1-OUNCE SERVINGS)

NUTRITION PER SERVING

Calories	96	Total fat	0g
% from fat	0	Saturated	0g
Carbohydrates	25g	Cholesterol	0mg
Fiber	<1g	Sodium	4mg

Mint Jelly

This subtle but delicious classic has endless possibilities.

2 cups apple juice or cider

2 bags peppermint tea, or 8 tablespoons (½ cup) fresh peppermint leaves

1½ cups sugar

3 tablespoons fresh lemon juice, strained

¼ teaspoon butter or margarine

1–3 drops all-natural green food coloring (optional)

3 ounces liquid pectin

1. In a heavy 5-quart saucepan, bring the apple juice and tea bags to a full boil, and then let the tea steep for 10 minutes. If you use fresh mint, strain the liquid after cooking.

2. Remove the tea bags and add the sugar, lemon juice, butter, and food coloring, if using. Bring to a boil over high heat, stirring constantly.

3. Add the liquid pectin and return the mixture to a boil, timing it for exactly 1 minute and stirring constantly.

4. Remove from the heat and ladle into clean jars, leaving ¼ inch of headspace. Cap and seal.

5. Process in a boiling-water-bath canner for 5 minutes. Adjust for altitude (page 40), if necessary.

Note: Try using 2 tablespoons of dried mint leaves instead of tea bags; strain the finished mixture through a coffee filter before ladling into jars for processing.

YIELD: 2 PINTS (THIRTY-TWO 1-OUNCE SERVINGS)
NUTRITION PER SERVING

Calories	53	Total fat	<1g
% from fat	1	Saturated	0g
Carbohydrates	14g	Cholesterol	0mg
Fiber	<1g	Sodium	6mg

Recycling "Failed" Fruit Spreads

Sometimes the best efforts result in runny fruit spreads. If this happens, don't throw out your runny jams or jellies. Instead, use them as sauce for pound cake, waffles, pancakes, or ice cream. Or add them to plain yogurt for a treat. They still taste great.

Ginger Jam

This recipe gives new meaning to tea and toast.

2 lemons

8 medium-sized tart apples, peeled, cored, and sliced (about 7 cups)

2½ cups water

1 teaspoon ground ginger

6 cups sugar

½ cup chopped crystallized ginger

1. Peel the lemons, reserving the zest. Cut the peeled lemons in half and squeeze the juice. Reserve the juice.

2. In an 8-quart saucepan, cook the apples, water, lemon zest, lemon juice, and ground ginger until the apples are soft. Add the sugar and stir until it is dissolved.

3. Boil the mixture rapidly for 15 minutes, stirring frequently, until a candy thermometer reaches 220°F.

4. Remove the pan from the heat and stir in the crystallized ginger. Skim off any foam and let stand for 10 minutes.

5. Pour it into clean jars, leaving ½ inch of headspace. Cap and seal.

6. Process for 10 minutes in a boiling-water-bath canner. Adjust for altitude (page 40), if necessary.

YIELD: TEN ½-PINTS (EIGHTY 1-OUNCE SERVINGS)
NUTRITION PER SERVING

Calories	68	Total fat	0g
% from fat	0	Saturated	0g
Carbohydrates	17g	Cholesterol	0mg
Fiber	<1g	Sodium	1mg

Carrot and Orange Marmalade

This spread is something of a mystery — your family will never guess that it has carrots in it!

6 cups water

4 cups raw carrots, peeled and grated

4 medium lemons, 2 rinds grated, then all 4 juiced and strained

2 medium oranges, 1 rind grated, then both juiced and strained

4 cups sugar

⅛ teaspoon salt

1. In a 4-quart saucepan, combine the water, carrots, and zest of two lemons and one orange. Cook, covered, until tender, about 30 minutes.

2. Add the strained lemon and orange juices to the citrus zest and carrots. Measure the mixture. There should be about 6 cups.

3. Add ⅔ cup of the sugar for each cup of the mixture. Stir over medium heat until the sugar has dissolved.

4. Boil, uncovered, until the mixture reaches 220°F on a candy thermometer or sheets off a spoon (see page 186). This should take 30–45 minutes. Stir and watch the pot so the mixture does not burn.

5. Add the salt and remove the mixture from the heat.

6. Pour the marmalade into clean, hot jars. Leave ¼ inch of headspace. Cap and seal.

7. Process in a boiling-water-bath canner for 10 minutes. Adjust for altitude (page 40), if necessary.

YIELD: FOUR ½-PINTS (THIRTY-TWO 1-OUNCE SERVINGS)
NUTRITION PER SERVING

Calories	107	Total fat	<1g
% from fat	<1	Saturated	0g
Carbohydrates	28g	Cholesterol	0mg
Fiber	<1g	Sodium	14mg

Summer Squash Conserve

When yellow squash are abundant, try this recipe. It is a great accompaniment to lamb, chicken, or pork.

2 pounds small, tender yellow squash, peeled and sliced

5 cups sugar

1 can (13½ ounces) crushed pineapple in its own juice, drained

Juice of 2 lemons

2 tablespoons chopped crystallized ginger

1 teaspoon grated lemon zest

1 package (1¾ ounces) powdered pectin

1. Combine the squash, sugar, pineapple, lemon juice, ginger, and grated lemon zest in a heavy saucepan. Bring to a simmer, lower the heat, and cook, uncovered, for about 15 minutes, stirring frequently.

2. Remove the pan from the heat and add the powdered pectin, stirring well. Return the mixture to a boil for exactly 1 minute. Remove the pan from the heat.

3. Pour the hot mixture into clean jars, leaving ¼ inch of headspace. Cap and seal.

4. Process for 15 minutes in a boiling-water-bath canner. Adjust for altitude (page 40), if necessary.

YIELD: 5 PINTS (EIGHTY 1-OUNCE SERVINGS)
NUTRITION PER SERVING

Calories	57	Total fat	<1g
% from fat	<1	Saturated	0g
Carbohydrates	14g	Cholesterol	0mg
Fiber	<1g	Sodium	2mg

Horseradish Jelly

Serve this aromatic sweet-and-tart jelly with your next roast of beef — or mix it with low-fat cream cheese and eat it with vegetable sticks or crackers.

2 cups white wine vinegar

1 bottle (6 ounces) prepared horseradish (not cream style)

6 cups sugar

2 cups water

6 ounces liquid pectin

1. Heat the vinegar in a nonreactive saucepan and pour it into a clean 1-quart jar.

2. Add the horseradish, cover the jar, and let stand for 24–48 hours at room temperature.

3. Strain through a wire strainer into a 2-quart saucepan. The mixture will measure 2 cups.

4. Add the sugar and water, stirring to dissolve the sugar. Bring to a full boil.

5. Add the liquid pectin and boil the mixture for exactly 1 minute, stirring constantly.

6. Pour the jelly into clean jars, leaving ¼ inch of headspace. Cap and seal.

7. Process in a boiling-water-bath canner for 10 minutes. Adjust for altitude (page 40), if necessary.

YIELD: SEVEN ½-PINTS (FIFTY-SIX 1-OUNCE SERVINGS)
NUTRITION PER SERVING

Calories	95	Total fat	0g
% from fat	0	Saturated	0g
Carbohydrates	25g	Cholesterol	0mg
Fiber	<1g	Sodium	10mg

Quick Jalapeño Chile Jelly

This jelly is great with meats or mixed with cream cheese and spread on crackers.

¼ cup (4–6 medium) seeded, chopped jalapeño chiles (wear rubber gloves)

6 cups sugar

2½ cups cider vinegar

1 medium-sized green bell pepper, chopped

6 ounces liquid pectin

1. Prepare the chiles while wearing rubber gloves, then mince in a food processor.

2. Combine the sugar, vinegar, chiles, and bell pepper in a heavy saucepan. Bring to a full boil over high heat, stirring constantly.

3. Remove from the heat and stir in the liquid pectin. Return to a full boil. Boil for exactly 1 minute.

4. Remove from the heat and skim off any foam with a metal spoon.

5. Ladle into sterile jars, leaving ¼ inch of headspace. Cap and seal.

6. Process for 5 minutes in a boiling-water-bath canner. Adjust for altitude (page 40), if necessary.

YIELD: SEVEN ½-PINTS (FIFTY-SIX 1-OUNCE SERVINGS)
NUTRITION PER SERVING

Calories	94	Total fat	0g
% from fat	0	Saturated	0g
Carbohydrates	26g	Cholesterol	0mg
Fiber	0g	Sodium	6mg

Five-Pepper Jelly

Serve this jelly with corn bread or over cream cheese as an appetizer. Try prepared pineapple cream cheese, available at supermarkets.

2 large red bell peppers, seeded and chopped

1 large green bell pepper, seeded and chopped

1 small onion, peeled and finely chopped

4 jalapeño chiles, seeded and very finely chopped (wear rubber gloves)

2 teaspoons salt

2½ teaspoons cumin seeds, toasted

1 whole, small red chile

5 cups sugar

1½ cups red wine vinegar

½ cup fresh lemon juice

¼ teaspoon chili powder

¼ teaspoon cayenne pepper

6 ounces liquid pectin

1. Combine the red and green peppers, onion, jalapeño chiles, and 1 teaspoon of the salt in a colander. Let stand for about 3 hours. Drain well and press the mixture with the back of a spoon to remove moisture. (Wear rubber gloves.)

2. Make a spice bag of the cumin seeds and red chile.

3. Combine the pepper mixture, sugar, spice bag, vinegar, lemon juice, chili powder, cayenne, and remaining salt. Bring to a boil in a 6-quart saucepan. Stir and simmer for 10 minutes.

4. Add the pectin and return to a boil. Boil for exactly 1 minute. Remove from the heat. Remove the spice bag.

5. Ladle into sterile jars, leaving ¼ inch of headspace. Cap and seal.

6. Process for 5 minutes in a boiling-water-bath canner. Adjust for altitude (page 40), if necessary.

YIELD: SEVEN ½-PINTS (FIFTY-SIX 1-OUNCE SERVINGS)
NUTRITION PER SERVING

Calories	42	Total fat	0g
% from fat	<1	Saturated	0g
Carbohydrates	11g	Cholesterol	0mg
Fiber	<1g	Sodium	42mg

Tomato Marmalade

*After all, tomatoes are in the fruit family. When combined with citrus,
they make a remarkable marmalade.*

1 medium orange, peeled (reserve the zest and cut into strips)

1 lemon, peeled (reserve the zest and cut into strips)

5 pounds tomatoes, peeled, cored, and chopped (about 8 cups)

3 cups sugar

¼ cup cider vinegar

1½ teaspoons ground allspice

1½ teaspoons ground cinnamon

½ teaspoon ground cloves

1. Carefully remove and discard the white membrane from the citrus and chop the fruit.

2. Combine the citrus and tomatoes in a heavy 8-quart nonreactive saucepan.

3. Add the sugar, vinegar, and spices to the saucepan and bring to a boil over high heat. Lower the heat and simmer, uncovered, for 1 hour or more, or until the mixture is reduced to about 4 cups. Stir frequently and be careful not to burn.

4. Ladle into sterile jars, leaving ¼ inch of headspace. Cap and seal.

5. Process for 10 minutes in a boiling-water-bath canner. Adjust for altitude (page 40), if necessary.

YIELD: FOUR ½-PINTS (SIXTEEN 2-OUNCE SERVINGS)
NUTRITION PER SERVING

Calories	93	Total fat	<1g
% from fat	1	Saturated	0g
Carbohydrates	24g	Cholesterol	0mg
Fiber	<1g	Sodium	6mg

Tomato Jam

Try this on a garlic bagel with cream cheese.

8 pounds tomatoes, peeled, cored, and chopped in a food processor

2 tablespoons sugar

2 teaspoons salt

¼ cup apple cider vinegar

¼ cup firmly packed light brown sugar

1 teaspoon ground cinnamon

½ teaspoon ground white pepper

1. Combine the tomatoes, sugar, and salt in a 4-quart saucepan. Bring to a boil over medium heat, and then simmer for about 30 minutes.

2. Skim off the foam as it rises with a metal spoon.

3. Add the vinegar, brown sugar, and spices and simmer until thick, about 30 minutes longer, or until the mixture mounds up on a cold spoon.

4. Ladle into sterile jars, leaving ¼ inch of headspace. Cap and seal.

5. Process for 15 minutes in a boiling-water-bath canner. Adjust for altitude (page 40), if necessary.

6. Store for 2 weeks before using to allow the flavors to marry.

YIELD: FOUR ½-PINTS (THIRTY-TWO 1-OUNCE SERVINGS)

NUTRITION PER SERVING

Calories	37	Total fat	<1g
% from fat	4	Saturated	0g
Carbohydrates	9g	Cholesterol	0mg
Fiber	1g	Sodium	143mg

Yellow Tomato Jam

This jam is delicious on a bagel, bran muffin, or warm piece of corn bread.

4 cups sugar

¾ cup water

6 cups tiny pear-shaped yellow tomatoes*

3 jalapeño chiles, seeded and finely chopped (wear rubber gloves)

3 tablespoons chopped fresh basil leaves

3 tablespoons fresh lemon juice

2 tablespoons distilled white vinegar

Note: Don't substitute red cherry tomatoes, as they are more acidic and less sweet.

1. In a 6-quart saucepan combine the sugar and water. Bring to a boil over medium heat and simmer until the syrup reaches 234°F on a cooking thermometer.

2. Remove from the heat and add the tomatoes, mixing well. The syrup may change consistency, but continue stirring and eventually the tomatoes will mix evenly.

3. Return to the heat and add the chiles, basil, lemon juice, and vinegar. Simmer, uncovered, on very low heat until the mixture thickens, about 1½–2 hours. Stir often, being careful not to burn. The jam will darken.

4. Ladle into clean jars, leaving ¼ inch of headspace. Cap and seal.

5. Process for 15 minutes in a boiling-water-bath canner. Adjust for altitude (page 40), if necessary.

YIELD: FOUR ½-PINTS (THIRTY-TWO 1-OUNCE SERVINGS)

NUTRITION PER SERVING

Calories	108	Total fat	<1g
% from fat	<1	Saturated	0g
Carbohydrates	28g	Cholesterol	0mg
Fiber	<1g	Sodium	4mg

Ginger Shallot Marmalade

. . . .

Serve this remarkable condiment with steamed vegetables, grilled chicken, or pork.

10 shallots, sliced

2 tablespoons peeled and julienned ginger root

2 tablespoons unsalted butter

1 clove garlic, sliced

½ cup chicken broth

⅓ cup balsamic vinegar

¼ cup honey

¼ teaspoon salt

¼ teaspoon freshly ground black pepper

1. In a heavy skillet, sauté the shallots and ginger in the butter until they are tender, about 10–12 minutes. Add the garlic and sauté, stirring constantly, about 1 minute longer. Do not let the garlic brown.

2. Stir in the remaining ingredients and increase the heat, stirring frequently, until the mixture thickens and most of the liquid has been absorbed.

3. Store in a clean refrigerator container for up to 2 weeks.

. . . .

YIELD: 1 CUP (EIGHT 1-OUNCE SERVINGS)
NUTRITION PER SERVING

Calories	85	Total fat	3g
% from fat	32	Saturated	2g
Carbohydrates	15g	Cholesterol	8mg
Fiber	<1g	Sodium	169mg

. . . .

Garlic Jelly

Use this condiment as a flavorful accompaniment to lamb, pork, or chicken.

3 cups white wine vinegar

½ cup fresh garlic, peeled and finely chopped (about 50 cloves)

6 cups sugar

2 cups water

6 ounces liquid pectin

1. In a 2½-quart saucepan, simmer the vinegar and garlic for about 15 minutes. Remove the pan from the heat and cool slightly.

2. Pour the liquid into a clean 1-quart glass jar. Cover the jar and let stand at room temperature for 24–48 hours.

3. Strain the vinegar and garlic through a wire strainer into a 6-quart kettle. Measure 2 cups of liquid. Add more uncooked white wine vinegar, if necessary.

4. Add the sugar and water to the vinegar, stirring to dissolve the sugar. Bring to a full rolling boil over high heat.

5. Stir in the liquid pectin and return the mixture to a boil for exactly 1 minute, stirring constantly.

6. Skim off any foam with a metal spoon.

7. Pour the jelly into hot, clean jars, leaving ¼ inch of headspace. Cap and seal.

8. Process in a boiling-water-bath canner for 10 minutes. Adjust for altitude (page 40), if necessary.

YIELD: THREE ½-PINTS (TWENTY-FOUR 1-OUNCE SERVINGS)

NUTRITION PER SERVING

Calories	96	Total fat	0g
% from fat	0	Saturated	0g
Carbohydrates	25g	Cholesterol	0mg
Fiber	0g	Sodium	7mg

Preserved Lemons

· · · · · · · · · · · ·

Serve these as a tangy flavor enhancer for fish, lamb, or chicken.

5 small organically grown lemons

⅔ cups canning salt

1 cup fresh lemon juice (about 6 lemons)

½ cup olive oil

1. Scrub the lemons under cold water. Dry and cut each into four wedges.

2. Toss the lemon wedges with the salt in a decorative airtight glass jar.

3. Add the lemon juice and mix well.

4. Store at room temperature (72°F) for 7–10 days. Stir or shake the jar each day to remix the salt and juice.

5. Add the oil to cover the lemon mixture and store in the refrigerator for up to 6 months.

6. Before using, rinse each slice under cold running water. Chop and sprinkle over baked fish or serve alongside roasted lamb or chicken. Delicious and beautiful.

Note: Lemons may darken as they age.

YIELD: 20 LEMON WEDGES (TWENTY SERVINGS)
NUTRITION PER SERVING

Calories	6	Total fat	0g
% from fat	0	Saturated	0g
Carbohydrates	3g	Cholesterol	0mg
Fiber	<1g	Sodium	3,411mg

Cranberry-Lime Curd

Spread this condiment on breads or use it as a sauce for chicken, turkey, or pork.
For more information on curds, see page 180. For a speedy shortcut,
try the canned cranberry version.

2 cups whole cranberry sauce, or
   1 can (16 ounces) cranberry sauce

4 eggs

½ cup (1 stick) butter, softened

½ cup fresh lime juice (about 4
   medium limes)

½ cup sugar

2 teaspoons grated lime zest

1. Purée all the ingredients in a food processor until smooth.

2. Pour the mixture into a double boiler over hot, not boiling, water. Stirring constantly, cook until the mixture is thick, smooth, and shiny. This should take about 20 minutes. Do not overcook.

3. Ladle into hot, clean jars, leaving ½ inch of headspace. Cap and seal.

4. Process in a pressure canner at 10 pounds of pressure for 10 minutes. Adjust for altitude (page 40), if necessary. Store in the refrigerator; use within 3 months.

Whole Cranberry Sauce

To make your own cranberry sauce, combine:

1 cup sugar
1 cup water
½ pound whole cranberries

Boil for 5–7 minutes in an uncovered saucepan, stirring constantly, until thick and clear.

YIELD: THREE OR FOUR ½-PINTS (TWENTY-FOUR TO THIRTY-TWO 1-OUNCE SERVINGS)
NUTRITION PER SERVING

Calories	77	Total fat	4g
% from fat	44	Saturated	2g
Carbohydrates	10g	Cholesterol	35mg
Fiber	<1g	Sodium	45mg

Pear Butter

....

Here is a great new way to enjoy an old-fashioned favorite.
Energy saving and speedy, this pear butter will delight all who try it.

12 ripe Bosc or Bartlett pears, peeled and
    chopped

¾ cup sugar

  Juice of 1 lemon

¼ cup water

3 2-inch strips lemon zest, ¼ inch wide

1 vanilla bean

1. Combine all the ingredients in a heavy 8-quart saucepan. Cook over low heat for 2½ hours, until fruit is very soft. Be careful not to burn. Stir frequently.

2. Remove the vanilla bean and the strips of lemon zest.

3. Put the mixture through a food mill. Pour into sterile jars. Cap and seal.

4. Refrigerate immediately. This will keep for 2 weeks in the refrigerator.

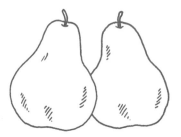

....

YIELD: TWO ½-PINTS (SIXTEEN 1-OUNCE SERVINGS)
NUTRITION PER SERVING

Calories	95	Total fat	<1g
% from fat	4	Saturated	0g
Carbohydrates	25g	Cholesterol	0mg
Fiber	2g	Sodium	0mg

....

PICKLES, RELISHES, AND CHUTNEYS are like jewelry — they accessorize the meal, adding zest and interest to the main course. Chutneys and relishes are kissing cousins to conserves and preserves and go well with such spicy foods as meat curry and grilled chicken with Cajun seasoning. A sandwich is never just a sandwich if a homemade sweet pickle is on the side. Chicken salad and tuna salad take on entirely new characters with 2 tablespoons of artichoke relish added.

In colonial America, particularly in Pennsylvania Dutch country, making relishes, chutneys, and pickles preserved the extra fruits and vegetables from the harvest. By chopping the fruits and vegetables, adding vinegar, spices, and perhaps sugar as available, they mixed the ingredients together until everything was "pickled." Commercially, as early as 1869, the H. J. Heinz Company bottled horseradish, at the time a great new convenience food.

Today, though the preserving processes have sometimes changed, we can count on enjoying our own concoctions of pesticide-free, additive-free condiments for a fraction of the cost of store-bought ones.

VARIETIES

Pickles and relishes are, alas, a far cry from nutritious, but they serve a spicy purpose: making food that *is* nutritious even more appealing. Many favorite recipes are included

Pickles, Relishes & Chutneys

here: refrigerator pickles; freezer pickles; fruit pickles; brined pickles; relishes and chutneys using cranberries, tomatoes, and peaches; and almost anything else you can imagine. I have also included recipes for low-salt, low-sugar pickles for people on special diets. Choose from among the four basic types:

Fresh-pack pickles. This kind of pickle is the least labor intensive. Essentially, the produce is pared, soaked, drained, packed, and processed with vinegar and spices. The vinegar, as well as the processing, acts as a preservative.

Fruit pickles. Fruit for pickling usually requires paring, then simmering in a sugar and vinegar syrup, packing, and processing.

Chutneys and relishes. These condiments are usually mixtures of fruits and vegetables, pared and cooked with vinegar and/or sugar, packed, and then processed.

Salt-cured or brined pickles. This method takes longer and requires daily tending and skimming of foam or scum as it forms. The vegetables are pared and soaked (or cured) in brine. The salty brine encourages fermentation and, therefore, acid levels become high enough to prevent spoilage. Pack and process in a boiling-water-bath canner as a recipe dictates.

INGREDIENTS

For the best pickles, relishes, and chutneys, start with the freshest produce: firm, ripe, and solid, with no yellowing or tough skins, and no damaged or moldy spots. Remove blossom ends and *cut* cucumbers from the vines rather than *pulling* them. It is a great rainy-day activity to put up pickles, but save the harvesting for a sunny day. Rain can drown the whole garden, waterlogging the cucumbers especially. Wait a day after a heavy rain to harvest. Handle the produce carefully to prevent bruising and wash it thoroughly, leaving no grit behind. Peaches and cucumbers especially need careful handling to prevent bruising.

Start with the best produce available.

Refrigerate the produce after picking and use it within 24 hours to ensure freshness and proper fermentation of pickles. To guarantee even pickling and cooking, it's a good idea to use produce similar in size, whether it's whole, chopped, or sliced.

SPICES AND HERBS

Spices and herbs have finally taken their rightful place again as valued medicines and cosmetics, as well as for cooking. In the last 50 years, modern science seemed to replace the significance and usefulness of herbs and spices with technology and pharmacology. Thankfully, the current thinking seems to combine the science of medicine and the art of herbal knowledge.

The value of herbs and spices lies in more than their medicinal applications, of course. Who hasn't smelled the strong perfume of fresh lemon balm when accidentally brushed against by the lawn mower? How about the essence of dried oregano wafting up to your nose when you open a jar of the season's recently dried leaves? Herbs and spices have the power to evoke everything from strong memories of childhood to anticipation of just plain mouthwatering goodness.

To make sure your labors are worthwhile, always use fresh herbs and spices purchased or preserved especially for that season. Never use anything more than a year old when beginning any pickling project. When adding the flavors of spices and herbs, tie them in a cheesecloth bag, and unless otherwise noted in your pickling recipe, remove them when you're packing the finished product. Leave spices and herbs in the jar only if the recipe specifies it. Leaving them in will darken the foodstuffs and intensify the flavor.

SWEETENERS

Use granulated white sugar for making relishes, pickles, and chutneys unless your recipe states otherwise. Brown sugar darkens the finished product and significantly changes the flavor.

Light-colored or flavored honey can be substituted for sugar. Remember that honey has *twice* the sweetening power of sugar. After boiling the vinegar, taste your pickle syrup as you sweeten it with honey; you may need considerably less than you expect. Unlike with recipes for fruit spreads, you can alter the amount of sugar or honey in a pickle recipe because, generally speaking, the sugar does not act as a preservative but is included for taste.

TIP
• • • • • • • •

Remember to add the substituted honey to the syrup after boiling. Honey that has been boiled for long periods of time may break down and cause significant flavor changes.

Help for Too-Tart Pickles
• •

Pickles that are too tart might seem to have too much vinegar in them, but that's not the ingredient to change the next time you make the recipe. Never alter the amount of vinegar called for in a pickling recipe, since the vinegar prevents the growth of bacteria. Instead, make your pickles less tart by adding more sweetener, either sugar or honey.

Vinegars

Vinegar, referred to in the Bible, has been used for thousands of years in a variety of helpful ways. As well as a cosmetic, a healing tonic, and a skin preparation, it is also the main ingredient in pickling. The word "vinegar" is French in origin and means "sour wine."

Actually, vinegar is made from any liquid that can be fermented into alcohol. Yeasts change the sugar in a liquid into alcohol. Afterward, bacteria present in the alcohol solution change the alcohol to acetic acid, the primary acid in vinegar.

Read labels carefully when buying vinegar. The best vinegars should be aged and should state this on the label. If it isn't mentioned, it means it was made by an inferior process. Also stated on the label will be the percent acidity, which is essential to know when pickling food. Look for vinegars with at least 5 percent acidity for pickling.

While red wine, white wine, and cider vinegars work well for pickling, fancy salad vinegars, such as balsamic, are not appropriate for pickles, relishes, and chutneys because they don't contain enough acetic acid. Cider vinegar can discolor or darken a light-colored vegetable like cauliflower, so you may wish to use another variety. Whatever kind of vinegar you choose, do not deviate from the amount specified in the recipe. Refer to chapter 7 (page 281) for more about vinegar.

Other Ingredients

Don't overlook the quality of the other ingredients for pickling just because they are commonplace.

Water. Use only drinking-quality water. If it isn't potable before pickling, it won't be better after pickling. If your water is too hard and full of minerals, use bottled distilled water.

TIP

The chemical interaction of vinegar or salt on metals can impart off flavors and discolor foodstuffs. Use only stainless steel or unblemished enamel for cooking pickling liquids.

Salt. Salt-brined pickles rely on salt as a *preservative.* Canning salt is plain and pure, coarse or fine, and available in most supermarkets. Avoid using sea salt, solar salt, kosher salt, and iodized or table salt in pickling. (See chapter 1, page 11 for a discussion of salt in canning.) For those on sodium-restricted diets, fresh-pack method pickles are quick and salt-free or salted sparingly for taste only. These can be just as crisp and are good for people on low-salt diets.

EQUIPMENT

Having all the equipment on hand and ready to use before you begin will make canning easier and help you feel more confident. If you have duplicates of kitchen equipment, keep them on the counter just in case you need them.

Equipment for Pickling

Before you begin pickling, have the following equipment in an accessible spot and ready to use.

Canning jars with screw rings
New rubber-edged vacuum
    lids
Jar lifter or tongs
Boiling-water-bath canner
Widemouthed canning
    funnel
Kitchen timer
Teakettle
Clean kitchen towels
Large wooden and slotted
    spoons
Nonmetallic spatula or
    wooden chopstick
Scrub brush
Sieve
Colander
Paring and chopping knives
Measuring cups and spoons
Large glass or ceramic bowls
Food processing equipment
    (grinder, blender, slicer, or
    food processor)
Heavy potholders or mitts

It's great to be able to reach for a clean set of measuring spoons instead of fumbling in the drawer in the middle of a recipe. Be organized and read over your recipe and the list of equipment in the box on the previous page before your pickling session.

Never use aluminum, brass, or copper bowls, pots, or utensils for pickling because of the off flavors or discoloration of the food resulting from the chemical interactions of the metal with the vinegar or salt. Cooking pans should be made of stainless steel or unblemished enamel, and mixing bowls should be made of ceramic, glass, stainless steel, or enamel.

Jars and Containers

The same cleaning and sterilization rules and requirements for jars and lids that apply to other kinds of canning apply to pickling as well. All canning jars must be short enough for the water bath to cover them by 1 to 2 inches before the water boils. They need an additional 2 inches of "boiling room" at the top of the pot after the water begins to boil, so plan to use jars that are at least 4 inches shorter than the height of your canner.

In pickling, as in other forms of canning, the screw ring holds the vacuum lid in place. Unlike the vacuum lid, a screw ring, kept in pristine condition, can be used year after year. Twenty-four hours after the pickling process, when the jars have cooled, remove the metal screw rings before you store your pickles in the pantry. Metal screw rings left on jars may rust. If a screw ring is stuck or stubborn, don't force it and risk breaking the seal; rather, leave the ring in place.

Other canning jars include European varieties, which can be quite attractive. But for safety's sake, don't buy any of these unless they include specific processing instructions that meet USDA guidelines.

Appropriate jars for pickling

Antique jars with porcelain-lined zinc caps, which require rubber rings, are available at flea markets, and you can purchase new rubber rings to fit them. However, rather than risk your hard work being foiled by jars not sealing, I recommend that you use these antique jars for dry storage for foods such as beans, pasta, and the like. The same goes for antique glass jars with bailed-wire seals. They look great, but use them for dry storage or short storage in the refrigerator for some of the fancy sauces or refrigerator jellies and pickles listed herein.

Crocks

For a brining or fermenting process, use a clean stoneware widemouthed jar, sometimes called a crock. A less glamorous but practical choice would be a glass or nonporous plastic bowl. You will also need a clean plate, which must fit inside the container and press directly against the food. Use a clean, unopened glass jar of last year's pickles — or any heavy, clean, nonmetallic object — to hold down the plate against the food in the crock.

Processing Pickled Foods

The boiling-water bath is the canning process used for pickling foods. Because of the high acidity level, foods that are pickled do not require the higher temperatures produced by the pressure-canning method to stay safe.

The boiling-water-bath method involves submerging the properly filled jars in a kettle of rapidly boiling water for a specified amount of time, ensuring that a vacuum forms inside the jar, thereby sealing the lids. See chapter 2 (page 27) for more information about this method of canning.

Boiling-Water-Bath Equipment

As noted in chapter 1, I recommend a new 21- or 33-quart boiling-water-bath canner with lid and jar rack.

A boiling-water-bath canner

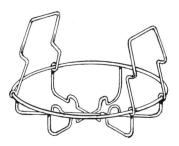

Wire rack for holding jars in a boiling-water-bath canner

The better ones are made of aluminum or porcelain-covered steel. The most expensive but durable ones are made of stainless steel. There are also many appropriate alternatives. Any large pot with a lid can be substituted as long as it is at least 4 inches higher than the jars — deep enough to allow 1 to 2 inches of water to cover the jars plus the 2 inches of boiling room. Use towels between the jars to prevent breakage during the canning process. You will need a wire rack for the bottom to hold jars away from the direct heat and to preven cracking. In lieu of a rack, connect metal screw rings with twist ties and place them on the bottom of the canner.

Prewashing Jars and Lids

If the processing time will be longer than 10 minutes, wash the empty jars in the dishwasher or submerge them in hot, soapy water. Thoroughly rinse the jars after you remove them from the dishwasher or dishpan. No soapy residue can remain. Keep the jar lids hot in gently boiling water. If you are reusing screw rings, put them in the boiling water, too. You should always read the manufacturer's instructions and follow them to the letter when washing and sterilizing jars for canning any kind of food.

Sterilizing the Jars

For processing times less than 10 minutes, sterilize clean, prewashed jars. Fill the clean jars with hot water and lower them onto the rack in the water-filled pot, making sure that there is at least 1 inch of water above the rims of the jars. At sea level, the jars should boil for 10 minutes. At higher elevations, boil 1 additional minute for each 1,000 feet of altitude. Using the jar lifter, remove and pack the sterilized jars one by one. (Save the boiling water for the canning process.)

Packing the Jars

Immediately after you remove each sterilized jar from the boiling-water-bath canner, fill it with the relish, chutney, or other food to be pickled. A widemouthed funnel and ladle are invaluable for this stage. Be careful of drips when you remove the funnel from the filled jar. Drips, if not wiped off, can spoil the seal.

If you're making pickles, be sure to pack the jar loosely enough for the liquid to circulate around the food, leaving the headspace indicated in the recipe. To get rid of bubbles that appear in the liquid, tap the side of the jar with a knife handle to help settle the contents. You can also run a clean plastic spatula along the sides in several places to help remove bubbles. Don't stir, which creates more bubbles.

Use a thin, clean, wet dish towel pulled over your index finger to rub around the rim of each jar. It picks up the smallest drip of liquid, and you can feel the slightest chip on the rim as well. A wet paper towel works for this job, too. (If you find a flaw, either put the ingredients in a new sterilized jar or place the damaged jar in the refrigerator for immediate use.) Place the lid and metal screw ring on the jar and secure the ring to the jar. Then fill the next jar until all are filled and ready for processing. Be sure to observe the proper headspace called for in the recipe.

PROCESSING PICKLED FOODS

Because of their acidity, pickled foods never require the pressure-canning method of processing. Follow these guidelines for successful boiling-water-bath processed pickles. The information is based on a bulletin from North Carolina State University.

1. Fill the canner halfway with water.

2. Preheat the water to 200°F, a simmer with bubbles.

3. Load the filled jars, fitted with lids, into the canner rack and use the handles to lower the rack into the simmering water. Or fill the canner, one jar at a time, with a jar lifter.

4. Add boiling water, if needed, so that the water level is at least 1 to 2 inches above the jar tops.

5. Cover the canner with the lid.

6. Set a timer for the minutes required for processing the food and begin timing immediately. Be sure to adjust for altitude (page 40).

7. Adjust the heat setting to maintain a simmer throughout the processing schedule.

8. Add more boiling water, if needed, to maintain the water level above the jars.

9. When jars have been boiled for the recommended time, turn off the heat and remove the canner lid.

10. Using a jar lifter, remove the jars and place them on a towel, leaving at least 5 to 6 inches of space between the jars while they cool.

Pickle-Processing Time

• • • • • • • • • • • •

The processing time for pickles begins as soon as you submerge the jars in the boiling-water bath. This ensures a crisp, processed pickle that is not soft or overcooked.

STORAGE

Storing home-canned foods requires just a shelf in a cool, dry, dark place. You can tuck canned pickles in all sorts of nooks and crannies in your house or apartment — just don't forget where you stored them. Keep a location chart taped to the inside of a cabinet or pantry door. Mark the jars off the list as you use them. As with other canned goods, the best storage temperature is between 50 and 70°F. Store your newest batches of pickles toward the back of the shelf so you will use the oldest pickles first. Any jar kept for longer than 1 year is probably too old to eat.

Refrigerate homemade pickles after opening, just as you would store-bought pickles.

SAFETY FIRST

Enough can never be said about canning safety. *Clostridium botulinum,* the bacterium that causes botulism, grows in the absence of air, making the vacuum in a jar of canned food the ideal environment. Vinegar is a preservative, and botulism is less of a threat in pickles than in low-acid canned foods, but *never* bend the rules when spoilage is suspected. *Clostridium botulinum* is deadly. Never taste even a tiny bit of canned food you suspect may be spoiled.

First, check the seals after 12 to 24 hours. Use your thumbs to test the seal of the metal lid. Press hard on the center. If the lid does not move downward or "give," your seal is intact. If a jar or two in the batch isn't sealed, you can save it in the refrigerator and consume it over the next day or two.

Another method is to try lifting your newly canned jar by its lid after the screw ring has been removed. Use the weight of the jar to test the weakness of the seal. (Protect yourself and the jar by doing this over the sink prepared with a towel to pad a possible fall.)

Questions to Ask Yourself after Pickling

To reduce your chances of ending up with jars that don't seal, don't try to cut corners, and make it a practice to be organized in advance.

1. Did I clean, pack, and process the jars exactly according to the recipe directions as well as the general directions for canning?

2. Did I fail to use the specified vinegar measurement in the recipe to prevent too tart a flavor, or did I correctly add a little sugar to overcome this problem instead?

3. Did I use clean equipment and have clean hands?

4. Did I regularly tend to the brining solution, faithfully removing all traces of scum each day?

5. Was my water too hard or full of minerals?

6. Did I prepare all the produce approximately the same size to ensure even processing?

7. Did I remove the spice bag from the jars before processing?

8. Did I check my finished cooling jars 24 hours after processing and test for incomplete seals and signs of spoilage? When in doubt or when you spot mold, spurting or cloudy liquids, gases, change in color, or change in texture — throw it away. Use the safe method of disposal described on page 47 of chapter 2.

9. Did I store the canned pickles in a cool, dark place?

Pickle Making

1. Scrub the cucumbers with a soft brush and slice off the blossom end.

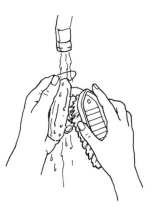

2. Pack the cleaned cucumbers loosely in the sterilized jars.

3. Using a widemouthed funnel, pour the hot brine over the cucumbers, allowing the proper headspace.

4. Using a nonmetallic spatula or wooden chopstick, press against the cucumbers to release all air bubbles.

5. Wipe the rim with a clean cloth to ensure a good seal.

6. Place the lid on the jar and tighten the screw ring.

7. Preheat the water to 200°F, a simmer with bubbles. Place the filled jars in the preheated canner. Add more boiling water until it is 1 to 2 inches above the jars.

8. Process for the time and at the temperature given in the recipe. Add more boiling water, if necessary, to keep it 1 to 2 inches above the jars.

(continued on page 252)

9. Remove the jars and place on a towel or rack to cool for 24 hours.

10. Remove the screw rings and test the seals. The center of the lid should be depressed. You can lift the jar by the lid and it should hold.

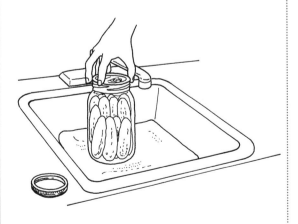

11. Wash the jars, label, and store unopened in a cool, dark place for at least 6 weeks before using.

RECIPES FOR PICKLES, RELISHES & CHUTNEYS

Bread and Butter Pickles

· · · · · · · · · · ·

This is an old-fashioned favorite. Use these pickles to dress up a plain sandwich.

Boiling-water-bath canner; seven 1-pint jars

- 6 pounds (about 4 quarts) medium-sized cucumbers, scrubbed and sliced ⅛ inch thick
- 1½ cups (about 1 pound) peeled and sliced small white onions
- 2 cloves garlic
- ⅓ cup salt
- Ice cubes
- 4½ cups sugar
- 2 tablespoons yellow mustard seeds
- 1½ teaspoons celery seeds
- 1½ teaspoons ground turmeric
- 3 cups distilled white vinegar

1. In a large mixing bowl, combine the cucumbers, onions, and garlic. Add the salt and mix thoroughly. Cover with ice cubes. Let stand for 3 hours.

2. Rinse well, thoroughly drain the mixture, and remove the garlic cloves.

3. Combine the sugar, mustard seeds, celery seeds, and turmeric; stir in the vinegar and heat to boiling in an 8-quart saucepan. Add the drained cucumber mixture and heat for 5 minutes.

4. Pour into sterilized jars, leaving ½ inch of headspace. Cap and seal.

5. Process for 10 minutes in a boiling-water-bath canner. Adjust for altitude (page 40), if necessary.

· ·

YIELD: 7 PINTS (FIFTY-SIX 2-OUNCE SERVINGS)
NUTRITION PER SERVING

Calories	74	Total fat	<1g
% from fat	2	Saturated fat	0g
Carbohydrates	19g	Cholesterol	0mg
Fiber	<1g	Sodium	611mg

· ·

Fresh-Pack Refrigerator Dill Pickles

Great for a small family, these pickles stay crisp for 6 weeks in the refrigerator if you can keep from eating them that long.

10–14 whole pickling cucumbers, approximately 2 inches long, scrubbed

3 sprigs dill

2 cloves garlic

½ cup fresh lemon juice

Cold water

1. Pack a sterilized jar with the cucumbers, dill, and garlic in alternating layers, leaving ¼ inch of headspace.

2. Pour the lemon juice over the cucumbers. Fill the jar with cold water.

3. Seal and refrigerate. These will keep for at least 6 weeks. Serve and enjoy!

YIELD: 1 QUART (SIXTEEN 2-OUNCE SERVINGS)
NUTRITION PER SERVING

Calories	33	Total fat	<1g
% from fat	7	Saturated fat	<1g
Carbohydrates	7g	Cholesterol	0mg
Fiber	2g	Sodium	6mg

Old-Fashioned Brined Dill Pickles

*Here is another one of my favorites. While these pickles need to sit in the crock for
3 weeks, plan ahead, and maintaining these pickles will only take
a few minutes each day. They're worth it.*

Boiling-water-bath canner; ten 1-pint jars

20 pounds (about ½ bushel) pickling
cucumbers, 3–6 inches long, scrubbed

¾ cup mixed pickling spice

3 large bunches fresh dill weed

2½ cups cider vinegar

2½ gallons water

1¾ cups salt

10 cloves garlic

1. In a 5-gallon crock, place half of the cucumbers, pickling spice, and dill, then layer again to within 3–4 inches of the top of the crock.

2. Mix the vinegar, water, and salt and pour over the cucumbers. Cover with a ceramic plate and place a heavy jar of last year's pickles on it to weight down the cucumbers.

3. Make sure the cucumbers are completely under the brine. Cover the crock loosely with a clean towel.

4. Keep the pickles at room temperature (80–85°F). I use my laundry room sink for this purpose.

5. In about 3 days, begin skimming off the foam. Do not stir the pickles. Keep them completely covered with brine throughout this process.

6. Check daily, removing scum and foam. In 3 weeks the cucumbers should be an olive-green color. White spots inside the cucumbers will disappear when processed.

YIELD: 10 QUARTS (ONE HUNDRED SIXTY 2-OUNCE
SERVINGS)

NUTRITION PER SERVING

Calories	10	Total fat	<1g
% from fat	15	Saturated fat	0g
Carbohydrates	2g	Cholesterol	0mg
Fiber	1g	Sodium	1,122mg

7. Pack the cucumbers in sterile quart jars. Add 1 clove of garlic to each jar and divide the dill sprigs evenly among the jars.

8. Strain the brine through a coffee filter into the jars, leaving ½ inch of headspace. Cap and seal.

9. Process for 15 minutes in a boiling-water-bath canner. Adjust for altitude (page 40), if necessary.

Note: Start timing the canning process as soon as the jars are put into the boiling water instead of waiting for the water to boil again. This will ensure a crisp, processed pickle without overcooking.

Mixed Pickling Spice

Use this in the same quantity as you would store-bought pickling spice.

2 tablespoons yellow mustard seeds

2 teaspoons whole allspice

2 teaspoons coriander seeds

2 teaspoons dill seeds

2 teaspoons whole black peppercorns

2 bay leaves, crumbled

2 dried red chiles
(2 inches long), crumbled
(wear rubber gloves)

1. Mix all the ingredients and store in an airtight jar in a cool, dark place.

2. Use in any pickle recipe.

YIELD: ⅓ CUP

Refrigerator Super-Sweets

· · · · · · · · · · ·

This is quick and easy and good for beginners and experienced cooks alike.

1 gallon (about 10–12 large) cucumbers, scrubbed and sliced

2 quarts distilled white vinegar

6 cups sugar

1 teaspoon whole mixed pickling spice

1 teaspoon salt (optional)

1. Place the cucumber slices in an 8-quart crock. Cover with the vinegar. Make sure the cucumbers are completely under the vinegar.

2. Cover the cucumbers with a ceramic plate and place a heavy jar of last year's pickles on it to weight it down. Let stand for 24 hours.

3. Drain and discard the vinegar. Add the sugar, pickling spice, and salt (if using) to the cucumber slices.

4. Mix gently to allow the sugar to dissolve somewhat. After several hours, stir again. The pickles are ready to eat when all the sugar has dissolved.

5. Pack the pickles in sterile canning jars and refrigerate before eating. These will keep for 2 months in the refrigerator.

Note: This is an adaptation of the N.C. Agricultural Extension Service recipe.

· ·

YIELD: 8 PINTS (SIXTY-FOUR 2-OUNCE SERVINGS)

NUTRITION PER SERVING

Calories	80	Total fat	0g
% from fat	0	Saturated fat	0g
Carbohydrates	21g	Cholesterol	0mg
Fiber	<1g	Sodium	34mg

· ·

Two-Day Mustard Pickles

This recipe is best made in early fall, when cauliflower is plentiful but before frost nips the tomatoes, green peppers, and cucumbers. Enjoy it all winter as an accompaniment to meat or sandwiches.

Boiling-water-bath canner; five 1-quart jars

- 1 head cauliflower, broken into florets (about 1½ quarts)
- 1 quart small white onions, peeled
- 1 quart small cucumbers, sliced
- 1 quart small green tomatoes
- 2 large green bell peppers, seeded and chopped (about 2 cups)
- 2 large red bell peppers, seeded and chopped (about 2 cups)
- 3 quarts cold water
- ½ cup pickling salt
- 2 quarts cider vinegar
- 1½ cups firmly packed light brown sugar
- 6 tablespoons prepared mustard
- ⅓ cup flour
- 2 tablespoons ground turmeric

1. Prepare the vegetables; place them in a large crock or a glass or ceramic bowl. Mix the water and salt, then pour over the vegetables. Cover; let stand for 24 hours.

2. Drain the brine from the vegetables, catching the vegetables in a colander and the solution in a saucepan. Heat the solution to boiling and pour over the vegetables in the colander. Drain.

3. Combine the vinegar, brown sugar, mustard, flour, and turmeric in a large nonreactive saucepan. Stir, then heat gradually, stirring constantly, until the mixture is thick and smooth. Add the vegetables and cook gently until they are tender but have not lost their individuality. Stir with a heavy wooden spoon to prevent scorching.

4. Pack into hot, clean quart jars, leaving ½ inch of headspace. Cap and seal.

5. Process in a boiling-water-bath canner for 10 minutes. Adjust for altitude (page 40), if necessary.

YIELD: 5 QUARTS (EIGHTY 2-OUNCE SERVINGS)
NUTRITION PER SERVING

Calories	29	Total fat	<1g
% from fat	3	Saturated fat	0g
Carbohydrates	8g	Cholesterol	0mg
Fiber	<1g	Sodium	658mg

Watermelon Rind Pickles

A real old-fashioned classic, perfect with a turkey sandwich. As a child, my sister-in-law called this her "favorite green vegetable."

Boiling-water-bath canner; three 1-pint jars

- 3 tablespoons slaked lime*

- 2 quarts water

- 8 cups watermelon rind (1 large melon), peeled and cut into 1-inch squares

- 3 cups firmly packed brown sugar

- 2 cups white distilled vinegar

- 1 lemon, thinly sliced

- 1½ cinnamon sticks, 2–2½ inches long

- 1 teaspoon whole allspice

- 1 teaspoon whole cloves

- 2 drops all-natural green food coloring (optional)

1. In a large glass or ceramic bowl, add the lime to the water. Soak the peeled watermelon rind in the lime solution for 8 hours.

2. Drain, then rinse well and drain again.

3. In a large saucepan, simmer the rind in clear water until tender, about 20 minutes.

4. Meanwhile, make a syrup of the sugar, vinegar, lemon, and spices (tied in cheesecloth). Boil for 5 minutes in an 8-quart saucepan. Add the rind to the vinegar solution and cook until the rind is clear and thin, about 10 minutes.

5. Pack clean jars with the rind and pour hot liquid over each one, leaving ½ inch of headspace. Cap and seal.

6. Process for 10 minutes in a boiling-water-bath canner. Adjust for altitude (page 40), if necessary.

Slaked lime, or pickling lime, is calcium hydroxide, which is found in health food and grocery stores.

YIELD: 3 PINTS (TWENTY-FOUR 2-OUNCE SERVINGS)
NUTRITION PER SERVING

Calories	124	Total fat	<1g
% from fat	1	Saturated fat	0g
Carbohydrates	32g	Cholesterol	0mg
Fiber	1g	Sodium	16mg

Note: Watermelon rind can be pared and stored in the refrigerator "as eaten" for up to 3 days. When you have accumulated 8 cups of rind, it's time to pickle them.

Spicy Frozen Cucumbers

Even after they've been thawed and stored in the refrigerator for up to a week, these pickles taste like Granny's homemade ones, but they are a lot easier to make. This recipe is frequently requested by friends.

4 cups (about 12–14) pickling cucumbers, 3–4 inches long, washed, unpeeled, and thinly sliced

2 large onions, peeled and thinly sliced

1 tablespoon salt

1 cup sugar

½ cup cider vinegar

1 tablespoon whole white mustard seeds

½ teaspoon ground turmeric

1. Combine the cucumbers, onions, and salt in a glass or ceramic bowl. Let stand for 2–4 hours to extract the moisture.

2. Rinse and drain the vegetables well, blotting them with paper towels to absorb all the moisture.

3. Combine the remaining ingredients and mix well until the sugar dissolves completely, about 10 minutes. Stir in the cucumbers and onions.

4. Pour the cucumber mixture into clean freezer containers, leaving 1 inch of headspace for expansion. Cap and seal. These will keep for up to 1 year in the freezer.

5. To use, thaw for about 4 hours in the refrigerator. Serve chilled!

YIELD: 5 PINTS (TWENTY 4-OUNCE SERVINGS)
NUTRITION PER SERVING

Calories	54	Total fat	<1g
% from fat	4	Saturated fat	0g
Carbohydrates	13g	Cholesterol	0mg
Fiber	<1g	Sodium	321mg

Green and Gold Refrigerator Pickles

These easy-to-make refrigerator pickles will disappear rapidly.

2 cups sugar

1 cup cider vinegar

3½ cups yellow summer squash, thinly sliced

3½ cups zucchini, thinly sliced

1 cup green bell peppers, finely chopped

1 cup red bell peppers, finely chopped

1 cup onions, thinly sliced

1 tablespoon dill seeds

1 tablespoon salt

1. Heat the sugar and vinegar in a nonreactive 4-quart saucepan until the sugar dissolves.

2. Add the remaining ingredients and chill overnight.

3. Transfer the vegetables to sterile quart canning jars. Cover with the vinegar mixture, cap, and seal. These will keep in the refrigerator for 2 months.

YIELD: 2 QUARTS (SIXTEEN 4-OUNCE SERVINGS)
NUTRITION PER SERVING

Calories	116	Total fat	<1g
% from fat	1	Saturated fat	0g
Carbohydrates	30g	Cholesterol	0mg
Fiber	1g	Sodium	402mg

Pickled Garlic

Not only is this good for what ails you and low in calories, but it's also a mellow and delicious appetizer. "Crab boil" seasoning can be found in most grocery stores in the seafood section. I use Old Bay.

¾ cup distilled white vinegar

½ cup water

2 teaspoons coarse salt

⅛ teaspoon crab boil seasoning

6 large bulbs garlic, separated, blanched, and skinned

Zest of 1 lemon, peeled in one continuous spiral

1 dill head, or ½ teaspoon dill seeds

1 small whole red chile

Substitute for Crab Boil Seasoning

If crab boil seasoning is not available, make your own, using a pinch each of celery seeds; ground cayenne pepper, cinnamon, ginger, allspice, yellow mustard, and paprika; and half a bay leaf.

1. In a saucepan, combine the vinegar, water, salt, and crab boil seasoning and bring to a boil. Add the garlic and let steep for 10 minutes over very low heat.

2. Line a clean 1-pint jar with the lemon zest and add the dill head and red chile.

3. Ladle in the garlic and enough liquid to cover. Cap and seal.

4. Cool at room temperature.

5. Allow the flavors to marry for 3–4 days before using. Refrigerate up to 4 weeks.

YIELD: 1 PINT (EIGHT 2-OUNCE SERVINGS)
NUTRITION PER SERVING

Calories	46	Total fat	<1g
% from fat	3	Saturated fat	0g
Carbohydrates	11g	Cholesterol	0mg
Fiber	<1g	Sodium	486mg

Pickled Brussels Sprouts

· · · · · · · · · · ·

Low in calories and high in taste and nutrients, this recipe can be used as a salad base for mixed lettuces or eaten alone on toothpicks as an appetizer.

Boiling-water-bath canner; four 1-pint jars

6 cups (about 2 pounds) Brussels sprouts

2½ cups vinegar

2½ cups water

3 tablespoons salt

1 teaspoon cayenne pepper

4 dill heads, or 2 teaspoons dill seeds

4 cloves garlic

1. Leave the Brussels sprouts whole but trim off old foliage. Boil them until tender. Drain and pack into clean jars.

2. Mix the vinegar, water, salt, and cayenne pepper in a heavy saucepan; boil for 5 minutes.

3. Pour the vinegar mixture over the Brussels sprouts, leaving ¼ inch of headspace.

4. Evenly distribute the dill heads and garlic among the jars.

5. Cap, seal, and process for 15 minutes in a boiling-water-bath canner.

· ·

YIELD: 4 PINTS (SIXTEEN ½-CUP SERVINGS)
NUTRITION PER SERVING

Calories	32	Total fat	<1g
% from fat	7	Saturated fat	0g
Carbohydrates	8g	Cholesterol	0mg
Fiber	2g	Sodium	1,215mg

· ·

Pickled Cauliflower

Pickle cauliflower in cool weather when it is plentiful.
This recipe is easy to make and low in calories.

Boiling-water-bath canner; six 1-quart jars

- 3 heads (about 10 pounds) cauliflower, washed and cut into small florets
- 8 cups distilled white vinegar
- 8 cups water
- ¼ cup salt
- ¼ cup yellow mustard seeds
- 12 cloves garlic
- 12 dill heads
- 12 small chiles

1. Steam the cauliflower florets over boiling water for 1 minute.

2. Simmer the vinegar, water, salt, and mustard seeds in a 5-quart saucepan for 5 minutes.

3. Pack each sterilized jar with 2 cloves of garlic, 2 dill heads, and 2 chiles. Pack the warm cauliflower in each jar, leaving ¼ inch of headspace.

4. Cover with the vinegar solution, leaving ¼ inch of headspace. Cap and seal.

5. Process for 15 minutes in a boiling-water-bath canner. Adjust for altitude (page 40), if necessary.

6. Store the jars for 3 weeks before using to allow the flavors to develop.

YIELD: 6 QUARTS (NINETY-SIX 2-OUNCE SERVINGS)
NUTRITION PER SERVING

Calories	8	Total fat	<1g
% from fat	14	Saturated fat	0g
Carbohydrates	2g	Cholesterol	0mg
Fiber	<1g	Sodium	268mg

Pickled Asparagus

Remember spring as you serve these on lettuce leaves in the middle of winter;
garnish with hard-boiled egg slices and mustard mayonnaise.

Boiling-water-bath canner; two 1-quart jars

3   cups distilled white vinegar

3   cups water

¼   cup sugar

2   teaspoons salt

3   pounds (about 8 cups) asparagus
    spears, washed and trimmed

4   cloves garlic, peeled

2   teaspoons pickling spice

12 whole black peppercorns

1. Combine the vinegar, water, sugar, and salt in a 2-quart saucepan and heat to a boil.

2. Pack the asparagus in two 1-quart jars, leaving ½ inch of headspace.

3. Divide the garlic, pickling spice, and peppercorns between the two jars. Pour the hot vinegar mixture over the asparagus, leaving ½ inch of headspace. Cap and seal.

4. Process for 20 minutes in a boiling-water-bath canner. Adjust for altitude (page 40), if necessary.

YIELD: 2 QUARTS (SIXTEEN 4-OUNCE SERVINGS)
NUTRITION PER SERVING

Calories	45	Total fat	<1g
% from fat	5	Saturated fat	<1g
Carbohydrates	12g	Cholesterol	0mg
Fiber	2g	Sodium	272mg

Sweet Pickle Relish

· · · · · · · · · · ·

Colorful and delicious, this remarkable relish will delight your picnic guests.

Boiling-water-bath canner; nine 1-pint jars

- 3 quarts cucumbers, scrubbed and chopped

- 3 cups green bell peppers, seeded and chopped

- 3 cups red bell peppers, seeded and chopped

- 1 cup onions, chopped

- 8 cups water

- 4 cups ice cubes

- ¾ cup salt

- 4 teaspoons ground turmeric

- 4 teaspoons whole allspice

- 4 teaspoons yellow mustard seeds

- 1 tablespoon whole cloves

- 6 cups distilled white vinegar

- 2 cups sugar

1. In a 12-quart saucepan, combine the vegetables, water, ice, and salt; let stand for 4 hours. Drain and re-cover with fresh ice and water for 1 additional hour. Drain thoroughly.

2. Combine the spices in a cheesecloth bag. Place the spice bag, vinegar, and sugar in a nonreactive 4-quart saucepan and heat to boiling.

3. Pour the vinegar syrup over the vegetables and refrigerate for 24 hours.

4. Heat the mixture to boiling and ladle into sterile jars, leaving ½ inch of head-space. Cap and seal.

5. Process for 10 minutes in a boiling-water-bath canner. Adjust for altitude (page 40), if necessary.

Note: A food processor can be used to chop the vegetables in batches by pulsing the motor.

· ·
YIELD: 9 PINTS (SEVENTY-TWO 2-OUNCE SERVINGS)
NUTRITION PER SERVING

Calories	31	Total fat	<1g
% from fat	4	Saturated fat	0g
Carbohydrates	8g	Cholesterol	0mg
Fiber	<1g	Sodium	1,068mg

· ·

Red Refrigerator Relish

This recipe can serve as a garnish for the standard hamburgers and hot dogs, but it's also delicious as a slaw with barbecue.

½ cup cider vinegar

½ cup water

⅓ cup sugar

1 tablespoon yellow mustard seeds

1½ teaspoons celery seeds

⅛ teaspoon cayenne pepper

6 medium tomatoes, chopped and drained

1 small head green cabbage, shredded

½ small head red cabbage, shredded

1 cup chopped dill pickles

1 large green bell pepper, seeded and chopped

1 large red onion, diced

1. Combine the vinegar, water, sugar, mustard seeds, celery seeds, and cayenne pepper in an 8-quart saucepan. Simmer, uncovered, for 5 minutes. Cool.

2. Add the remaining ingredients to the pan, cover, and refrigerate for 8 hours. Serve chilled. Keeps for 3–5 days in the refrigerator.

YIELD: 10 CUPS (TEN 1-CUP SERVINGS)

NUTRITION PER SERVING

Calories	89	Total fat	<1g
% from fat	8	Saturated fat	<1g
Carbohydrates	20g	Cholesterol	0mg
Fiber	3g	Sodium	331mg

Sweet Onion Relish

Make a hot dog a festive occasion with this relish. It is easy to prepare and adds zest to any meat.

Boiling-water-bath canner; five 1-pint jars

- 5 pounds sweet onions, chopped (about 10 cups)
- 2¼ cups distilled white vinegar
- 1 cup sugar
- 2 tablespoons celery seeds
- 2 tablespoons salt

1. Combine all the ingredients in a heavy 8-quart saucepan. Bring to a boil.

2. Reduce the heat and simmer for 10 minutes, stirring occasionally.

3. Ladle the relish into clean jars, leaving ½ inch of headspace.

4. Cap and seal.

5. Process for 10 minutes in a boiling-water-bath canner. Adjust for altitude (page 40), if necessary.

YIELD: 5 PINTS (FORTY 2-OUNCE SERVINGS)
NUTRITION PER SERVING

Calories	40	Total fat	<1g
% from fat	3	Saturated fat	0g
Carbohydrates	10g	Cholesterol	0mg
Fiber	<1g	Sodium	322mg

Refrigerator Corn Relish

*A quick version of Granny's corn relish, this is a great favorite
on hot dogs and hamburgers.*

1½ cups distilled white vinegar, 5% acidity

¾ cup sugar

2¼ teaspoons salt

¾ teaspoon mustard seeds

¼ teaspoon celery seeds

¼ teaspoon Tabasco sauce

12 large ears corn, or about 8 cups corn kernels

1 small green bell pepper, seeded and chopped

1 small red bell pepper, seeded and chopped

3 scallions, sliced

1. Combine the vinegar, sugar, salt, mustard seeds, celery seeds, and Tabasco sauce in a heavy 8-quart nonreactive saucepan. Boil, uncovered, over medium heat for about 5 minutes.

2. Combine the vegetables. Distribute equally into four sterilized pint jars. Pour the vinegar mixture over the vegetables.

3. Cover tightly and refrigerate. Consume within 1 month. Delicious!

YIELD: 4 PINTS (THIRTY-TWO 2-OUNCE SERVINGS)
NUTRITION PER SERVING

Calories	42	Total fat	<1g
% from fat	5	Saturated fat	0g
Carbohydrates	10g	Cholesterol	0mg
Fiber	1g	Sodium	154mg

Black-Eyed-Pea Refrigerator Relish

In the South, black-eyed peas are traditionally served on New Year's Day to bring good fortune. What a great New Year's gift for friends! But don't forget, this relish is delicious served all year long.

½ pound dried black beans, cooked until barely tender (al dente)

½ pound dried black-eyed peas, cooked until barely tender (al dente)

2 ears yellow corn, blanched, kernels removed

1 red bell pepper, seeded and finely chopped

½ red onion, finely chopped

½ yellow onion, finely chopped

½ orange, sectioned and seeded

2 scallions (including green tops), finely chopped

SIMPLE VINAIGRETTE

1 cup extra-virgin olive oil

⅓ cup red wine vinegar

1 teaspoon chopped fresh parsley

1 teaspoon chopped fresh tarragon

¼ teaspoon dry mustard

¼ teaspoon salt

⅛ teaspoon freshly ground black pepper

1. Combine all the ingredients in a 4-quart ceramic bowl. Pour the Simple Vinaigrette dressing over the warm vegetables.

2. Cover the bowl and refrigerate overnight.

3. Ladle the relish into 6 sterile canning jars. Cap and seal. This will keep for 3 days in the refrigerator.

YIELD: 3 PINTS (TWENTY-FOUR 2-OUNCE SERVINGS)
NUTRITION PER SERVING

Calories	163	Total fat	9g
% from fat	50	Saturated fat	1g
Carbohydrates	16g	Cholesterol	0mg
Fiber	3g	Sodium	27mg

Green Tomato Chutney

This chutney can be heated and thickened with cornstarch to complement Chinese vegetables or rice.

Boiling-water-bath canner; seven 1-pint jars

- 16 cups slightly pink green tomatoes, cored and chopped
- 8 cups coarsely chopped green cabbage
- 2 cups coarsely chopped green bell peppers
- 1 cup chopped onion
- ½ cup salt
- 4½ cups cider vinegar
- 1½ cups firmly packed brown sugar
- 3 cloves garlic, peeled and sliced
- 2 tablespoons mustard seeds
- 4 teaspoons celery seeds
- 1 tablespoon prepared horseradish (not cream style)

1. In a large bowl, combine the tomatoes, cabbage, peppers, and onions.

2. Sprinkle the salt over the chopped vegetables and let stand for 4–5 hours.

3. Transfer the salted vegetables to a colander. Press them with the back of a broad spoon, removing as much moisture as possible. Drain well.

4. Combine the vinegar, sugar, garlic, spices, and horseradish. Simmer for 15 minutes in a heavy nonreactive 12-quart saucepan.

5. Add the drained vegetables to the saucepan and bring the mixture to a boil.

6. Pack into clean jars, leaving ¼ inch of headspace. Cap and seal.

7. Process for 10 minutes in a boiling-water-bath canner. Adjust for altitude (page 40), if necessary.

YIELD: 7 PINTS (FIFTY-SIX 2-OUNCE SERVINGS)
NUTRITION PER SERVING

Calories	45	Total fat	<1g
% from fat	5	Saturated fat	0g
Carbohydrates	11g	Cholesterol	0mg
Fiber	1g	Sodium	926mg

Basil-Shallot Mustard

* * * * * * * * * * *

Turn a plain sandwich into a feast with this mustard.

⅔ cup apple juice

⅔ cup red wine vinegar

½ cup dry mustard

⅓ cup water

¼ cup light mustard seeds

3 tablespoons chopped fresh basil

2 tablespoons minced shallots

2 tablespoons packed light brown sugar

1 teaspoon salt

¼ teapoon ground allspice

1. Combine the apple juice, vinegar, dry mustard, water, and mustard seeds in a glass or ceramic bowl and stir, mixing well.

2. Cover the bowl with plastic wrap and let stand for 4–6 hours, stirring occasionally.

3. Process the mixture in the bowl of a food processor until the mustard seeds are coarsely ground.

4. Cook the mixture in a double boiler over simmering water, adding the basil, shallots, sugar, salt, and allspice. Cook for 20–25 minutes. The mustard will thicken as it cooks.

5. Pour into sterile jars. Cap and seal.

6. Allow the flavors to marry for 2–3 days before using. Will keep in the refrigerator for 2–3 months unopened.

YIELD: FIVE ½-PINTS (FORTY 1-OUNCE SERVINGS)
NUTRITION PER SERVING

Calories	15	Total fat	1g
% from fat	33	Saturated fat	0g
Carbohydrates	2g	Cholesterol	0mg
Fiber	<1g	Sodium	54mg

Raisin Refrigerator Relish

It wouldn't be Thanksgiving without this relish on our table. But we love it with pork and ham as well.

½ cup white wine vinegar

1½ tablespoons sugar

3 cloves garlic, minced

2 teaspoons fresh ginger root, peeled and minced

½ teaspoon cayenne pepper

½ teaspoon yellow mustard seeds

¼ teaspoon salt

1 cup dark raisins

1 cup golden raisins

1. Heat the vinegar and sugar. Add the garlic, spices, and salt.

2. Pour the warm vinegar over the raisins in a 1-pint sterile canning jar.

3. Cap, seal, and refrigerate. Will keep for 3–5 days in the refrigerator.

YIELD: 1 PINT (EIGHT 2-OUNCE SERVINGS)

NUTRITION PER SERVING

Calories	131	Total fat	<1g
% from fat	2	Saturated fat	<1g
Carbohydrates	35g	Cholesterol	0mg
Fiber	2g	Sodium	72mg

Colorful Pear Relish

* * * * * * * * * *

*This recipe is a perfect way to preserve the delicious taste of fresh pears
while they are plentiful.*

**Boiling-water-bath canner;
fourteen 1-pint jars**

12½ pounds ripe pears, peeled, cored,
and chopped

8 jalapeño chiles, seeded and chopped
(wear rubber gloves)

6 green bell peppers, seeded and
chopped

6 red bell peppers, seeded and
chopped

6 medium onions, chopped

5 cups distilled white vinegar

5 cups sugar

1 tablespoon celery seeds

1 tablespoon salt

1. Combine all the ingredients in a heavy
10-quart saucepan. Mix well and bring to a
boil. Reduce the heat.

2. Simmer, uncovered, for approximately
20–30 minutes, stirring frequently and
being careful not to burn.

3. Ladle the hot relish into clean pint jars,
leaving ½ inch of headspace. Cap and seal.

4. Process in a boiling-water-bath canner
for 20 minutes. Adjust for altitude (page
40), if necessary.

*Note: You may use the food processor to chop the
fruit and vegetables in batches, pulsing the motor.*

* * * * * * * * * * * * * * * * * * *
YIELD: 14 PINTS (ONE HUNDRED TWELVE 2-OUNCE
SERVINGS)
NUTRITION PER SERVING

Calories	70	Total fat	<1g
% from fat	3	Saturated fat	0g
Carbohydrates	18g	Cholesterol	0mg
Fiber	2g	Sodium	58mg

* * * * * * * * * * * * * * * * * * *

Rhubarb Chutney

· · · · · · · · · · ·

Try this chutney with poultry, pork, or lamb.

Boiling-water-bath canner; eight ½-pint jars

- 2 large oranges
- 2½ pounds rhubarb, washed and cut into 1-inch pieces
- 5⅓ cups firmly packed light brown sugar
- 4 cups cider vinegar
- 2 cups golden raisins
- 2 medium onions, peeled and chopped
- 1 tablespoon yellow mustard seeds
- 12 whole allspice berries
- 12 whole black peppercorns

1. Grate the zest from both oranges and set aside.

2. Halve and then section both oranges as you would a grapefruit, removing the white membranes. Place in a 2-quart bowl.

3. Chop the orange sections coarsely. Squeeze any remaining juices out of the orange halves into the chopped sections.

4. Combine the rhubarb, oranges, sugar, vinegar, raisins, and onions in a 4-quart saucepan.

5. Tie the spices in a cheesecloth bag and add to the pan. Slowly bring the mixture to a boil, stirring to dissolve the sugar.

6. Simmer uncovered until thick, about 1–1½ hours, being careful not to burn and stirring often. Remove the spice bag.

7. Ladle into hot, clean jars, leaving ¼ inch of headspace. Cap and seal.

8. Process for 10 minutes in a boiling-water-bath canner. Adjust for altitude (page 40), if necessary.

· ·

YIELD: EIGHT ½-PINTS (THIRTY-TWO 2-OUNCE SERVINGS)

NUTRITION PER SERVING

Calories	199	Total fat	<1g
% from fat	2	Saturated fat	<1g
Carbohydrates	52g	Cholesterol	0mg
Fiber	2g	Sodium	20mg

· ·

Refrigerator Plum Chutney

*Baste grilling pork or chicken with this rich chutney during the last stages of cooking.
Then serve the rest as a side dish. Delicious.*

2½ cups (about 1 pound) red plums,
     washed, pitted, and chopped

¼ cup chopped red onion

¼ cup sugar

3 tablespoons golden raisins

3 tablespoons orange juice

2 tablespoons distilled white vinegar

2 cloves garlic, minced

½ teaspoon ground allspice

¼ teaspoon salt

1. Combine all the ingredients in a
2-quart saucepan with a lid. Bring to a boil,
covered, then reduce the heat to medium.
Simmer, covered, for 20–30 minutes.

2. Uncover and cook for 8–10 minutes
longer, until the moisture disappears, being
careful not to burn.

3. Pour into three ½-pint sterile canning
jars, leaving ¼ inch of headspace. Cap; seal.

4. Refrigerate and consume within
1 week.

YIELD: THREE ½-PINTS (TWELVE 2-OUNCE SERVINGS)
NUTRITION PER SERVING

Calories	60	Total fat	<1g
% from fat	5	Saturated fat	0g
Carbohydrates	15g	Cholesterol	0mg
Fiber	1g	Sodium	45mg

Southwestern Cranberry Sauce

· · · · · · · · · · ·

A variation on a theme, this cranberry sauce tastes fresh even after being frozen or refrigerated. Serve with lamb or turkey cutlets.

1 package (12 ounces) fresh cranberries, rinsed and picked over

¾ cup sugar

1 scallion, coarsely chopped

1 medium jalapeño chile, seeded and quartered (wear rubber gloves)

3 teaspoons fresh cilantro

¼ teaspoon ground cumin

1. Coarsely chop all the ingredients in a food processor, pulsing the motor.

2. Pour into three sterile 1-cup canning jars, leaving 1 inch of headspace.

3. Allow the flavors to develop in the refrigerator overnight. This will keep for 1 week in the refrigerator or 2 months in the freezer.

4. To use frozen cranberry sauce, thaw in the refrigerator.

Note: For a quick version of this recipe, combine one 16-ounce can of whole cranberry sauce with ½ cup of Five-Pepper Jelly (see page 228). Melt together in a saucepan over medium heat until combined. Cool, then serve. This will keep for 2 weeks in the refrigerator.

· ·

YIELD: THREE 3 ½-PINTS (TWELVE 2-OUNCE SERVINGS)
NUTRITION PER SERVING

Calories	67	Total fat	<1g
% from fat	1	Saturated fat	0g
Carbohydrates	17g	Cholesterol	0mg
Fiber	2g	Sodium	3mg

· ·

Pickled Mixed Vegetable Chunks

A great accompaniment to all meats and sandwiches.

Boiling-water-bath canner; ten 1-pint jars

4 pounds pickling cucumbers, washed and thickly sliced

2 pounds small onions, peeled and quartered

4 cups celery, sliced into 1-inch pieces

2 cups carrots, peeled and thickly sliced

2 cups cauliflower florets

2 cups red bell peppers, cut into 1-inch pieces

Ice cubes

6 cups distilled white vinegar

3½ cups sugar

¼ cup salt (or more to taste)

¼ cup prepared mustard

3 tablespoons celery seeds

2 tablespoons yellow mustard seeds

½ teaspoon whole cloves

½ teaspoon ground turmeric

1. Combine the vegetables in an 8-quart ceramic bowl and cover with the ice cubes. Refrigerate for 4 hours.

2. Combine the vinegar, sugar, salt, mustard, seeds, and spices in a heavy 8-quart saucepan. Bring to a boil.

3. Drain the vegetables. Pack into sterile jars, leaving ½ inch of headspace.

4. Ladle the vinegar syrup over the vegetables, leaving ½ inch of headspace. Cap and seal.

5. Process for 10 minutes in a boiling-water-bath canner. Adjust for altitude (page 40), if necessary.

YIELD: 10 PINTS (EIGHTY 2-OUNCE SERVINGS)
NUTRITION PER SERVING

Calories	50	Total fat	<1g
% from fat	4	Saturated fat	0g
Carbohydrates	12g	Cholesterol	0mg
Fiber	<1g	Sodium	657mg

Baby Carrots with Honey and Dill

Try this with poultry or fish or as a low-calorie appetizer.

2 packages (1 pound each) peeled baby carrots (4 cups)

⅔ cup white wine vinegar

½ cup honey

2 tablespoons whole light mustard seeds

1 teaspoon salt

2 tablespoons minced fresh dill

1. Cook the carrots in a large pot of salted boiling water until tender but still crisp, about 5 minutes. Drain.

2. Combine the vinegar, honey, mustard seeds, and salt in a 2-quart bowl. Add the hot carrots to the vinegar mixture. Stir to cool.

3. Cover and store in the refrigerator for 3–5 days. Serve at room temperature sprinkled with the fresh dill.

YIELD: 5½ CUPS (ELEVEN ½-CUP SERVINGS)
NUTRITION PER SERVING

Calories	91	Total fat	1g
% from fat	9	Saturated fat	<1g
Carbohydrates	21g	Cholesterol	0mg
Fiber	2g	Sodium	225mg

CHAPTER 7

Vinegars & Seasonings

I REMEMBER, YEARS AGO, the first time I visited Harrod's food hall in London. It was, and remains today, the granddaddy of all food halls in the world. The aisles overflowed with pyramids made of tins of dry mustard and other foods. Overhead displays were laden with sassy bunches of dried herbs tied with ribbon and raffia bows. And a mosaic mural of dried cloves, allspice, dried beans, and other spices adorned the walls. It was an art gallery of food!

In the midst of all this, I found culinary magic in bright, crystal-clear bottles of vinegar, which had suspended inside fruit larger than the bottleneck. I pondered this for years, wondering how they had gotten the fruit into the bottle. Later, I learned that they had threaded the bottleneck over a small, immature, growing peach. They had chosen fruit from a bottom branch, somewhat shaded from the sun, easy enough to reach. Then they removed all the leaves from the branch and tied the bottle over the immature fruit.

After learning how those fruited vinegars at Harrod's had been created, my husband and I tried this process. We tied our bottles over peach and apple branches and checked them often as the fruit grew. Of course, you don't want to do this with fruit trees that have been sprayed. It took us many bottles tied to many branches to actually get one completed peach inside. At that stage, all we had to do was shake the branch and the fruit fell off, caught in the bottle. We then followed a recipe for fruit vinegar and ended up with a real conversation piece. In fact, we almost had more fun talking about it than we did eating it.

Looking back, we had many failures but great fun. It's no wonder the fruited vinegar in Harrod's was so expensive. But you can make your own flavored vinegar using much simpler methods and ingredients. Give it a try. Flavored vinegars make a meal interesting by providing a little of the unexpected to an otherwise ordinary dinner. Look upon these condiments and seasonings as your helpmates in making good food delicious.

Vinegar

Is it a medicine, cosmetic, preservative, flavor enhancer, cleanser, disinfectant, beverage, or digestive aid? While modern science has had to prove vinegar's antibacterial and antiseptic powers, inhabitants of the ancient Mediterranean already knew of its qualities. In the Old Testament, reference is made to the medicinal qualities of wine and vinegar. The many flavored, refined vinegars of today are used mostly to enhance and enliven cuisines around the world.

Vinegar, which contains acetic acid, is the natural outcome of fermented fruit juices and grains. Oxygen and the alcohol of wine combine with organisms known as acetobacters to produce vinegar. Each grain or fruit used imparts its own special flavor to the vinegar. The flavor range seems endless. Appreciating the subtle and not-so-subtle vinegar flavors is a full-time occupation. Age, flavoring, and the acidity contribute to the taste and character of vinegars.

Modern vinegar production has been speeded greatly by mechanization — though aged balsamic vinegars are still being produced today, as they were in ancient Italy.

Vinegar is the single most effective vehicle for low-caloric flavoring of meats and vegetables. Sometimes vinegar is identified as containing a certain "grain," which specifies the proportion of acetic acid to water. A 40-grain vinegar means that it is 40 percent acetic acid. Read the label carefully to determine acidity when you purchase vinegar. For cooking purposes, 4 to 6 percent acidity is ideal. Once you

Vinegar Varieties

Balsamic. Once produced as an art form by family for private use; true *aceto balsamico* is made only in the Emilia-Romagna region of Italy near Modena. It has been fermented and sometimes aged for hundreds of years. Today's balsamic vinegar, controlled by the Italian government, is aged at least 12 years. It is fruity and thick, rich and dark brown, and ideal for meats, marinades, and salads.

Champagne. Technically speaking, this vinegar is made only in the Champagne district of France. Delicate in flavor and expensive in price, it is best used in seafood sauces or with mild herbs.

Cider. Made from apples and aged from pure apple cider, it is best used with strong, pungent herbs or spices. Great for pickling, it can also be used in salad dressings and marinades.

Malt. The intense flavor of malt vinegar, which is fermented from beer (grains), stands up best in pickles and other relishes. Malt vinegar is sprinkled over fried potatoes and fried fish in the United Kingdom to create the classic fish and chips.

White rice. Very distinct in taste and fairly sweet, this Japanese vinegar complements rice and makes an excellent sauce base, combining well with seafoods and vegetables. Chinese white rice vinegar, which is a mild sweet vinegar, enhances sweet-and-sour dishes.

Sherry. Slightly sweet and nutty, sherry vinegar comes from Spain. It can be used lavishly in cooking with strong herbs and spices. It stands up well in cream- and tomato-based sauces and has a more intense flavor than rice vinegar.

White wine. Pair this delicately flavored vinegar with other subtle flavors, such as mild herbs and seafoods.

Red wine. Stronger in character, this vinegar stands up well in dark meats, heavier vegetable salads, and dark marinades that may contain soy sauce or Worcestershire sauce.

have learned about the differences in flavors, aged versus nonaged, and variations in acidity, you will want to choose the full-bodied, aged vinegars over the pale grocery store varieties every time. Distilled white vinegar is perfect for pickling, but not for making flavored concoctions to enhance your menu.

While homemade vinegar is great for flavoring your meals, do not use homemade vinegar in canning. Usually the acidity of homemade vinegar is much lower than that of commercial varieties, and measuring the exact acidity percentage of your homemade brew is difficult to do. Another

Store flavored vinegars in decorative glass bottles or cruets.

After the steeping process, filter the vinegar into clean, narrow-necked bottles for final bottling.

problem with using homemade vinegar in canning is that it often contains the "mother" of vinegar, a jellylike, cloudy substance that contains the bacteria used for making vinegar. You don't want the mother clouding your pickles.

Wine Vinegar

Wine vinegar contains no alcohol, which is oxidized in the process of turning wine into vinegar. All the vinegars listed here are suitable in flavor and acidity for our purposes, but always read labels carefully to check acidity before buying.

Flavored Vinegar

Is it a kitchen decoration, gift-giving idea, culinary essential, or the perfect suspension medium for those summer herbs that grow in such abundance? Flavored vinegar does it all. In addition to herbs and spices, you can flavor vinegar with fruits, flowers, and vegetables singularly or in combination.

For today's cook, it is easy to buy a good-quality vinegar and use your energy and ideas for creative flavor combinations. Remember, poor-quality vinegar cannot be elevated by adding a few herbs to it — always choose the best in the beginning.

Making Flavored Vinegar

The process of bottling flavored vinegars is simple compared to that of canning fruits or vegetables. Because of its high acidity, vinegar prevents the growth of bacteria, eliminating the need for processing with heat. Nevertheless, all the usual rules of cleanliness apply.

Make sure you are prepared and organized before you begin bottling. Use hot, soapy water to wash the bottles and utensils, removing all the soap with hot water. Drain all the washed equipment on clean tea towels. Pour boiling water into the clean bottles and let stand for 10 minutes. The individual recipe will give instructions for steeping or otherwise combining ingredients.

I find it most convenient to steep the vinegar ingredients in a clean, widemouthed jar. Many recipes call for removing the spices and herbs before the final bottling, and this kind of jar allows you to do that easily. If you steep the ingredients in a narrow-necked bottle, it may be difficult to remove the spices and herbs later. Spices and herbs that remain in the vinegar after bottling continue to impart their flavors. Sometimes this is desirable, as with Lemon-Thyme Vinegar (page 296). Sample your wares after a few days of steeping and decide for yourself. It is a matter of taste. You may choose to leave the seasonings intact. Sometimes the suspended seasonings are quite beautiful and add to the effect of your creation. Often it is a judgment call by the cook. Herbs such as garlic, when left in the vinegar, could eventually overpower the other flavors. So after the herbs and spices have steeped in the vinegar, filter the vinegar through a coffee filter into clean, narrow-necked bottles for final bottling.

Equipment

Most of the equipment you need for flavoring vinegar can be found in your kitchen (see box at right). The bottles

The basic equipment for making flavored vinegars can be found in your kitchen.

Equipment for Making Flavored Vinegars

• • • • • • • •

Use only ceramic, glass, stainless steel, or enameled equipment. Never use reactive metals, such as aluminum.

Large widemouthed jars, for steeping
Long-necked jars and corks, recycled or new, for storage
Water
Bottle brush
Sealing wax
Paraffin or candle wax
Ribbon of your choice, to ornament your creation
Long-handled spoon
Potholders
Glass measuring cups
Plastic measuring spoons
Heavy 4–5 quart saucepan (nonreactive)
Coffee filters, jelly bag, or supply of muslin or cheesecloth
Plastic funnel
Plastic wrap, to cover the steeping vinegar

for steeping and storing the vinegar are possibly the only things you will have to search for. Keep your eyes open throughout the year for interesting reusable bottles and jars. Rosé and white wine bottles are best, as they are clear. Pick up a package of generic corks in different sizes the next time you see them at the hardware store and have them on hand for "bottling season." Of course, you can always buy ornamental glass bottles as well. The upscale home-furnishings stores carry quite an array of them.

STORAGE

Always store your finished product in a cool, dark place. Some light, but certainly not direct light, is okay while the solution is steeping. It is tempting to store vinegars in plain view of guests because the fancy varieties can be quite attractive, but unless you keep your living room dark and cool, don't do it. Fancy flavored vinegar will keep for 6 months, fruit vinegar for 3 months.

MAKING HERB-FLAVORED VINEGAR

Herbal vinegars are delightfully attractive, wonderfully flavorful, and extremely easy to make. Experiment with different herbs and vinegars to create a diversity of flavors for use in cooking and salads. All vinegars can be paired with herbs, but red wine vinegar and white wine vinegar are the most versatile. More delicate varieties, such as champagne vinegar, are best suited for lemony herbs. Apple cider vinegar and malt vinegar pair well with oniony herbs, such as chives and garlic.

1. Gather the herbs before the midmorning sun hits the leaves but after the dew has evaporated. Clean off all the grit and blot the herbs dry with clean towels or paper towels.

2. Remove the leaves from the stems and measure 1 cup of leaves to 2 cups of vinegar. If you are using dried herbs, choose one-half the amount, or ½ cup of herbs to 2 cups of

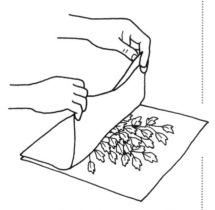

Clean the herbs and then blot them dry on clean towels.

vinegar. It may seem to be too strong a ratio of herbs to vinegar, but don't be put off. The solution must be strong enough to be effective even after steeping and straining.

3. Put the leaves into a clean jar and fill with vinegar. Cover the jar and store it in a dark, cool place. Shake or stir the solution every few days and taste it after about 1 week. If the flavor is intense enough and to your liking, it is ready.

4. Strain the vinegar infusion into a clean bottle using cheesecloth, muslin, a clean jelly bag, or a coffee filter. Cork or cap, label, and store in a dark, cool place.

Making Spice-Flavored Vinegar

While heat is not recommended for other kinds of flavored vinegars, it enhances the flavor of spiced vinegar by releasing the essential oils in the spices. All types of vinegar work well with spices. Experiment to find your favorite combinations by trying allspice, cardamom, cinnamon, ginger, juniper, nutmeg, peppercorns, and peppers. Use the seeds of herbs, such as anise, caraway, celery, coriander, cumin, dill, and mustard.

1. Use whole spices, not the ground form, which could cloud the finished product. You may wish to bruise them slightly or crush them, using a mortar and pestle or a food processor.

2. Heat 2 cups of vinegar to 110°F, being careful not to let it overheat. Remove the pan from the heat and let it cool slightly.

3. Put up to 4 tablespoons of the bruised spices in a clean widemouthed jar along with the 2 cups of vinegar. Cover the jar and store it in a dark, cool place. Shake or stir the solution every few days and taste it after about 1 week. If the flavor is intense enough and to your liking, it is ready.

4. Strain the vinegar infusion into a clean bottle using cheesecloth, muslin, a clean jelly bag, or a coffee filter. Cork or cap, label, and store in a dark, cool place.

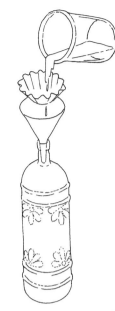

Use a cheesecloth or coffee filter to strain the vinegar infusion.

TIP

• • • • • • • • •

For a sparkling vinegar concoction to give as a gift, include your favorite oil and vinegar salad dressing recipe on a card tied to the bottleneck.

Making Fruit-Flavored Vinegar

The hardest part of making fruit-flavored vinegar is deciding which fruit to use. The possibilities are nearly endless. Most fruit vinegars fare well with milder red or white wine vinegar as a base to match the delicacy of the fruit flavors. Make sure the vinegar has at least 5 percent acidity.

1. Wash and blot the fruit dry; pit it, if necessary; and peel, if desired.

2. Mash slightly or cut up the fruit and place the prepared fruit in a clean jar with the vinegar. Don't heat the vinegar for flavoring with fruit; it's too hard on the fruit, as a rule. The 2-to-1 ratio of vinegar to fruit is good here. Cover with vinegar and place in a cool, dark place to let the flavors marry.

3. After a few days to a week, taste the solution. At this point, you can strain out the fruit and add newly prepared fruit for a more intense flavor. Let the mixture steep for another week or two. Repeat the steeping process until the taste is to your liking.

4. Strain the mixture into a nonreactive saucepan. For each 2 cups of flavored vinegar, add ⅛ cup to ½ cup of sugar, or use 1½ tablespoons to ⅓ cup of honey. Simmer but do not boil the mixture, stirring as the sweetener dissolves, for about 3 minutes. If foam develops, skim it off.

5. Let the vinegar cool and pour it into a clean bottle. Add a fruit slice to the bottle for beauty. Cork or cap, label, and store in a cool, dark place.

Making Floral-Flavored Vinegar

The main thing to remember when making floral vinegar is to use nonpoisonous flowers and only those that have not been sprayed with dangerous chemicals. Never use florist flowers. Know your sources or use your own flowers.

Using herbs that have "bolted" in the hot sun of late summer is a great way to flavor vinegars, because the flowers

---

Flowers to Use

• • • • • • • • • • • •

Anise	Marjoram
Basil	Mint
Borage	Nasturtium
Calendula	Oregano
Carnation	Pinks
Chamomile	Primrose
Chive	Rose
Dill	Rose-scented
Elder	geranium
Fennel	Thyme
Lavender	Violet
Lovage	

add delicate flavor. If you're flavoring with roses, though, use only the petals, never the whole rose, and use the inner petals, not the sepal or outer green petals. No matter what kind of flower you use, make sure the petals are clean, dry, and free of insects.

1. Choose a mild white vinegar such as champagne, white rice, or white wine. Use 1 cup of petals to 2 cups of vinegar. With some flowers, such as violets, this could end up requiring a very large supply of plant material. Combine the ingredients in a clean, widemouthed jar, then cap and store in a cool, dark place.

2. As with other flavored vinegars, steep for about a week and then taste. Continue to steep a few more weeks if you want a stronger flavor.

3. Strain the vinegar into a clean, small-necked bottle; add a fresh flower, if desired; cork or cap, seal, and label.

Seasoning Mixes

How easy it is to turn all your everyday dishes into something spectacular with herb blends and seasonings. Keep on hand your own mix of herbs, spices, and other seasonings. What a luxury to enliven your fresh, steaming-hot produce with a vegetable seasoning right before serving, or to add sparkle to that pot of soup with a spoonful of soup-seasoning blend. Most of these recipes add no calories to your dishes, and they are easy to combine and keep on hand.

TIP

Use your own pesticide-free flowers for cooking.

Steep the petals in a mild vinegar in a sealed container.

Flavored Oils

Flavored oils are wonderful for adding zest and body to a recipe. Use them instead of butter on breads and in recipes. But to be safe, they must be refrigerated as soon as the flavoring is added, and they must be used within 1 day of flavoring. Clostridium botulinum, the deadly bacterium that causes botulism, can quickly develop in oil. Never use flavored oils that have been left standing on a table or shelf.

RECIPES FOR FLAVORED VINEGARS AND SEASONINGS

Spiced Sherry Vinegar

This hearty vinegar stands up well to grilled pork and beef when used as a marinade ingredient.

1 teaspoon whole black peppercorns

1 teaspoon whole cloves

1 small whole red chile

1 1-inch-piece dried ginger root

2 cups sherry vinegar

1. Combine all the ingredients except the vinegar in a large widemouthed jar.

2. Heat the vinegar just to boiling in a non-reactive 2-quart saucepan over medium heat.

3. Pour the vinegar into the spice-filled jar and let steep until cool.

4. Tightly cover the jar and store in a cool, dark place.

5. Check the flavor after 1 week. Decant from the widemouthed jar through a coffee filter into a narrow-necked bottle. Cork or cap and store in a cool, dark place.

YIELD: 1 PINT

Provençal Vinegar

This herb vinegar has a wonderfully light, fresh flavor imparted by a bit of orange peel. Use as is over fresh raw summer vegetables, or add a dash of olive oil.

1 pint red wine vinegar

1 strip orange zest, 1 inch by 4 inches

1 sprig fresh rosemary

1 sprig fresh thyme

1 bay leaf

1 large garlic clove, peeled

1. Combine all the ingredients in a clean 2-cup jar.

2. Seal the jar and store at room temperature in a dark place for about 1 month before using.

3. Filter into a clean 1-pint bottle.

4. Store at room temperature, tightly sealed, for up to 6 months.

YIELD: 1 PINT

French-Blend Herb Vinegar

Serve this lovely vinegar drizzled over sliced fresh tomatoes or cucumbers.

1 quart red wine vinegar

4 sprigs fresh oregano

3 large stems fresh basil

2 sprigs parsley

2 sprigs fresh rosemary

2 teaspoons whole black peppercorns

1 clove garlic, peeled

1. Combine all the ingredients in a large widemouthed jar.

2. Tightly cover the jar and store in a cool, dark place. Check the flavor after 1 week.

3. Decant from the widemouthed jar through a coffee filter into a narrow-necked bottle.

4. Cork or cap; store in a cool, dark place.

YIELD: 2 PINTS

Spiced Vinegar

This recipe makes a large quantity, so plan to give some as gifts.

6 quarts cider vinegar

2 cups sugar

6 tablespoons whole black peppercorns

¼ cup fresh ginger root, peeled and sliced

¼ cup whole allspice

¼ cup whole cloves

¼ cup yellow mustard seeds

3 tablespoons celery seeds

3 tablespoons turmeric

2 tablespoons mace

1. Combine all the ingredients in a nonreactive 10-quart saucepan.

2. Heat slowly, stirring until all the sugar has dissolved.

3. Pour into two 1-gallon jars, dividing the spices evenly. Cover and let steep for about 3 weeks in a cool, dark place.

4. Strain through a coffee filter into six sterile quart jars. Cap, seal, and store in a cool, dark place.

YIELD: 6 QUARTS

Ginger-Pepper Rice Vinegar

This vinegar is a wonderful ingredient in stir-fry sauces.

1 cup fresh ginger root, peeled and sliced

1 tablespoon whole black peppercorns

1½ cups rice wine vinegar, heated to 110°F

1. Place the ginger and peppercorns in the steeping container. Press them with the back of a spoon to release the flavor.

2. Add the vinegar. Screw on the lid tightly and store in a cool, dark place. Stir the mixture or shake the jar every other day.

3. Check the flavor after 1 week. Let steep longer, if desired. When the ginger flavor is to your liking, strain the vinegar and use. It will keep for 3–6 months.

YIELD: 1½ CUPS

Using Fresh Ginger

Look for smooth-skinned ginger. Wrinkled or cracked skins indicate older ginger.

To peel ginger: *Holding the ginger root firmly, use a vegetable peeler to peel the tough skin, being careful not to remove much of the flesh.*

Mint Vinegar

Marinate fresh tomatoes in this vinegar concoction.

1½ cups fresh mint leaves

6 cups white wine vinegar

½ cup honey, or 1 cup sugar

Zest of 3 lemons

3 fresh mint leaves

1. In a half-gallon container, bruise the mint leaves with the back of a spoon.

2. Add the remaining ingredients and stir.

3. Store in two 1-quart jars, capped and sealed, at room temperature for about 2 weeks.

4. Filter into three clean containers and add a fresh mint sprig for beauty. Store tightly sealed in a cool, dark place for up to 6 months.

YIELD: 6 CUPS

Tarragon Vinegar

A base for almost any sauce or dressing, tarragon vinegar is a tried-and-true favorite. Combine 1 part vinegar with 3 parts olive oil for a delicious salad dressing.

20 sprigs fresh tarragon

4 cups white wine vinegar

1. In a widemouthed 1-quart jar, bruise the tarragon, using the back of a spoon.

2. Pour the vinegar over the herbs and seal the jar.

3. Store in a dark place for 2–4 weeks, or until the flavor has reached the desired intensity.

4. Remove the herbs by straining the vinegar (or use a coffee filter) into a 1-quart decorative bottle. Cork or cap and make sure the bottle has an airtight seal.

YIELD: 1 QUART

Basil Balsamic Vinegar

Sprinkle this over fresh sliced tomatoes and cucumbers.

4 sprigs fresh basil

1 clove garlic, peeled

1 teaspoon whole black peppercorns

1 pint balsamic vinegar

1. Combine all the ingredients except the vinegar in a large widemouthed jar.

2. Pour the vinegar into the jar and cover tightly.

3. Store the jar in a cool, dark place. Check the flavor after 1 week.

4. Decant from the widemouthed jar through a coffee filter into a narrow-necked bottle.

5. Cork or cap, label, and store in a cool, dark place.

YIELD: 1 PINT

Spicy Dill Vinegar

Try this vinegar with fish or boiled potatoes.

6 sprigs fresh dill

2 fresh dill heads, or ½ teaspoon dill seeds

1 tablespoon yellow mustard seeds

1 clove garlic, peeled

1 quart white wine vinegar

1. Combine all the ingredients except the vinegar in a large widemouthed jar.

2. Heat the vinegar to 110°F.

3. Pour the vinegar into the jar and let the herbs steep until cool. Tightly cover the jar and store in a cool, dark place. Check the flavor after 1 week.

4. Decant the vinegar from the widemouthed jar through a coffee filter into a narrow-necked bottle.

5. Cork or cap, label, and store in a cool, dark place.

Yield: 2 pints

Fresh Herb Vinegar

This large quantity is perfect to make when the garden is rampant, then give away as welcome gifts.

1 dozen shallots, peeled

8 sprigs fresh rosemary

8 sprigs fresh thyme

¾ cup fresh tarragon leaves

½ cup fresh parsley leaves

¼ cup chopped fresh chives

2 dozen black peppercorns

3 gallons cider vinegar

3 cloves garlic

1. Combine the herbs and divide the mixture into three 1-gallon jars.

2. Pour vinegar into each jar. Add 1 clove of garlic to each jar and let steep for 24 hours.

3. Remove the garlic. Seal the jar and place in a cool, dry place for 2 weeks.

4. Strain or pour through a coffee filter into twelve 1-quart bottles. Cap, seal, and label. Store in a dark, cool place.

Yield: 12 quarts

Lemon-Thyme Vinegar

· · · · · · · · · · ·

Try to peel the lemon in one continuous spiral. "Thread" it into the bottle in a spiral fashion. Beautiful!

2 cups white wine vinegar

1 lemon, peeled in one spiral

2 sprigs fresh thyme

2 teaspoons white peppercorns

8–10 fresh cranberries (optional)

1. Combine all the ingredients in a sterile decorative bottle.

2. Seal and store for 1 month in a cool, dark place before use.

YIELD: 1 PINT

Note: I like to thread about 8–10± fresh cranberries on a wooden skewer and insert the skewer through the neck of the bottle. It's challenging and fun to try to get the skewer in the center of the lemon spiral. Like building a ship in a bottle, your friends will wonder how you did it!

Lime Vinegar

· · · · · · · · · · ·

This is remarkable on fresh fruit.

1 tablespoon coriander seeds

Zest of 1 lime

1 clove garlic, peeled

1 quart white wine vinegar

1. Combine the coriander, zest, and garlic in a large widemouthed jar.

2. Heat the vinegar to 110°F.

3. Pour the vinegar into the jar; let cool.

4. Tightly cover and store in a cool, dark place. Check the flavor after 1 week.

5. Decant from the widemouthed jar through a coffee filter into a narrow-necked bottle. Cork or cap, label, and store in a cool, dark place.

YIELD: 2 PINTS

Cranberry Vinegar

· · · · · · · · · ·

Use this vinegar as a dressing base for cole slaw. Add two chopped apples to your favorite slaw recipe. Different and delicious!

1½ cups fresh cranberries, rinsed and picked over

1¼ cups white rice vinegar

3 tablespoons honey

1. Heat the ingredients in the top of a double boiler over simmering water for 10 minutes.

2. Cool and store in a clean pint jar for 3 weeks in a cool place.

3. Strain the vinegar through a coffee filter, pressing out all the fruit juices.

4. Funnel into a clean 1-pint bottle.

YIELD: 1 PINT

Strawberry Vinegar

· · · · · · · · · ·

Use this vinegar in slaw, as a base for pork marinade, or heated slightly with olive oil for a different salad dressing.

2 pints strawberries, rinsed, stemmed, and halved, ¼ cup reserved

1 quart cider vinegar

1 cup sugar

1. In a large 4-quart nonreactive saucepan, combine the berries and vinegar. Let stand for 1 hour.

2. Add the sugar to the saucepan and heat to a slow boil to dissolve the sugar. Simmer for 10 minutes.

3. Use a coffee filter to strain into three sterile 1-pint bottles. Press out as much juice from the berries as possible.

4. Add some of the reserved strawberries to each bottle. Cap, seal, and label. Store in a cool, dark place for 2 weeks before use.

YIELD: 3 PINTS

Herbes de Provence

This is my version of the famous French herb blend. But if you are feeling patriotic, rename it for your local area! This is especially excellent for grilling meats. Sprinkle on lamb chops, chicken, or beef while they cook on the grill.

½ cup dried rosemary

½ cup dried thyme

¼ cup dried marjoram

¼ cup dried oregano

¼ cup dried savory

2 tablespoons dried fennel seeds

2 tablespoons dried lavender leaves

1. Combine all the ingredients and store in an airtight container in a cool, dark place.

2. This will stay fresh for 2 months.

YIELD: 2 CUPS

TIP

Save your grocery store spice jars with shaker-style lids. They are convenient dispensers for many of these blends.

Popcorn Shaker Mix

Sprinkle about ½ teaspoon of this spicy seasoning on each cup of buttered popped corn, adjusting to taste. The butter helps it stick to the popcorn, but if you wish to eliminate the fat, sprinkle the blend on hot unbuttered popcorn and stir often to keep it mixed together.

¼ cup ground cumin

3 tablespoons dried oregano

1 tablespoon cayenne pepper (or less to taste)

1. Combine the ingredients and pour into a salt shaker. Sprinkle over hot buttered popcorn to taste.

2. This will keep for 6 weeks in a cool, dark place. Keep tightly sealed.

YIELD: ½ CUP

Dill Blend

Dried herbs keep this recipe uncomplicated. This blend is terrific with fish or as a seasoning for fresh tomatoes and cucumbers. Try it on baked potatoes or in soups for a change of pace.

¼ cup dried dill weed

2 tablespoons dried lemon-balm leaves

1 tablespoon garlic powder

1. Combine all the ingredients and store in an airtight jar away from heat and light.

2. Sprinkle on foods according to taste.

YIELD: ½ CUP

Vegetable Seasoning Mix

This mix of favorite dried summer herbs is good for seasoning fresh vegetables, and when you sprinkle a little on pasta, it becomes a special-occasion meal.

8 tablespoons dried parsley

4 tablespoons dried chives

1 teaspoon dried basil

1 teaspoon dried oregano

1 teaspoon dried sage

1 teaspoon dried thyme

1 teaspoon garlic powder

½ teaspoon celery seeds

1. Combine all the ingredients and store in an airtight container away from heat and light. The garlic can sink to the bottom of the container, so stir well before each use.

2. Sprinkle on vegetables, buttered pasta, salads, or soups, as desired.

YIELD: ¾ CUP

Southwestern Spice Mix

Dried red pepper flakes give this spice mix an extra kick. Use this blend anytime you want a southwestern flavor for cream cheese dip, chicken salad, tangy soup, or chili. Good with any recipe calling for chili powder.

3 tablespoons chili powder

2 tablespoons ground cumin

1 tablespoon freshly ground black pepper

1 tablespoon garlic powder

1 tablespoon salt

1½ teaspoons dried red pepper flakes

1. Mix all the ingredients thoroughly in a small bowl.

2. Store in an airtight container in a cool, dry place for up to 3 months.

YIELD: 8½ TABLESPOONS

Asian Seasoning Blend

This combination gives rice a hot, complex, wonderfully seasoned Thai flavor. Use it for stir-fried vegetables as well.

4 tablespoons dried mint leaves

2 tablespoons dried lemon zest

1 tablespoon ground white pepper

2 teaspoons dried lemon verbena leaves

½ teaspoon cayenne pepper

¼ teaspoon ground cumin

1. Combine all the ingredients in a blender and pulverize to a fine powder.

2. Store in an airtight container away from heat and light. Add to rice or stir-fried vegetables according to taste.

YIELD: ABOUT ½ CUP

Seasoned Butters

· · · · · · · · · · ·

Herbs and spices give vegetables and other foods a new dimension. Start with ½ cup (1 stick) of softened butter, and then add one of the combinations below. Seasoned butters will keep for several days in the refrigerator.

ROSEMARY-THYME BUTTER SEASONING

1 teaspoon dried rosemary, crushed

1 teaspoon dried thyme, crushed

¼ teaspoon ground white pepper

ALL-PURPOSE BUTTER SEASONING

2 teaspoons dried basil, crushed

¼ teaspoon freshly ground black pepper

¼ teaspoon onion powder

SPICY BUTTER SEASONING

¼ onion, finely minced

½ teaspoon ground cumin

½ teaspoon dried oregano, crushed

¼ teaspoon cayenne pepper

ITALIAN BUTTER SEASONING

2 teaspoons dried oregano, crushed

2 cloves garlic, peeled and minced

¼ teaspoon freshly ground black pepper

Seasoned Butter on French Bread

· · · · · · · · · · ·

1. *Slice a loaf of French bread lengthwise.*

2. *Blend one of the seasoning mixtures with ½ cup of softened butter and spread on each slice of bread.*

3. *Reassemble the loaf and wrap in foil.*

4. *The buttered French bread can be stored in the freezer for 1 week.*

5. *To use, remove the bread from the freezer, defrost it in the refrigerator, and bake it at 425°F for 15 minutes, or until it's heated through.*

Note: Make one loaf of bread for dinner that night and one for the freezer.

· ·

YIELD: ½ CUP (EIGHT 1-TABLESPOON SERVINGS)
NUTRITION PER SERVING

Calories	100	Total fat	11
% from fat	99	Saturated fat	7g
Carbohydrates	0g	Cholesterol	31mg
Fiber	0g	Sodium	116mg

· ·

CHAPTER 8

Cold Storage

COLD STORAGE IS THE SIMPLEST FORM of preserving. It involves placing food in a cool, dark environment with varying amounts of humidity. Some foods require moist air, while others prefer dry; some need warmer temperatures and others, colder. All these factors must be taken into account when deciding on the proper form of cold storage for each food.

A root cellar takes advantage of the cool, moist temperatures of the earth to prevent food from decomposing. Old houses with dirt floors in their basements, for example, provide the ideal environment for storing food. The temperature in a root cellar needs to remain above 32°F but below 40°F. Humidity of at least 80 percent is important, too. Most house foundations have air ducts that can be opened and closed as needed to vary the temperature and humidity. If your furnace is in the same area of your basement as your root cellar, the temperature may not stay low enough. Monitor it frequently during a cold spell to make sure the temperature stays low enough.

Keeping vegetables and fruits in a root cellar basically differs from refrigeration only in humidity. Refrigeration does provide a dark environment with controlled, cool temperatures, but there the similarity stops. Air in a refrigerator dries food quickly — consider what happens to unwrapped cheese — while the humidity in a root cellar is higher. The added moisture works with the cool temperature to help produce stay fresh.

Bruises can be the start of the rotting process. With gentle handling and proper storage, your cold-stored produce will nourish you throughout the winter months.

Produce for Cold and Dry Storage

As with any form of preserving, always start with unblemished, good-quality produce. Handle it gently as you harvest and prepare it for storage. While many varieties of produce adapt well to the root cellar, many do not. You can store the following produce without *any* processing.

Produce	Ideal Storage Temperature	Humidity*	Air Circulation	Shelf Life (in Months)
Cold Storage				
Apples	32°F	medium moist	medium	4–6
Beets	32–40°F	moist	low	3–5
Cabbage	32°F	medium moist to moist	low	2–4
Carrots	32–40°F	moist	low	6
Cauliflower	32°F	medium moist	low	1½–2
Celery	32°F	medium moist to moist	low	1½–4
Endive	32°F	medium moist to moist	medium	2–3
Grapefruit	32°F	medium moist	low	1–1½
Grapes	32°F	medium moist	low	1–2
Horseradish	32°F	moist	low	4–6
Kohlrabi	32–40°F	moist	low	2–3
Leeks	32°F	medium moist	medium	1–3
Parsnips	32°F	moist	low	4–6
Pears	32°F	medium moist to moist	low	2–6
Potatoes, white	35–40°F	medium moist	low	4–6
Radishes	32°F	moist	low	2–4
Rutabagas	32°F	moist	low	3–4
Turnips	32°F	moist	low	2–4
Dry Storage				

These vegetables prefer drier conditions and should not be stored in the classic root cellar, which tends to be too moist. These good "keepers" like cool ambient temperatures but not moisture.

Produce	Ideal Storage Temperature	Humidity*	Air Circulation	Shelf Life (in Months)
Onions	32°F	dry	medium	4–6
Pumpkins	55°F	medium dry to dry	medium	4–6
Squash, winter	55°F	dry	medium	4–6
Tomatoes, green	55–70°F	medium moist	medium	1–1½

*dry = 70% or less; medium dry = 70–80%; medium moist = 80–90%; moist = 90–95%

Choosing a Location

Many places in a home can work for cold storage of produce. The requirements are higher-than-average humidity of 80 percent or more, temperatures of between 32°F and 40°F, proper ventilation, and low light. The earth's unprotected surfaces freeze and thaw with the cold temperatures of winter to a depth of 18 inches or more, depending on the severity of the weather. An unheated basement or cellar protected by a house is deep enough to be unaffected by the changes in surface temperature and will remain above 32°F and below 40°F, which is perfect for root storage.

Brainstorm to find an area in or around your house that meets these requirements. Ask yourself:

1. Does your basement have a dirt floor? You can wet down a dirt floor periodically for added moisture if it's needed. Or you can keep pans of water in various locations.

2. Is your basement cool to cold, or does the furnace heat it up? Use a thermometer to test.

3. Does your basement have an outside entrance? The steps to the outside door are great for lining up baskets of produce.

TIP

Store each kind of vegetable separately so that the gases and flavors of different foods won't mingle.

Produce for Drier Conditions

Some produce won't last long in the cool, moist air of most root cellars. Pumpkins, squash, and onions prefer drier air and warmer temperatures — from 50 to 55°F with humidity at about 70 percent. You can sometimes find these conditions near the ceiling of your basement root cellar, closer to the main floor of the house. Hang a thermometer and a humidity gauge from a beam in the ceiling of your basement to determine whether these vegetables will last if stacked above other produce in your root cellar.

Drier, warmer conditions can sometimes exist in an attic, too, but monitor the temperature there vigilantly because temperatures in an attic tend to exhibit a wider range than those in a cellar.

4. Could your garage be a good place with the right amount of moisture and cold-enough temperatures? Will exhaust fumes be absorbed by the fruits or vegetables that you intend to store there?

5. Do you have an old lightweight ice chest (Styrofoam with a lid) that could serve as a "mini" root cellar for a month or so? The unheated space of a garage is a good spot to store a cooler filled with the end-of-the-season green tomatoes, onions, pumpkins, or squash, all of which prefer a drier climate and slightly warmer temperatures than those found in most basement root cellars. Use a thermometer first to test for below-freezing temperatures inside the garage.

6. Do you have a window well that could be adapted as a root cellar to take advantage of below-earth temperatures and moisture? Top off the window well with hardware cloth to discourage rodents and a wooden cover to seal in the right conditions. If severe cold comes, you can open the basement window to allow "heat" from the basement to raise the ambient temperature of the well.

7. Does the area have proper ventilation to keep mold and bacteria from forming?

Classic Built-in Basement Root Cellar

Old houses had basements with dirt floors, which helped keep the temperatures low and steady and the air moist. A built-in basement (about 8 feet by 10 feet) is plenty large for storage purposes for today's gardeners. You can use your basement even if it has a cement floor. If it's the right temperature, you can keep the floor moist by sprinkling water on it periodically or by keeping pans of water in the basement.

Check the temperature frequently before selecting a final spot. To build a small storage area in your basement, select a spot away from the heat of the chimney and fur-

TIP
. . . .

A garage is usually a convenient location for produce storage. When you are in a hurry to prepare dinner, you'll find it easy to access.

TIP
. . . .

Don't wash produce before storing it in a root cellar. Even if it then dries before storage, the added moisture is sometimes enough to encourage mold and therefore spoiling. Instead, wipe each dirty piece gently with a clean cotton-gloved hand. Treat all produce tenderly.

Old industrial packing pallets are great for elevating containers from a dirt or gravel basement floor.

TIP

· · · · · · · ·

When it's first harvested, store produce in the refrigerator to remove the ambient heat. This takes the cooling "load" off your root cellar. The cool shade of a north-facing porch or garage works well, too.

nace, since air close to heat sources is warmer. The north wall, I usually find, is best. The northeast corner walls are the very coldest, and if your partition is in the corner, you need only construct two walls to make your storage room.

Be sure to include a foundation vent in the room to regulate the temperature. In the fall or spring, when outside temperatures shoot up during the day, keep the vent to the outside closed to prevent warm air from raising the temperature too much. When outside temperatures suddenly drop to freezing, close the vents immediately.

Obviously, a thermometer is a necessity in a root cellar. Train yourself to check the temperatures outside and inside the root cellar frequently.

The walls and ceiling should be made of nonporous materials so you can clean them easily. Bins and storage shelves should be removable for cleaning. Take them outside on a dry summer day and dry brush them, or scrub them with soapy water. Make certain they are completely dry before replacing them in the root cellar. Open all the air vents and the door and let the breeze blow through the entire room.

OTHER KINDS OF COLD STORAGE

If you don't have a root cellar and aren't in a position to build one, try another method of storing your produce. There are many easy and economical ways to keep food during the winter months that don't require elaborate measures.

OUTSIDE STAIRWAY

The outside basement steps can be a simple storage area for root crops. Construct an inside basement door at the bottom of your steps to prevent the heat from your basement from warming the stairwell area. As long as you make room to walk up and down them, the steps themselves make great shelves for storing containers of produce. If the outside air gets too cold, you can open the basement door at the bottom of the steps to warm up the stairwell. As you go down the steps to the basement, and away from the outside door, the temperature will be warmer. Set pans of water on the steps to keep the air moist, if necessary. This works well for most vegetable root crops and for apples and pears. Remember, however, not to store apples, pears, cabbage, or turnips near other produce. The fruit will emit gases that will spoil other produce, and the vegetables give off odors that spoil other produce.

Ice Chest

A Styrofoam ice chest is a perfect cooler for crops such as apples and green tomatoes. As long as you have an unheated place that does not actually freeze, these coolers can work well for short periods of time.

The benefit of using something as portable as an ice chest is the ease of moving it. This is especially helpful when you want to keep foods in separate areas.

Window Well

A window well is protected by the house itself and the ground. Beets store particularly well in this kind of space. Store food in covered baskets, buckets, wooden boxes, coolers, or cans and place the container in the window well. Although it is not as constant in temperature as a cellar storage room, you can vary the temperature by opening and closing the window, allowing the heat from the basement to warm up a snow-covered well in the most severe weather. I like to cover the well with pieces of wood, although screening works, also. Wood usually keeps out sunlight and large pests and helps buffer the outside temperatures. However, wood will not keep out field mice or other rodents.

An outside basement stairwell makes an excellent root cellar, as long as access is not blocked.

. . . .

Prolonging the harvest is an easy and exciting way to "store" the hardier root vegetables. We once had newly dug potatoes for Christmas dinner! This method works best, however, in milder climates.

As the temperature falls, cover your root vegetables with a 6-inch layer of straw. Good drainage is essential. In late winter, dig up the root crops and prepare them for storage in your root cellar. Leave leeks in the ground long into the winter and dig them up as needed. Carrots, beets, and potatoes will keep this way, too.

UNDERGROUND STORAGE

Burying produce is another way to preserve food over the winter, and it is successful even in areas with harsh winters. The buried or partially buried produce containers should be kept separate from one another, and if snow is likely to make them hard to find, you should mark their location. It's also important that water drain away from the containers. Sturdy covered wooden boxes, barrels, or plastic garbage containers provide good protection for underground storage. A large cylindrical piece of tile or drainage pipe can also be used.

When you dig the hole, remove any large stones that would touch your underground storage container, as stones conduct frost.

Regardless of what kind of container you choose, put 3 inches of clean sand in the bottom and a finishing layer on top for insulation. Layer produce between 3-inch layers of clean sand. Produce of different types can be stored in the same containers in a pinch, except for cabbage, turnips, apples, and pears.

Partially bury a wooden barrel, sloping the ground away from it to prevent groundwater from running in, then cover with plastic sheeting to keep rain out. Top with 6 inches of straw for insulation.

A wooden box wrapped in hardware cloth to keep pests out can be completely buried, creating a protected pit for the produce. Slope the ground away to avoid groundwater runoff. Cover the box with a secure wooden lid.

Buried galvanized garbage cans also provide effective storage. These metal cans are pest-proof and work well as long as you treat the produce kindly, store it in layers of clean sand, and keep groundwater away. Cover the top with plastic sheeting and 6 inches of straw, depending on how cold your climate is. You may need to cover it with more straw for colder winter weather. Use the straw later in the spring for mulch.

STRAW-BALE STORAGE

Without the protection of the earth, storing produce aboveground requires another method of insulation. Straw-bale storage does just that while allowing easy access to food. Straw bales can be a wonderful insulating material for aboveground storage. However, this method is practical only in areas that have fairly mild winters. The insulation straw provides is not enough to protect produce from consistently very cold temperatures. Straw is superior to hay, because bales of hay have seeds in them that will germinate and cause problems later in the spring.

When using straw bales for food storage, choose a well-drained location. Play it safe by digging a trench around your straw-bale aboveground storage site to prevent rain water from running in. Build a rectangle of straw bales approximately two bales long and one bale wide. Lay the bales end to end, and line the "floor" with about 3 inches of loose straw. Line the hole created by the bales with hardware cloth or place the food to be stored in covered wooden boxes to keep small animals from making a meal of your produce. Carefully place the produce in the hole or boxes, separating each layer with about 3 inches of loose straw. Top off the produce with another layer of loose straw. Close the pit or box with either more hardware cloth or a wooden top. Place two straw bales over the top, and prop them up with bricks or stones to let a little air circulate. If the weather turns severely cold, remove the bricks or stones and close the extra air vent created by the elevated bales. The baled straw will provide enough ventilation as is. When the warmer weather of spring arrives, you can again prop up the top bales with stones or bricks for added ventilation.

The straw-bale storeroom is simple to construct and makes it very easy to remove needed produce. It is ideal for carrots, beets, potatoes, and turnips. Use the straw for mulching your garden in the spring.

MATERIALS FOR COLD STORAGE

Fortunately, root cellaring requires no expensive or specialized equipment. The beauty is that you can use what you already have — your home, commonly found containers, produce from your garden — and creatively choose a natural way of preserving simply by putting your food to rest after harvest in just the right spot.

Consider how much produce you'll need to store, first of all, and be aware of the size restrictions of your storage sites. You don't want to save more than you'll be able to accommodate. Then get in the habit of collecting containers and packing materials throughout the year, wherever you come across them. Wooden fruit crates or banana cartons can stack in out-of-the-way corners for use in the fall, and most can be reused from year to year.

Make sure the storage container you choose is free of any substance that would affect the quality of the food you store. Contamination from diseased vegetables will spoil your produce, and the odor and scent of gasoline, cedar, or any other strong-smelling substance can be absorbed by vegetables. Wash plastic and metal containers before using them for storage, and make sure they are dry before you pack produce in them.

Many types of containers are appropriate for cold storage.

Cold Storing Fruits and Vegetables

The following list contains the produce that I have had the best experience with storing in a root cellar. If you don't see a fruit or vegetable listed, it probably is not a good keeper for root cellars. No need wasting valuable produce or your energy on items that will have an unsatisfactory outcome. Start small the first year and keep notes on successes and failures for the next year.

Never bring a big load of just-harvested produce into your root-cellar area. The warmth of all that extra bulk will certainly change the temperature of the root cellar. If at all possible, chill the produce first. Refrigerators will do this quickly, of course, but it's impractical for some folks to use up all their refrigerator space to chill produce for a day. Instead, try cooling the produce in stages. Store it in a cool garage for a day or so, then move it to the root cellar. Two drawbacks are that the garage can have gas and oil fumes, and the temperature in a garage can't always be controlled, but for a day or so, if the temperature remains cooler than outdoors, precooling there can work quite well. Find other spots around your home that remain cooler than the average outdoor temperature, such as a porch on the north side or a shaded spot.

Preparing Fruits for the Root Cellar

If at all possible, keep the fruit in your root cellar well away from your vegetables. Apples and pears give off ethylene gas, which causes potatoes to sprout.

The fruits listed here are the best for storing in a root cellar. Refer to the index in this book for alternative preservation methods if you don't see your fruit of choice listed here.

Apples. Wrap apples in newspaper or nest them in straw or clean, dry leaves. Apples "breathe" more than most other fruits and give off a pungent aroma, so keep them away from other produce. Store in boxes or barrels, trash cans or buckets. Cover with 2 inches of packing material on top.

Nest apples in layers of clean straw.

Grapefruit. No wrap is needed for grapefruit. Store them in boxes, cartons, baskets, or coolers with no covering.

Grapes. Cut into very small bunches and cushion them with straw between layers. Use cartons, boxes, or bins and cover with a top layer of packing material. Be sure to use a shallow storage container — too many grapes on top of each other can crush the bottom layer.

Pears. Store while still green. Wrap pears in newspaper or nest them in straw or clean, dry leaves. Store in boxes or barrels, trash cans or buckets, covering with 2 inches of packing material on top. Store pears away from other fruits and vegetables.

PREPARING VEGETABLES FOR COLD STORAGE

If you're new to cold storage, start with the most commonly stored root vegetables: beets, carrots, potatoes, rutabagas, and turnips. If a particular fruit or vegetable is not listed here, check the index for other methods of preserving it.

Remember to keep vegetables separate from the fruits in your root cellar if at all possible. Cabbage and turnips can emit permeating odors for fruits like apples and pears.

Beets. Harvest after nights reach 30°F. Cut off most of the green tops and leave the tails intact. Use boxes, cans, baskets, coolers, or buckets, all lined with a plastic bag. Layer the beets with sawdust or moist sand; use peat moss or straw for outside storage, such as window wells. Beets prefer higher humidity, as much as 95 percent. You can also leave the beets in the ground covered with 6 inches of straw and harvest as needed.

Cabbage. Remove the outer leaves and roots and wrap in newspaper. Store in boxes or cartons in your basement, or leave the roots on and store in damp sand in an outside area, such as a window well.

Carrots. Cut off most of the green tops. Use boxes, cans, or buckets lined with a plastic bag. Layer the carrots with sawdust or moist sand; use peat moss or straw for outside

Layer beets with sawdust or moist sand.

window-well storage. You can also leave carrots in the ground, cover them with 6 inches of straw, and then harvest them as needed.

Cauliflower. Cut off the roots and leave the leaves intact. Use covered boxes or baskets with moist sand layers.

Celery. Leave on the roots and leaves; stand upright in very moist sand.

Endive. Leave on the roots; stand upright in very moist sand.

Horseradish. Harvest after nights reach 30°F. Cut off most of the green tops and leave the tails intact. Use boxes, cans, or buckets lined with a plastic bag. Layer the horse-radish with sawdust or moist sand; use peat moss or straw for outside storage, such as window wells.

Kohlrabi. Harvest after nights reach 30°F. Cut off most of the green tops and leave the tails intact. Use boxes, cans, or buckets lined with a plastic bag. Layer the kohlrabi with sawdust or moist sand; use peat moss or straw for outside storage.

Leeks. Harvest after nights reach 30°F. Cut off most of the green tops and leave the tails intact. Use boxes, cans, or buckets lined with a plastic bag. Layer the leeks with sawdust or moist sand; use peat moss or straw for outside storage. You can also leave leeks in the ground, cover them with 6 inches of straw, and harvest as needed.

Onions. Condition onions by letting them dry after digging. Put them outside in the shade on newspaper, turning them several times, for about 10 to 14 days. If the weather turns wet, bring the onions inside on newspapers. Let them "harden off," or dry, somewhat. As the tops dry, braid them together for hanging or place them in old stockings, tying a knot between each onion, and store in a cool, dry place. Hang near the ceiling of the root cellar (the driest place) or in the attic, where it's cool but dry.

Parsnips. Harvest after nights reach 30°F. Cut off most of the green tops and leave the tails intact. Use boxes, cans, or buckets lined with a plastic bag. Layer the parsnips with sawdust or moist sand; use peat moss or straw for outside storage. Parsnips love the frozen ground

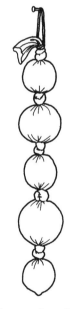

Hang onions in old stockings.

Store potatoes in a covered box in a dark, very moist location.

TIP

. . . .

If produce begins to sprout, your root cellar is too warm.

of a dormant garden (no wonder they are so popular in northern Europe). Try leaving them in the ground and digging them up as you need them. Beware of a warm spell, though, because you don't want them to thaw and then freeze again.

Potatoes. Dig after the vines have been dead about 2 weeks, or dig when it's no hotter than 70°F and not raining. Allow the potato skins to toughen in moist 70°F air in a nonwindy place (not in the sun) for about 2 weeks. Store at about 40°F with dirt on the skins in covered boxes or cartons in a dark, very moist place. The cover will keep out light and, therefore, prevent green skins or sprouting, which indicates the presence of a poisonous alkaloid that has formed due to exposure to light. (Dispose of those potatoes.) Storage at 40°F helps prevent sugars from forming and thereby changing the taste. Store potatoes away from other produce, especially apples. You can also leave potatoes in the ground, cover them with 6 inches of straw, and harvest as needed.

Pumpkins. Harvest when very mature, before frost, with the stems attached. Let them cure for about 2 weeks in 70°F temperatures so the skins will toughen. Wash pumpkins with a mild bleach solution to prevent mold from forming during storage. Another method that works well is to wipe them with a soft cloth moistened with vegetable oil to deter molds. Store on a shelf in a dry, 55°F place. Don't pile them up, as their weight may crush the bottom layer. Try storing them on the top shelf near the ceiling of the root cellar if it's dry.

Radishes. Cut off most of the green tops and leave the tails intact. Use boxes, cans, or buckets lined with a plastic bag. Layer the radishes with sawdust or moist sand; use peat moss or straw for outside storage.

Rutabagas. Cut off most of the green tops and leave the tails intact. Use boxes, cans, or buckets lined with a plastic bag. Layer the rutabagas with sawdust or moist sand; use peat moss or straw for outside storage. You may also keep rutabagas in an inside root cellar. Wrap them in plastic wrap to prevent their strong odor from permeating other produce. (This takes the place of the layer of wax almost always found on supermarket rutabagas.)

Winter squash. Harvest when very mature, before frost, with the stems attached. Let them cure for about 2 weeks in 70°F temperatures so the skins will toughen. Wash squash with a mild bleach solution to prevent mold from forming during storage. Another method that works well is to wipe them with a cloth moistened with vegetable oil to deter molds. Store on a shelf in a dry, 55°F place. Don't pile them up, as their weight may crush the bottom layer. Try the top shelf near the ceiling of the root cellar if it's dry.

Green tomatoes. Harvest before the first frost without the stems attached. Wash and dry thoroughly; store in shallow cartons or boxes packed with straw, leaves, or shredded paper to prevent the weight of the top layer from crushing the bottom layer. Put in a cool place, such as the attic or an enclosed back porch, where the temperature range is between 55°F and 70°F.

Turnips. Cut off most of the green tops and leave the tails intact. Use boxes, cans, or buckets lined with a plastic bag. Layer the turnips with sawdust or moist sand; use peat moss or straw for outside storage. You may also keep turnips in an inside root cellar. Wrap them in plastic wrap to prevent their strong odor from permeating other produce. (This takes the place of the layer of wax almost always found on supermarket turnips.)

Cleaning and Maintenance of Root Cellars

Clean and air out your storage area before each season begins. Scrub all containers with hot, soapy water and place them in the open air for a few days in the warm sun.

During the winter, check your cellar frequently. Remove overripe produce and use immediately, if possible. If it

To keep out rodents, stuff cracks or holes in a cellar wall with steel wool.

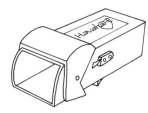

You may wish to try a live mouse trap.

TIP
· · · · · · · · ·
To discourage smaller pests, such as insects, sprinkle bay leaves on the storage shelves.

shows signs of spoiling — such as soft spots, drainage, shriveling, mold, mildew, off odor, or other decay — dispose of it at once. It makes a good addition to your compost pile.

A Word about Pests

Be sure to watch out for rodents and other critters that would like to feast on your "rooty booty."

Mice can be a real problem. Obviously, you'll want to fill in every crack and cranny of your root cellar's walls with steel wool. Try not to exterminate mice, since rodents are the favorite entrée of many wild birds, reptiles, and other animals and do serve a useful purpose on the food chain. What a disappointment, though, when rodents eat away at your cellar bounty — not to mention the safety and health hazards of runaway breeding mice.

The kindest way of dealing with this problem is a live trap. This is great for capturing an occasional creature that comes in from the cold in fall's first freeze.

Mouse bait also works for a larger infestation, but, of course, is not as environmentally kind. The poison makes the rodent very thirsty and, theoretically, it leaves the premises looking for water before dying. But the mouse could simply wander to a dark corner or find shelter in your walls before expiring, resulting in the pungent odor of decomposition.

Folklore has it that borax sprinkled around the shelves and floors of root cellars can help control pests. However, the Environmental Protection Agency has not approved borax for this purpose and therefore does not recommend using it.

My recommendation for keeping your root cellar free of pests is to get a mousetrap on legs — a cat. A country cat can be a real joy. When hunting rodents, cats are following their intended purpose in life!

CHAPTER 9

Gifts of Preserved Food

A HOMEMADE JAR OF FOOD given in love is one of the finest gifts available. And the pleasure when you take the time to decorate it creatively rewards both the maker and the receiver. Use the ideas that follow as a springboard for your own creations. Creativity is really the art of seeing. Teach yourself to look at different containers, for example, and not be locked into only putting beans in a bean pot, or only serving tea or coffee in a cup and saucer.

Once you learn to think this way, you'll never view life in the same way again. You are broadened and expanded by creative thinking rather than diminished. The more expansive your thinking, the more you share with others, then the more that begins to come back to you. It is like priming a pump. I used to marvel at how my dad could add just a little water to the hand pump at his fish camp and, after a few tries, the water would come gushing out of the spout. I realize now that this is a metaphor for life. Give and you will receive — but save a little for yourself so the water will come out of the pump the next time!

PLANNING FOR GIFT GIVING

I start at the beginning of the calendar year, right after the holidays, to organize my ideas for the coming season. I set aside a special closet in which to store ideas, containers, and decorations as I come across them. When you set aside items as the year unfolds instead of doing crisis-intervention

Save items you can use for decorating gifts.

shopping in December or the middle of canning season, creating gifts becomes a joy, not a drudgery.

When it is too cold to garden, you can learn a lot about produce by reading the colorful seed catalogs that begin arriving right after Christmas. It's fun, when there's snow on the ground, to begin planning your springtime garden and anticipating the harvest. Think how rich you will feel to have jars ready for filling when the harvest season comes. Then think how marvelous it will be to have your Christmas shopping completed long before the deadline! When the next holiday season rolls around, you may have more leisure time to celebrate with your family, to consider the real meaning of the holidays, or to just plain relax and enjoy yourself.

Not only is it rewarding to share, I believe it also must be just as rewarding to receive, judging from the reactions of people who receive my produce or gift of prepared food. Of course, you wouldn't want to give a basketful of zucchini to a fellow gardener in August. And you might not want to give a basket of homemade jams to a neighbor who makes fruit spreads. However, there are plenty of folks who don't garden or preserve their food who would love to receive some as a gift.

Gift giving can become a way of life. Because I am a cyclical-thinking person, nothing pleases me more than growing the food, harvesting it, cooking it, and then giving it away to friends or preparing it for my family. Nature is my biggest ally when I'm searching for suitable decorations for gift packages of food. You can ask my friends in my walking group, because I rarely walk without stopping to pick up something — a cone, an acorn, a thistle — that can be used to decorate a gift package. I'll admit that it takes storage space to save all the items, but the pleasure of collecting and the savings in storing far outweigh the disadvantages.

COLLECTING CONTAINERS

Store jars you collect in a cardboard box in the garage or attic. As you finish your canned goods from last season, clean the jars and place them in the box for the coming season. Neighbors frequently return canning jars after they have consumed your food offerings. Flea markets and garage sales have all kinds of containers available.

Don't limit yourself to canning containers. Look at potential containers with other preserving processes in mind, such as storage for dried foods or no-process preserving, such as pickles or chutneys. Even the simplest baby-food jar can be spruced up for gift giving.

Train your eye to spot unusual containers that can be recycled — a maple syrup bottle with distinctive handles, a purchased preserves jar in that octagonal shape with a "gingham"-printed lid, a cheese crock. These make good containers for gifts that need only refrigeration.

After you've collected your containers, soak off the labels, clean them thoroughly, and sterilize them.

Here are some other ideas for attractive containers for your preserved-food gift:

Decorate jars and bottles to make wonderfully unique gift packages.

- Be on the lookout in hardware stores for cork assortments to use as stoppers for small-necked bottles you have saved.
- Use cheese crocks for herbal butters or other flavored spreads.
- Long-necked bottles with attached lids, such as grolsch bottles, make perfect containers for flavored vinegars or other homemade dressings.
- Spray the lids of junior baby-food jars a colorful shade of nontoxic paint and use the jars for spicy mustards.
- Save the aluminum pie plates that are given to you or that come with grocery store goods. Recycle them for a freezer casserole, tied in colorful wrap, to give to an under-the-weather friend.

You can use a variety of containers for packaging preserved foods.

Save Fabrics and Other Items

I never throw away even a small piece of ribbon left over from the end of a project. Sometimes it's just the right size to tie around the neck of a bottle of flavored vinegar. Who says the ribbon has to have a bow? A knot is just as effective when it has a dried flower tucked in it.

Fabric scraps can be a great source of decoration for food gifts. If you don't sew, ask a friend who does. Most folks who sew have more scraps than they know what to do with and are grateful to recycle them for creative use.

What follows are other ideas you can use to spur your creativity with things that are left over or no longer usable for their original purpose.

Glue dried acorns or other seedpods to a lid and spray the lid and acorns gold. Add a matching bow.

- Save a dried flower or cut a piece of holiday greens from your garden to incorporate in a bow.
- For an old-fashioned lid cover, recycle those hand-crocheted coasters or doilies Aunt Lil made years ago.
- Cut out circles of brown paper bags, then carve a pattern in a potato, dip it in paint, and press it firmly onto the paper for a fun decoration. Tie raffia around the lid to hold down the circle.
- Brown lunch bags can be decorated and used to hold your gift. Dress up the bag by pasting cutout photos from magazines that relate to what's inside.
- Glue alternating colors of yarn around the lid of a jar, and use the same colors to attach a gift tag. Glue yarn into a pattern on top of the lid.
- If you have the time, you can sew lace or other edging on your cloth covers for a frilly finished look.
- Have a scrap party with friends to get a good assortment of fabrics. Everyone can bring one or two pieces of clothing that are being discarded and share a variety of fabric circles to decorate food jars.

CREATIVE LABELS

No matter what you give, be sure your preserved food is clearly labeled with the contents, the date preserved, your name, the date by which it should be consumed, and how it should be stored. If the food needs to be used in a particular way or is especially good in a specific recipe, be sure to include instructions for that as well.

Hunt for colorful labels in stationery, gardening, and hardware stores. Sometimes the labels that are the most fun are not intended to be labels at all. Whatever you use for a label, I recommend attaching it with rubber cement. Here are some other creative ideas for labeling.

Cut a circle of fabric 2 inches wider than the diameter of the jar top. Use pinking shears for a finished look.

- How about a manila old-style tag found in office supply stores to use as a label? Write with a colorful marker or glue it on a colorful sticker. Suspend the tag with colored string that comes with the tag or add your own ribbon.
- Use your local copy store for photocopying snapshots of the family to use as labels for gifts of food.
- Don't underestimate the appeal of a plain brown paper bag torn into an interesting shape and used as a label. This is inexpensive and convenient as well.
- Include recipes for a meal that features the food gift. This can provide extra enjoyment for someone who loves to cook.
- Stencil borders around labels, varying the colors.
- You may want to print your own labels; a number of computer programs generate them, and it's an inexpensive solution. Cut them out and use rubber cement to attach to the jar. Color them with magic markers, if you wish.
- If you have access to a color copier, you can use magazine pictures to create labels.

Secure the fabric circle with a rubber band.

Add a ribbon and a bow to cover the rubber band.

Gifts of Food

In Spain I once saw a proverb on a restaurant wall that, loosely translated, means: "Wine is better in a beautiful glass." How true that is of many gifts of food, as well. Presentation can be half the fun. Let the ideas that follow get your imagination going.

- When you make that special mustard and ladle it into a decorative recycled crockery jar, tie a wooden spreader or serving spoon to the lid with decorative ribbon or raffia. For that really special someone, include a homemade picnic sausage along with the mustard. Elaborate on this theme and place it in a picnic basket packed for two to celebrate a special anniversary.

Give a picnic basket filled with homemade food as an anniversary gift.

- Sealing wax, available in stationery and gift stores, will make your bottle of flavored vinegar look very expensive. It's great fun to use, and it smells good as well. If you can't find sealing wax, you may want to try dripping candle wax over the cork topping the bottle.
- Ribbon ideas are endless. Try raffia, green garden twine, or the short end from another project. Even a 6-inch piece of leftover grosgrain ribbon can usually do for the neck of a small bottle.
- Harvest a living tossed salad from your garden as a special treat. Use a large clay pot and replant it with several heads of bibb lettuce, roots and all, a parsley plant, and a parcel of fresh chives or an oregano plant. Include a bottle of mustard vinaigrette and a couple of fresh tomatoes. For the finishing touch, copy the dressing recipe on an index card. What a welcome surprise this will be!

A living tossed salad makes a novel gift.

- Fill a basket with lettuce from your garden for a neighbor's dinner. Stack it root-end down in a recycled peach basket. Be sure to cut it just before you give it, for it will wilt in an hour or so. Include a jar of herbal vinegar to go with it.

- That decorative jar that bubble bath came in, once it has been thoroughly cleaned, will make a wonderful container for your favorite herbal-blend tea. You can enjoy the container twice as long and save money as well.
- When you dry your Italian tomatoes, pack some in oil as a gift. Although flavored oils must be used immediately, a jar of Italian dried tomatoes in oil and a box of angel-hair pasta could make the basis of a delicious dinner that very day the oil was made.
- My friend Marion packs her dried apples in a quart jar to give as a gift the whole family enjoys. I left the filled jar out on the counter and the apples disappeared very quickly as snacks. Of course, other dried fruits work just as well. Marion just happens to live in an apple orchard. Add a refrigerator magnet in an apple motif to the metal top of the jar.
- Save the little spice and herb bottles that come from the grocery store. These containers make great resources for your own dried herbs the next season.
- One use for stale bread is to make giant plastic bags of herb-flavored croutons for salads or soups. Tie the bags with a bow of your choice. Croutons can be frozen, but they will also keep on the shelf for a week or so. To make the croutons, sauté bread cubes in an oil of your choice and sprinkle with garlic powder plus a variety of dried herbs, such as parsley, thyme, oregano, and rosemary.
- Layer colorful beans in a quart jar that is decorative but not safe for the canning process and create a wonderful New Year's gift. Be sure to include black-eyed peas and the recipe for Eight-Bean Soup (see page 108).
- Try a frozen fruit apple pie (see page 172) as a gift the whole family will enjoy.
- Thoroughly clean the little baskets that berries come in, add a waxed doily (from a craft or candy-making supply store), and fill with an assortment of dried fruits.

TIP

Recycled aluminum pans are wonderful for storing frozen gifts. Reusing the aluminum pans makes it easy for the receiver. No need to return the dish later: The receiver can recycle the already-recycled aluminum pan if it is in good shape.

A Little Something Extra

Whether or not your primary gift is food, the items from the store of preserved foods on your shelves, in your freezer, or from your root cellar can provide a unique addition to presents for any occasion. The time you spent creating something special that can't be purchased anywhere in the world adds value to your gift and will be appreciated. Here are some ideas to get you started.

- Accompany a set of special steak knives with a jar of your Corn and Zucchini Salsa (see page 57). Add a gift certificate for a selection of prime steaks from a mail-order source, if you wish.
- Your favorite grill chef will welcome a jar of your Barbecue Sauce (see page 59) along with colorful protective mitts and a new set of grilling tools. Be sure to include a long-handled brush for spreading the sauce.
- Pair a family-size pasta bowl or a set of individual bowls and the latest Parmesan cheese grater with a jar of your own Tomato Sauce (see page 62) or Spaghetti Sauce with Meat (see page 63). If the bowl is big enough, a choice of pastas could be included.
- A jar of elegant, honey-sauced Pineapple Spears (see page 73) will add just the right touch to a gift of holiday dessert plates or bowls. If you are hand carrying the gift, you could bring a plain cheesecake or some gourmet vanilla ice cream for the recipient to enjoy with the pineapple.
- Giving a glass fruit compote or soufflé dish? Fill it with a variety of your colorful homemade Fruit Leather (page 88), with the rolls standing on end. Or layer it with your home-dried fruit slices to be reconstituted for a dessert or balanced atop a pastry for a restaurant-style dried fruit garnish.
- Pack your Herb Cheese Appetizer (see page 109) with some flavorful crackers (include a frozen cold pack if you are traveling far) and present it along with a set of

martini glasses and a shaker. A jar of your Green Tomato Dip (see page 54) could be added to this cocktail party gift.

- Fill the jars of an herb and spice rack with a selection of your own dried herbs (see pages 90–93) before wrapping as a gift. Be sure to add a jar of your Herb Butter Blend (see page 99), Vegetable Seasoning Mix (see page 299), or Southwestern Spice Mix (see page 300).

- Tuck a jar of your Herbed Rice Mix (page 100) into the perfect saucepan or set of pans for a useful wedding shower gift that will give the new bride a head start on dinner for a busy night.

- Give an evening's entertainment to the Italian opera lover on your list. In a basket, tuck a well-wrapped container of Rosemary Paste for Angel-Hair Pasta (see page 143), along with the recipe, some imported pasta, a bottle of wine, and a gift of the latest CDs.

- A china or earthenware tureen makes a unique gift. It will be immediately useful if you add a container of your frozen Gazpacho (see page 148) in the summertime or Pumpkin Soup (see page 152) or Lentil and Sausage Soup (see page 154) in the winter.

- Wrap a loaf of Laura's Banana Bread (see page 170) in clear plastic wrap and place on a wooden bread board or metal bread tray. Then wrap the whole present in colorful cellophane and finish with a bow.

- Fasten an envelope containing tickets to the next antiques show around the neck of a jar of your old-fashioned Strawberry Rhubarb Jelly (see page 201). A depression-era glass or other antique jelly dish would be another perfect partner for the jelly.

- For a special surprise, add a jar of your classic Red Raspberry Preserves (see page 205) to a gift of an automatic bread maker. When the first loaf of aromatic homemade bread is baked, the perfect accompaniment will be waiting.

- Select a classic English teapot to accompany a jar of your Lime Marmalade (see page 206). You could add a flowered, quilted tea cozy and a tin of leaf tea to fill out the package, if desired.

- Give friends a Hawaiian vacation without leaving home. Pair a jar of your Lemon-Pineapple Preserves (see page 208) with a pound of Kona coffee and two individual plunger coffee makers for a tropical breakfast basket.

- Too special to hide in a peanut-butter and jelly sandwich, your Grape Jelly (see page 211) will sparkle alongside a footed glass jelly dish with a little silver spoon. Or pair it with a silver bread tray accompanied by a lace-trimmed linen liner.

- For a friend who loves to garden, arrange a potted nutmeg-scented geranium plant or two and a jar of your Nutmeg-Scented Geranium Jelly (see page 221) in a gardening basket. Add some tools and heavy-duty gardening gloves for an extra touch.

- For your favorite baker, accompany a jar of your Cranberry-Lime Curd (see page 235) with a variety of miniature tart pans. Tuck in a pastry cloth and a rolling pin stocking to make rolling out the pastry for the tart shells that much easier.

- Create a cookout kit around a jar of your Bread and Butter Pickles (see page 254). Select a good-quality disposable tablecloth, napkins, dinner and dessert plates, and tableware in coordinating colors. You can include a jar of Easy Tomato Ketchup (see page 58) or a chilled jar of homemade Basil-Shallot Mustard (see page 273) at the last minute as a bonus. Pack the items in a harvest basket that can be used to hold hamburger rolls, or place them on a sturdy matching tray that can be used for the condiments.

- Your Watermelon Rind Pickles (see page 260) are the perfect flavor partner for a traditional stew. Add a jar or two to the gift of a heavy enameled or stainless steel Dutch oven. For an additional personal touch, include several recipes for your favorite stews as well as the recipe for the pickles.

- Make up a fresh batch of your Popcorn Shaker Mix (see page 298), package it in an attractive jar with a tight lid, label it, and tie with a bow to a wrapped popcorn popper or microwave popcorn maker. The label on the jar will give a clue to what's inside.
- A jar of your home-dried Herbes de Provence (see page 298) is the ideal addition to the gift of a tablecloth, napkins, placemats, an apron, a quilted shopping bag, or a pocketbook made from a colorful Provençal fabric.
- Add a jar of your Basil Balsamic Vinegar (see page 294) to any gift of Tuscan pottery. Or make enough vinegar to fill a clear wine bottle, top it with an ornamented wine cork, and package it in an earthenware wine cooler. The addition of your personal label (see page 321) will be a plus.
- A new salad bowl is always a welcome gift. Fill a large glass or wooden salad bowl with a jar of your Fresh Herb Vinegar (see page 295) and a selection of olive oils. A set of a salad spoon and fork and a fabric lettuce bag or tea towel can be added if there is room.
- Although a beautiful jar of your Cranberry Vinegar (see page 297) could be presented at a Fourth of July party as well as at a Thanksgiving dinner, it would be the perfect gift to add to a turkey-shaped candle or a cranberry-scented candle for a November hostess gift.

APPENDIX A

· · · · · · · · · · ·

GLOSSARY OF TERMS

Acetobacters. Organisms that help convert the alcohol in fermented fruit juices into vinegars.

Acidified water. Used as a pretreatment to prevent browning in peeled or sliced fruits and vegetables, acidified water is made by combining 1 teaspoon of ascorbic acid or lemon juice per gallon of water.

Altitude adjustment. Processing times for both boiling-water bath and pressure canning are assumed to be at altitudes below 1,000 feet. Because water boils at lower temperatures as altitude increases, it is necessary to increase processing times when canning at altitudes above 1,000 feet. See page 40 for guidelines.

Ascorbic acid. Found naturally in tart fruits, ascorbic acid can be purchased either as vitamin C tablets or in crystalline form. Use it to prepare acidified water for preventing discoloration in fruits and vegetables as they are being prepared for preserving.

Bacteria. Naturally occurring microorganisms that can produce spoilage in preserved foods. Processing temperature must be high enough to destroy bacteria for successful preservation.

Blanch. To steam or dip foods in boiling water before preserving. The heat slows or stops enzymatic action, which causes ripening and browning in foods, and makes it easier to remove the skins of fruits and vegetables.

Boil. Water boils at 212°F at sea level. Canning times are based on the assumption that boiling will maintain that temperature for the prescribed processing time.

Boiling-water-bath canner. A large kettle (ideally 21–33 quarts) fitted with a jar rack and lid that is used to submerge jars of high-acid foods in boiling water for preserving.

Botulism. Extremely serious food poisoning resulting from the toxin produced when the spores of *Clostridium botulinum* are allowed to grow in the absence of air. Canned foods must be heated to a high enough temperature to destroy these spores. The presence of acid in the food retards the development of the spores, making it possible to process high-acid foods for shorter periods of time.

Citric acid. Found naturally in citrus fruits, citric acid is used to prepare acidified water for pretreating fruits and vegetables. It can also be purchased to add to tomatoes to increase their acidity for canning.

Dicalcium phosphate. A calcium salt that must be used when preparing low-sugar jams and jellies using low-methyl pectin.

Dry pack. Frozen foods that are packaged without added liquid or sugar. They are often frozen on trays as separate pieces and repackaged so that they are not frozen together.

Freezer burn. The loss of moisture, color, and flavor that occurs when foods are not wrapped in airtight packaging for freezing.

Full rolling boil. The point at which water or other liquids have been heated until the entire surface is covered with bursting bubbles. It is important to maintain this condition in boiling-water-bath canning in order to maintain the proper water temperature and in jam and jelly making to reduce the mixture by the evaporation of moisture.

Gel tests. Traditional methods used (instead of a thermometer) to tell when jams and jellies prepared without pectin have cooked long enough. See page 186 for directions.

Headspace. The space left between the top of the food and the top of the jar in canning. It must be great enough to allow room for the food to expand when heated and small enough that all air is expelled in the canning process. The required space varies because foods expand differently. Be sure to leave the proper amount of headspace as directed in the recipe.

High-acid food. Foods that contain enough naturally occurring acid to have a pH lower than 4.6. Tomatoes and most fruits are high acid and may be canned in a boiling-water-bath canner.

Hot pack. When foods have been precooked slightly before canning. This reduces shrinkage during processing and usually prevents "floating fruit."

Low-acid food. Foods that contain little naturally occurring acid and therefore have a pH higher than 4.6. Most vegetables, meats, and prepared dishes are low acid and must be processed in a pressure canner in order to be safe.

Low-methyl pectin. Derived from citrus peel, this form of pectin, with the addition of dicalcium phosphate, will gel jams and jellies without the addition of sugar. Sugar may be added for flavor only.

Mason jar. In the mid-nineteenth century, John Landis Mason designed the canning jar that we still use today. The shoulder on the jar made it easier to expel the air from it and the screw lid made it easier to produce a secure seal. Today, Mason jar has become a generic term for canning jars.

Mold. Naturally occurring fungi that thrive on fruits and vegetables. Mold was a problem when jams and jellies were preserved by coating with paraffin, but since they are easily destroyed by heat, the boiling-water-bath processing of jams and jellies recommended today has eliminated that problem.

Nonreactive. A descriptive term for cooking equipment that won't interact with acid or salt solutions to produce toxins or off flavors in the foods being prepared. Glass, enameled steel, enameled iron, and stainless steel are nonreactive and may be used for pickled and salted foods. Never use uncoated iron, copper, or aluminum cooking equipment when preparing high-acid or high-salt foods.

Open kettle. The canning of foods by heating them to boiling and placing them in a sealed sterile jar with no further processing. This is considered unsafe because it creates an atmosphere without air but does not heat the mixture high enough to destroy *C. botulinum* spores.

Pectin. The substance found in some fruits that produces a gel when cooked with sugar. Commercially prepared powdered and liquid pectin can be purchased for faster jam and jelly making, and homemade pectin solutions can be prepared from tart apples or citrus fruits.

pH. The measurement of acidity used by chemists, pH means "potential of hydrogen." Mixtures that have a high pH are low in acid; those with a low pH are high in acid. Foods with a high pH must be processed in a pressure canner in order to be safe.

Pickling lime. Also known as calcium hydroxide, pickling lime may be purchased in powdered form to use in pickling. It reacts with acid and produces crisp pickles.

Pretreatment. Preparing foods for canning or freezing, usually by blanching or soaking in acidified water to prevent browning.

Rancidity. The off flavor that develops in fats when stored in the presence of oxygen. This can be a problem in frozen meats, particularly those high in salt. For this reason, frozen meats should be dated and used within the directed storage time. See page 134 for more information.

Raw pack. The canning method in which raw foods are packed in canning jars and then processed. This is faster than precooking the foods but often causes shrinkage and floating once processed.

Rehydration. The addition of water or another liquid to dried foods to soften and restore some of their former texture and volume before using them in cooking.

Scald. Similar to blanching, scald means to dip in boiling water. It is used to loosen the skins of fruits and vegetables for peeling and to set the enzymes so the food doesn't discolor.

Screw ring. The threaded metal band that holds the vacuum lid in place before and during processing and is removed before storage. If not rusted, screw rings may be reused year after year.

Shelf life. The length of time foods will maintain their quality when stored. This varies greatly depending upon the type of food, storage method, storage temperature, and presence or absence of light and humidity.

Simmer. Gentle cooking in which the surface of the liquid barely moves. This occurs at temperatures between 180 and 200°F and is used for fragile foods, for precooking foods before processing, and in other cases where it is not necessary to heat the food to 212°F.

Spice bag. A selection of whole spices tied in cheesecloth or muslin and cooked with pickles, fruits, jams, and jellies, then removed before the products are jarred for processing. Since the spices would continue to add flavor during processing and storage and might darken the product as well, this method makes it possible to control the flavor of the final product.

Steam-pressure canner. A heavy kettle with a screw-on or other tight-fitting lid that contains a pressure gauge, a steam vent, and a safety valve, so that a vacuum can be produced within the kettle. As the pressure increases, the temperature of the steam rises above that in the normal atmosphere, thus superheating the foods and destroying the bacteria that would otherwise cause spoilage in low-acid foods.

Sterilization. Jars, lids, and other equipment are sterilized before use by submerging them in boiling water for 10 minutes to destroy any bacteria that might be present.

Stock. A flavored liquid made by long simmering meat, vegetables, fruit, or fruit peelings. The mixture is usually strained and added to fresh foods to provide increased flavor.

Syrup. A boiled mixture of sugar and water used as the liquid in canned and frozen fruits.

Vacuum lid. The rubber-rimmed replacement lid that provides the seal in canning. Vacuum lids must be new in order to safely seal. Used lids should be discarded once the jar has been opened.

Vacuum seal. The absence of air pressure that occurs in jars of canned foods once they have been processed. The vacuum keeps the jar sealed and keeps contaminants out.

Venting. The process of exhausting or forcing the air out of a canning jar during processing or out of a pressure canner before building up the pressure inside it.

Yeast. Naturally occurring fungi that cause fermentation. They are useful in the production of alcoholic beverages and breads but can cause spoilage in preserved foods. They are inactivated by freezing and destroyed by boiling-water-bath processing.

Additional definitions are found on pages 180 and 283.

Resources

All Season Homestead Helpers, Inc.
802-287-4788
www.homesteadhelpers.com
Squeezo strainers, pressure canners, and other hard-to-find canning equipment

Bernardin
Newell Brands
Fax: 905-731-3384
www.homecanning.ca
Canadian source for mason jars and other canning supplies and equipment; provides a canning help service by fax or mail and canning information on their website

Canning Pantry
Highland Brands, LLC
www.canningpantry.com
Pressure, water bath, and steam canners; pressure cookers; and other canning supplies

Cumberland General Store
800-334-4640
www.cumberlandgeneral.com
Old-time general merchandise since 1974

Kitchen Krafts, Inc.
563-535-8000
www.kitchenkrafts.com
A source of ClearJel and almost anything else you could need for preserving

Lehman Hardware & Appliances, Inc.
877-438-5346
www.lehmans.com
Serving the Amish and others without electricity with products for simple self-sufficient living since 1955

National Presto Industries, Inc.
800-877-0441
www.gopresto.com
Presto pressure canners; canning information by phone and on their website

Newell Brands
www.newellbrands.com
Producers of the Ball and Kerr lines of canning products

APPENDIX C

· · · · · · · ·

TABLE OF EQUIVALENTS

Apples . . . . 1 pound = 3 medium = 2½ cups peeled and sliced

Apricots . . . . 1 pound fresh = 8 to 10 medium = 2 cups sliced
1 pound dried = 3 cups

Asparagus . . . . 1 pound = 12 to 16 stalks = 3½ cups (in pieces)

Avocados . . . . 1 medium = 1 cup cubes

Bananas . . . . 3 to 4 = 2 cups sliced = 1½ cups mashed

Beets . . . . 1 pound = 2 cups sliced

Blueberries . . . . 1 pint = 2 cups

Broccoli . . . . 1-pound head = 2 cups florets

Cabbage . . . . 1 pound = 4½ cups raw, shredded or sliced
1 pound = 2½ cups cooked

Carrots . . . . 1 pound = 6 or 7 = 3 cups sliced or shredded

Cauliflower . . . . 1½ pounds = 2 cups cooked

Celery . . . . 1 stalk = ½ cup sliced or chopped

Cherries (fresh) . . . . 1 pound = 2 cups pitted

Chicken . . . . 3½ pounds, whole = 3 cups cooked meat
1 large boned breast = 2 cups cooked meat

Corn . . . . 1 plump ear = ½ cup kernels

Cranberries . . . . 1 12-ounce bag = 3 cups
(fresh or frozen) 2 ounces dried (by weight) = ¼ cup

Cucumbers . . . . 1 medium = 1½ cups sliced

Currants . . . . ¼ pound fresh = 1 cup
⅓ pound dried = 1 cup

Eggplant . . . . 1½ pounds = 2½ cups diced

Garlic . . . . 2 medium cloves = 1 teaspoon minced

Grapefruit . . . . 1 medium = ½ pound = 1 cup sections

Grapes . . . . 1 pound = 2½ cups

Ginger (fresh) . . . . 1-inch piece = 2 tablespoons grated or chopped

Green beans . . . . 1 pound = 3 cups fresh = 2½ cups cooked

Herbs (general) .... 1 tablespoon fresh = 1 teaspoon dried

Lemons .... 1 medium = 3 tablespoons juice, 2 teaspoons grated zest

Lentils .... 1 cup dried = 3 cups cooked

Limes .... 1 medium = 1½ to 2 tablespoons juice, 1 teaspoon grated zest

Mushrooms (fresh) .... ½ pound = 2 cups sliced

Nectarines .... 1 pound = 3 or 4 = 2 cups peeled and sliced

Okra .... 1 pound = 22 to 28 small pods = 5 cups

Onions .... 1 medium = ¾ cup sliced or chopped

Oranges .... 1 medium = ⅓ cup juice, 2 to 3 tablespoons grated zest

Peaches .... 1 pound = 4 medium = 2 cups peeled and sliced

Pears .... 1 pound = 3 medium = 2 cups peeled and sliced

Peas .... 1 pound pods = 1 cup shelled
1 cup or ½ pound dried split = 2½ cups cooked

Peppers (bell) .... 1 large = 1 cup chopped

Pineapple (fresh) .... 1 medium = 3 cups peeled and diced

Plums .... 1 pound = 8 medium = 2½ cups pitted

Pumpkin .... 1 pound = 1 cup cooked and puréed

Raisins .... 1 pound = 3 cups

Raspberries .... 1 pint = 1¾ to 2 cups

Rhubarb .... 1 pound = 2 cups cooked

Scallions .... 1 bunch = ⅓ cup chopped (whites only)

Shallots .... 1 large = 1 tablespoon minced

Squash (summer) .... 1 pound = 3½ cups sliced

Squash (winter) .... 1 pound = 1 cup cooked and puréed

Strawberries .... 1 pint = 2 cups sliced

Sugar, granulated .... 1 pound = 2¼ cups

Sugar, brown .... 1 pound = 2¼ cups (firmly packed)

Sweet potatoes .... 3 medium = 1 pound = 3 cups sliced

Tomatillos .... 1 pound = 10 to 12

Tomatoes .... 1 pound = 3 medium = 1½ cups peeled, seeded, and chopped

Zucchini .... 1 pound = 3½ cups sliced

APPENDIX D

• • • • • • • • • • •

Converting U.S. Recipe Measurements to Metric

Use the following formulas for converting U.S. measurements to metric. Since the conversions are not exact, it's important to convert the measurements for all of the ingredients to maintain the same proportions as those in the original recipe.

When the Measurement Given Is	Multiply It By	To Convert To
Teaspoons	4.93	milliliters
Tablespoons	14.79	milliliters
Fluid ounces	29.57	milliliters
Cups (liquid)	236.59	milliliters
Cups (liquid)	.237	liters
Cups (dry)	275.31	milliliters
Cups (dry)	.275	liters
Pints (liquid)	473.18	milliliters
Pints (liquid)	.473	liters
Pints (dry)	550.61	milliliters
Pints (dry)	.551	liters
Quarts (liquid)	946.36	milliliters
Quarts (liquid)	.946	liters
Quarts (dry)	1,101.22	milliliters
Quarts (dry)	1.101	liters
Gallons	3.785	liters
Ounces	28.35	grams
Pounds	.454	kilograms
Inches	2.54	centimeters
Degrees Fahrenheit	$\frac{5}{9}$ (temperature − 32)	degrees Celsius (Centigrade)

While standard metric measurements for dry ingredients are given as units of mass, U.S. measurements are given as units of volume. Therefore, the conversions listed above for dry ingredients are given in the metric equivalent of volume.

INDEX

Page references in *italic* indicate charts; those in **bold** indicate recipes.

P

Packaging
    for cold storage, 310
    dried foods, 85
    frozen foods, 115–16, 131, 132
Paraffin, perils of, 181, 189
Parsnips, *21, 303*, 313–14
Pasta and rosemary paste, **143**
Pasteur, Louis, 23
Pasteurizing foods
    and canning, 23–24, 32, 42
    and drying, 84–85
    and freezing, 85
    by heat, 85
Pâté of Chicken Livers, **141**
Peaches
    canning of, *10, 51*
    drying of, *81, 86–87*
    freezing of, *127*
    jam, spiced, **210**
    juicing of, *183*
    and pectin, *178*
    pie, filling, **76**
    preserves, old-fashioned, **209**
    preserving methods for, *18*
Pears
    butter, **236**
    butter, spiced, **138**
    canning of, *10, 51*
    cold storage of, *303,* 312
    drying of, *86–87*
    and pectin, *178*
    preserving methods for, *18*
    relish, **275**
Peas
    canning of, *10, 50*
    drying of, *86–87*
    freezing of, *121*
    preserving methods for, *21*
Pectin
    and fast-cook method, 178, 184
    in fruit, *178*
    and fruit spreads, 5, 176, 177–81

liquid or powdered, 178
low-methyl, 180–81, 193
making your own, 178, **179**
and ripeness, 177, 178, 180
and slow-cook method,
    177–78, 185–86
Peppers
    canning of, *10, 50*
    drying of, *86–87*
    and eggplant, in garlic oil, **55**
    freezing of, *121*
    preserving methods for, *21*
Pesticides, use of, 8
Pesto with green bell peppers,
    144
Pests, cold storage, 316
Pickled
    asparagus, **266**
    Brussels sprouts, **264**
    cauliflower, **265**
    garlic, **263**
    vegetable chunks, mixed, **279**
Pickles. *See also* Boiling-water-
    bath, canning; High-acid
    foods
    bread and butter, **254**
    crocks for, 244
    cucumbers, spicy frozen, **261**
    dill, brined old-fashioned, **256**
    dill, refrigerator fresh-pack, **255**
    equipment for, 242–43
    evaluation of, 249
    green and gold, refrigerator,
        262
    and headspace, 246
    and herbs, 239–40
    history of, 237
    ingredients for, 238–39
    jars, filling, 246
    jars, sterilization of, 246
    jars for, 243–44
    making of, **250**
    mustard, two-day, **259**
    recipes, **253**

relish, sweet, **267**
and salt, 242
and spices, 239–40
storage, 248
super-sweets, refrigerator, **258**
sweeteners, 240
varieties of, 238
water, 241
watermelon rind, **260**
Pickling
    salt, 11
    spice, mixed, **257**
Pies
    apple crumb, **172**
    apple filling, **75**
    cherry filling, **77**
    peach filling, **76**
Pineapples
    drying of, *81*
    freezing of, *127*
    sherbet, **171**
    spears, **73**
Plums
    canning of, *10, 51*
    chutney, refrigerator, **277**
    drying of, *86–87*
    freezing of, *127*
    juicing of, *183*
    and pectin, 5, *178*
    preserving methods for, *19*
Popcorn shaker mix, **298**
Pork
    Italian, marinated, **158**
    roll, Oriental, **157**
Potatoes, *21, 303*, 314
Poultry. *See* Meats
Preserves. *See also* Fruit spreads
    blackberry, **203**
    blackberry, cranberry, and pink
        grapefruit, **204**
    blueberry and cherry, **214**
    definition of, 180
    lemon-pineapple, **208**
    lemons, **234**

STOCK UP ON KITCHEN CREATIVITY WITH MORE BOOKS FROM STOREY

The Backyard Homestead Book of Kitchen Know-How by Andrea Chesman

Get the most from your homegrown foods with this friendly guide to gathering, preserving, and eating the fruits of your labor. You'll learn how to can fresh produce, mill flour, render lard, make butter and cheese, and much more!

Fermented Vegetables
by Kirsten K. Shockey & Christopher Shockey

Get to work making your own kimchi, pickles, sauerkraut, and more with this colorful and delicious guide. Beautiful photography illustrates methods to ferment 64 vegetables and herbs, along with dozens of creative recipes.

Fiery Ferments
by Kirsten K. Shockey & Christopher Shockey

Expand your fermented repertoire with more than 70 recipes for spicy sauces, mustards, chutneys, and relishes from around the globe. An additional 40 recipes for breakfast foods, snacks, entrées, and beverages highlight many uses for the hot ferments.

The Harvest Baker by Ken Haedrich

These 150 delicious recipes put a fresh spin on baking. With savory options including quiches, tarts, pot pies, pizza, calzones, and hearty yeast breads in addition to sweet cakes, pies, cookies, and bars, there's something for every taste.

Home Sausage Making, **4th Edition**
by Charles G. Reavis and Evelyn Battaglia, with Mary Reilly

Detailed directions for popular charcuterie techniques such as dry curing and smoking plus 100 mouthwatering recipes ranging from breakfast sausage to global favorites like mortadella, liverwurst, chorizo, kielbasa, and more make this the only sausage-making reference you need.

Put 'em Up! by Sherri Brooks Vinton

This comprehensive guide to preserving gives you bright flavors, flexible batch sizes, and modern methods. The simple instructions and more than 150 delicious recipes cover freezing, drying, canning, and pickling.